A Brief History
of Great Britain

A BRIEF HISTORY OF GREAT BRITAIN

WILLIAM E. BURNS

Facts On File
An imprint of Infobase Publishing

A Brief History of Great Britain

Copyright © 2010 by William E. Burns

All rights reserved. No part of this book may be reproduced or utilized in any form or by any means, electronic or mechanical, including photocopying, recording, or by any information storage or retrieval systems, without permission in writing from the publisher. For information contact:

Facts On File, Inc.
An imprint of Infobase Publishing
132 West 31st Street
New York NY 10001

Library of Congress Cataloging-in-Publication Data

Burns, William E., 1959-
  A brief history of Great Britain / William E. Burns.
    p. cm. — (Brief history)
  Includes bibliographical references and index.
  ISBN 978-0-8160-7728-1
  1. Great Britain—History. 2. Ireland—History. I. Title.
  DA30.B88 2009
  941—dc22   2009008217

Facts On File books are available at special discounts when purchased in bulk quantities for businesses, associations, institutions, or sales promotions. Please call our Special Sales Department in New York at (212) 967-8800 or (800) 322-8755.

You can find Facts On File on the World Wide Web at http://www.factsonfile.com

Text design by Joan M. McEvoy
Composition by Hermitage Publishing Services
Maps by Patricia Meschino
Cover printed by Art Print, Taylor, Pa.
Book printed and bound by Maple-Vail Book Manufacturing Group, York, Pa.
Date printed: December, 2009
Printed in the United States of America
10 9 8 7 6 5 4 3 2 1

This book is printed on acid-free paper.

Dedicated to the Frobish crew, Bill, Jerry, and Jim

CONTENTS

LIST OF ILLUSTRATIONS

LIST OF MAPS

ACKNOWLEDGMENTS

My principal thanks for this volume go to my mentors, friends, and colleagues in British history, including the late B. J. T. Dobbs, Ray Kelch, Margaret Jacob, Kathryn Brammall, Bruce Janacek, Art Williamson, Dane Kennedy, Jon Tetsuro Sumida, Lori Anne Ferrell, Deborah Harkness, Norma Landau, Florene Memegalos, and Lorraine Madway. My editor at Facts On File, Claudia Schaab, helped make this a better book, as did my copy editor, Elin Woodger. I also thank the Gelman Library of George Washington University, the Folger Library, the Library of Congress, and Julie Brazier.

INTRODUCTION

L ike that of all nations, the history of Great Britain is conditioned by
its geographic setting. The plethora of geographical and political
factors found in Britain can be overwhelming and reflects the ebb and
flow of power over the centuries.

Geography, Climate, and Natural Resources

Great Britain, which includes the constituent units of England, Wales,
and Scotland, is the world's ninth-largest island. It covers about 80,823
square miles (209,331 square kilometers) and extends about 600 miles
(966 kilometers) from north to south and about 300 miles (483 kilometers) from east to west. Britain is the largest island of the British Isles,
an archipelago—that is, a group of islands.

Despite Britain's position in the northern latitudes of Europe—the
same distance from the equator as the southern parts of the cold
countries of Norway and Sweden—the presence of the warm waters
of the Gulf Stream makes the archipelago much warmer than the corresponding areas in North America or Scandinavia. (Some fear that
global warming will alter the course of the Gulf Stream away from the
British Isles; thus, paradoxically, some British worry that it will make
their islands much colder.) The climate is very wet, and rainfall is pretty
evenly distributed and frequent, meaning that British farmers have little
need for the elaborate irrigation systems characteristic of drier climes.
Britain is seismically stable, and British earthquakes are small and very
rarely destructive.

Britain is well endowed with minerals, particularly tin, lead, iron,
and coal. The availability of iron and coal is one of the reasons why
Britain was the home of the Industrial Revolution. Its North Sea coastal
waters also have oil, but the supply is fast running out.

No place on the island of Great Britain is farther than 70 miles (113
kilometers) from the sea, and Britain's rivers and irregular coastline
provide numerous harbors, particularly facing south and east. The
British were not always great sailors, nor did they always have a strong
navy, but those powerful on the seas were a constant threat. Britain's

separation from the continent also means that most invaders of Britain were not entire peoples on the move but smaller groups of warriors. Successful invasions and conquests in British history have usually resulted in the imposition of a new ruling class rather than the introduction of an entirely new people.

Britain is marked by pronounced regional differences. The most basic division is that between highland areas and lowland areas. The "highland zone" is defined by being over 200 meters (656 feet) above sea level. Highland zones are found in Wales, much of Scotland, northern England, and parts of southwestern England, although lowland pockets exist in highland territories. The British highland zone is not really mountainous, as the highest mountains reach the modest height of roughly 4000 feet (1,219 meters). There is a much higher proportion of highland land in Scotland than in England, and the difference between the highlands and the lowlands and their inhabitants plays a central role in Scottish history and culture.

The highlands are marked by a greater emphasis on pastoralism, as they have mostly chalky soil and are too wet and cold for successful agriculture. The highlands are also much less densely populated than the lowlands, as it requires much more land to support a human being through pastoralism than through agriculture. Lowland areas are usually more fertile. The most fertile lowlands are in the south and southeast of Britain, where there is rich, heavy soil more suited to agriculture. Lowlanders can engage in raising either grains or livestock, depending on circumstances. In the Middle Ages much of the lowlands was turned over to the highly profitable production of wool. Lowlanders tended to live in villages, highlanders in small hamlets or isolated farmsteads, or to be nomadic.

Invasions of Britain had much less effect on the highlands than on the lowlands, which constituted the really valuable prize due to their greater agricultural productivity. Those regimes exercising power throughout Britain or the British Isles were usually based in lowland England, the only place capable of supporting them. The extension of power from the lowlands to the highlands was a difficult challenge due to the difficulty of the terrain. Mountainous Wales preserved its independence for centuries despite its poverty and its inability to unite politically. The only invaders to subdue Wales before the 13th century were the well-organized and disciplined Roman legions, and it took them years after the conquest of England. The less-organized Anglo-Saxons, Vikings, and Normans had a much harder time, and Wales was only permanently annexed to England in 1284.

United Kingdom

Shetland Islands
Mainland

Orkney Islands
Lewis and Harris
Mainland

Outer Hebrides

ATLANTIC OCEAN

Inner Hebrides

SCOTLAND
Aberdeen

North Sea

GRAMPIAN MTS.

Jura

NORTHERN IRELAND
Islay

Glasgow
Edinburgh

Londonderry

Belfast

HIGHLANDS

PENNINES

Isle of Man

York

Irish Sea

Humber R.

Liverpool

REPUBLIC OF IRELAND

Anglesey

ENGLAND
MIDLANDS

CAMBRIAN MTS.

Trent R.

LOWLANDS

WALES

London

Thames R.

Canterbury

Isle of Wight

N

Isles of Scilly

English Channel

Alderney
Channel Islands Herm
Guernsey
Jersey
Sark

FRANCE

0   500 miles
0   500 km

© Infobase Publishing

The greater poverty of the highlands meant that highlanders often raided lowlanders, creating hostility between the two. The highlands were also more culturally and linguistically conservative. Cultural innovations usually originated in the lowlands and spread to the highlands. The highlands were where the Celtic languages lasted the longest, as English and its offshoots, originally the language of Anglo-Saxon invaders, became the dominant tongue of the lowlands in the early Middle Ages. This cultural division further added to the hostility between highland and lowland peoples.

Other variations in land include those of open country, with lighter soils; forests with heavy, clayey soils; and fens and swamps. Britain in the earliest times was heavily forested and also contained many fens and swamplands. These areas were often associated with outlaws and people who lived freer but poorer lives. Over the course of millennia, much of this land has been developed into agricultural use.

There are no really large rivers in Britain due to the small size of the island. The most important is the Thames in the south; others include the Trent and the Tweed in the north. Despite the lack of good, waterborne internal communications, the ocean's proximity makes it relatively easy to move goods from place to place, as coal was moved from the north to London. In the 18th and early 19th centuries British entrepreneurs and landowners created a network of canals to make up for the relative lack of inland waterways. In the 19th and 20th centuries, railroads served a similar function.

Great Britain in the British Archipelago

Great Britain has usually been the archipelago's dominant political and cultural power, and it is certainly the most heavily populated island. The other big island is Ireland, whose history is closely connected with Britain's. Today Ireland is divided into a large, independent southern country, the Republic of Ireland, and a smaller section in the north, Northern Ireland, which along with Great Britain makes up the United Kingdom of Great Britain and Northern Ireland, called the United Kingdom for short. The United Kingdom is often commonly referred to as Britain, a political usage that differs from the geographical one. Connections between Ireland and Great Britain have included invasions across the Irish Sea in both directions, although the last Irish invasion of any part of Great Britain was in the early Middle Ages. There are long-standing connections of trade and migration between northwestern Britain and Northern Ireland. Christianity first arrived in northwestern Britain from Ireland.

The archipelago also includes many smaller islands. The Isle of Wight, about 147 square miles (381 square kilometers) in size, lies about 4 miles (6.5 kilometers) off the southern coast of Britain. The Isle of Wight's close proximity to south Britain has led its history to be part of south Britain's rather than one with its own identity. Today it is politically united with Britain, as it has been for centuries.

Another close island is the Welsh island of Anglesey, off the northern coast of Wales. The Menai Strait, which separates Anglesey from the mainland of Wales, is only about 273 yards (250 meters) at its narrowest point. Anglesey covers about 276 square miles (715 square kilometers). Its isolation made it a stronghold of Welsh tradition, the last area in Wales to fall to the Romans and currently one of the areas with the greatest density of Welsh speakers.

The Isle of Man, about 221 square miles (572 square kilometers), sits in the Irish Sea between Great Britain and Ireland and has a very different history and status, having belonged to England, Scotland, Ireland, and Norway. Unlike Anglesey and the Isle of Wight, the Isle of Man is not formally part of the United Kingdom but a separate Crown dependency.

Another Crown dependency is the Channel Islands, a chain of small islands between southern England and France in the English Channel. There are five inhabited islands—Jersey, Guernsey, Sark, Alderney, and Herm. The islands combine a French and British heritage, and their native language is a dialect of French. Their relationship to the European continent has been closer than that of the rest of the British Isles. During World War II (1939–45), the Channel Islands were the only part of the British Isles occupied by the Germans.

Another group of small islands in the south are the Isles of Scilly. Unlike the Channel Islands, they are not Crown dependencies but part of Great Britain. Their culture and history is most closely linked to that of Cornwall, a county in southwest England.

Several island chains have become part of Scotland. The Hebrides and the northern chains—the Shetlands and Orkneys—have also been linked to Scandinavia. The Hebrides are a large group of islands divided into the Inner Hebrides, off the coast of Scotland, and the Outer Hebrides, farther northwest. The larger islands of the Inner Hebrides include Jura and Islay. The major island of the Outer Hebrides is called Lewis and Harris. Contested for centuries between the Norwegian kings, various local rulers, and the kings of Scotland, the Hebrides were eventually incorporated into Scotland. Like Anglesey, they are a stronghold of Celtic speakers. The Celtic language of Scotland, Gaelic, is still spoken in the Hebrides.

Orkney is a small chain of islands immediately to the north of Scotland. It, too, was contested between Scotland and Norway, only becoming Scottish in the 15th century. Its largest island is called Mainland. The people of Orkney have a strong Scandinavian tradition and differ culturally from the Scottish mainland. Their language has a distinct Norse influence.

The British isles farthest to the north are known as Shetland. Again, the largest island is called Mainland, and its political and cultural history resembles that of Orkney; in fact, the two island groups have been politically and ecclesiastically united on several occasions.

England, Scotland, and Wales

For much of its history, Great Britain has been divided into three political and cultural units: England in the south; Wales, a peninsula to the west of England; and Scotland in the north.

The term *England* comes from the Germanic tribes known as Anglo-Saxons and does not apply to the southern area of Great Britain before the first Anglo-Saxon invasions in the fifth century C.E. Even then the Anglo-Saxons, or "English," were not politically united, and the Kingdom of England was not formed until the 10th century. However, southern Britain had a distinct identity before the coming of the English. The territory of the Roman province of Britannia was largely the same as that of modern England and Wales.

England is geographically the largest, the wealthiest, and demographically by far the largest of the four major regions of the British Isles, including Ireland. For much of its history, England has dominated Britain and the British Isles. England is mostly a lowland country, with more fertile land and a more temperate climate than its rivals. The most prominent mountain range in England is the Pennines, which extends from the northern Midlands—central England—to northern England and southern Scotland. The highest peak in the Pennines, Cross Fell, is only 2,930 feet (893 meters) high.

England's wealth has been a curse as well as a blessing, making it a tempting target for expansionist rulers on the European continent, including Roman emperors and Norman dukes. Mountainous and poor, Scotland and Wales have had less to fear from outsiders but more to fear from England itself.

One of the most important regional distinctions within England, affecting several phases of English history, is the division between northern and southern England. Southern England is made up primarily of fertile lowland areas, and it is more closely connected to the European continent. For many periods of English history, northern England has been a frontier region, closer to the Scottish border than the capital at London. The north contains a higher proportion of less agriculturally productive highland country. There is more raising and consumption of oats and barley as opposed to the wheat diet of the south. It is also more oriented to the North Sea in the east and the Irish Sea in the west rather than the English Channel in the south. The city of York in the northeast was one of the most important Viking strongholds in England, and Viking culture had far more impact on the north than the south. The culturally conservative north remained predominantly Catholic after the Protestant Reformation of the 16th century, led predominantly by southerners closely connected with the Protestant movement on the European continent. In the 18th century it was the north, with its abundant deposits of coal, that became the heartland of the Industrial Revolution rather than the richer south. In modern party politics the north is the land of Liberal and Labour rule, in opposition to the Conservative south.

Another distinct English region is Cornwall in the far southwest, inhabited by the only large non-English ethnic group within England itself for most of its history. The Cornish were originally Celtic speakers like the Welsh and the Gaels, but they were too small in number to resist being politically absorbed into England at an early stage. Some medieval and early modern documents and proclamations, however, refer to "England and Cornwall," and some Cornish nationalists have argued that Cornwall remains separate from England, although under the same government. The last speaker of Cornish as a native language died in the 18th century, but there have been modern efforts to revive it. For most of its history, Cornwall was dominated by fishing and tin mining. The first recorded contacts between the British Isles and the classical Mediterranean world was through Mediterranean traders visiting the tin mines of Cornwall, possibly as early as the sixth century B.C.E. They gave Britain the name *Isle of Tin*.

England's capital city, London, has been the largest city in England and the British Isles throughout its history since its founding by the Romans as Londinium around the year 50 C.E. Modern London, the largest city in Europe and a great center of world culture, is an agglomeration of urban units, including the core of medieval London—the City of London—as well as the administrative capital of the borough of Westminster and other cities, towns, and neighborhoods.

Wales is a term applied by the English, meaning "strangers" or "foreigners." Unlike England and Scotland, Wales never became a united kingdom. Its poverty and mountainous terrain made it impossible to establish a centralized government, although on some occasions one Welsh prince was able to dominate the entire country, taking the title Prince of Wales, but always failing to establish a royal dynasty. After encroaching on Wales's frontier for centuries, England conquered the country in the late 13th century, adopting the title Prince of Wales for the English king or queen's eldest son and heir. Wales was legally united with England, forming the Kingdom of England and Wales, in the 16th century, though the kingdom was usually referred to simply as "England," emphasizing Wales's subject position. Nonetheless, it retained a separate cultural and linguistic identity that persists to the present day. Religiously, it developed in the direction of sectarian Protestantism rather than the Church of England. Large areas of Wales are also major producers of coal.

Scotland remained a separate state through the Middle Ages and into the dawn of the 18th century. There were numerous wars between Scotland and England, basically caused by the conflict between the English desire to rule the whole island and the Scottish desire to remain independent. The border between England and Scotland varied before being established on its present course from the Solway Firth, an inlet of the Irish Sea, on the west to the Tweed River on the east. Like Wales, Scotland is relatively poor in good agricultural land compared to England. The conjunction of good harbors and fertile lowland with relative ease of transportation has made England (and Ireland) much more vulnerable to invasion by sea than Wales and Scotland, which were usually invaded from England. The most economically fertile area of Scotland for most of its history, and the heartland of the Scottish monarchy, is the lowland area to the southeast. No city dominates Scotland the way London does England, but its political capital has long been Edinburgh in the southeast. Other major Scottish cities include Glasgow in the south, one of Britain's great industrial centers, and Aberdeen in the north.

Scotland is geographically even more isolated than England from the main centers of development on the European continent, and it was often considered by continental Europeans and even the English to be remote. However, it is a crossroads of the North Atlantic, with easy access from the south of Britain, Ireland, and Scandinavia. The long-standing connection between Scotland and the north of Ireland plays an important role in British history. The original "Scots" were Irish immigrants, and many nobles held lands in both Scotland and Ireland. In the early modern period, many Scots settled in the northern parts of Ireland, becoming the ancestors of the modern Ulster Protestants.

The Terms *Great Britain* and *United Kingdom*

Although the island of Britain is sometimes referred to geographically as *Great Britain*, it is mostly a political term. *Great Britain* has been used as an identity that transcends that of English, Welsh, and Scottish, uniting all the peoples of the island in a common loyalty. It was first used as a title by James VI of Scotland, who inherited the English throne upon the death of Queen Elizabeth I in 1603. By calling himself "King of Great Britain," James tried, without much success, to dissolve the centuries-long animosities of his English and Scottish subjects.

In 1707 the Kingdom of England and Wales and the Kingdom of Scotland were joined together in the Act of Union to form a new Kingdom of Great Britain. (The English and Scottish parliaments each passed an Act of Union. The new kingdom had its capital at the English capital of London, and its institutions, such as Parliament, were basically continuous with those of England, so many Scots viewed it as an English takeover rather than a union of equals. So did many English.) While any hopes for the cessation of English and Scottish identities and enmities were doomed to disappointment, the term *British* did catch on for some things, most important the British Empire, a common creation of the island's peoples. However, there are some indications that the dissolution of the British Empire has had a corresponding impact on British identity. In the 21st century, British identity seems to be increasingly giving way to the older identities of English, Scots, and Welsh.

The *United Kingdom* is a political, not a geographical, term. It was originally the United Kingdom of Great Britain and Ireland, founded by the Act of Union between Great Britain and Ireland in 1801. The Act of Union abolished Ireland's separate parliament, incorporating Irish members in the British parliament as the 1707 act had incorporated the Scots, but with far less success. The term *United Kingdom* was meant to emphasize unity. After most of Ireland became the Irish Free State and eventually the Irish Republic, dissolving its ties with Britain, the remaining realm became known as the United Kingdom of Great Britain and Northern Ireland.

Administrative Boundaries of Great Britain

Orkney Islands

Na h-Eileanan an Iar (Western Isles)

Shetland Islands

Inset 1

Hertfordshire

Essex

Enfield

Barnet

Moray

Harrow

Haringey

Redbridge

Havering

Highland

Aberdeenshire

Brent 61 62 63 New Barking and Dagenham

Ealing 66 68 ham

Hounslow 64 65 67 Greenwich

Aberdeen

69 70 71 Bexley

Perth and Kinross

Angus

Merton

Richmond upon Thames

Sutton

Bromley

Kent

Clackmannanshire Fife

Stirling

Edinburgh City

Royal Borough of Kingston upon Thames

Croydon

Surrey

Argyll and Bute

East Lothian

Inset 2

North Ayrshire

South Lanarkshire

Midlothian

East Ayrshire

Scottish Borders

Northumberland

10

11

14 15 16 18

13

South Ayrshire

Dumfries and Galloway

Newcastle Upon Tyne

North Tyneside

12

17 21

19 20 22

Gateshead

South Tyneside

23

Sunderland

24

Darlington

Hartlepool

Cumbria

Stockton-on-Tees

Redcar and Cleveland

Middlesbrough

North Yorkshire

Lancashire

Bradford

York

East Riding of Yorkshire

Blackpool

Calderdale

Leeds

City of Kingston-upon-Hull

Sefton

Isle of Anglesey

Liverpool

Flintshire

Inset 2

25 26

27 28

29 30

North East Lincolnshire

Wirral

Cheshire

Derbyshire

Nottinghamshire

Lincolnshire

Conwy

31

32 33

Gwynnd

Wrexham

Staffordshire

Denbighshire

34 35 36

Leicestershire

Rutland 43

Norfolk

Shropshire

42

39

Ceredigion

40 41

Powys

37 38

Warwickshire

Worcestershire

Northamptonshire

Cambridgeshire

Suffolk

Rhondaa, Cyon, Taff

Hereford shire

44

Bedfordshire

Pembrokeshire

Carmarthenshire

Gloucestershire

Oxfordshire

Buckinghamshire

Hertfordshire

Essex

46 47 51

49

Thurrock

Swansea

50

48

52

Swindon

56

West Berkshire 57 58 60

Inset 1

Southend-on-Sea

Neath Port Talbot

Cardiff 53

54 55

Wiltshire

59

Surrey

Medway

Kent

Bridgend

The Vale of Glamorgan

City of Southampton

Hampshire

East Sussex

Somerset

West Sussex

Devon

Dorset

N

Cornwall

Poole

City of Portsmouth

City of Brighton and Hove

Isle of Wight

Isles of Scilly

City of Plymouth

Torbay

Bournemouth

| 0 | | 100 miles |
| 0 | | 100 km |

© Infobase Publishing

Britain and its Neighbors

Although a separate island, Britain is closely tied to Europe, which the English refer to as *the Continent*. The separation of Britain from the Continent began in roughly 9000 B.C.E. with the creation of the southern North Sea. The narrowest gap between Britain and Europe is at the eastern end of the English Channel. The gap is only 21 miles (34 kilometers), and the Kentish cliffs are visible from France on a clear day. Most successful invasions of Britain, and many unsuccessful ones, were launched from northern France and the Low Countries across the channel. There were many occasions when states controlled territory on both sides of the channel, as did the Roman Empire and the medieval Angevin Empire.

Another area of contact between Britain and the Continent is with western Scandinavia—Norway and Denmark—across the stormy North Sea. This took much longer than the English Channel connection to become a factor in British history as the distances were much greater and direct connections between Britain and Scandinavia had to wait for the development of improved shipping. However, from the coming of the Vikings in the late eighth century C.E. to the final exit of Norwegian

Key to Administrative Labels

1 West Dunbartonshire	25 Kirklees	50 Newport
2 East Dunbartonshire	26 Wakefield	51 Monmouthshire
3 Falkirk	27 Barnsley	52 South Gloustershire
4 Inverclyde	28 Doncaster	53 City of Bristol
5 Renfrewshire	29 Sheffield	54 North Somerset
6 Glasgow City	30 Rotherham	55 Bath and North East
7 North Lanarkshire	31 City of Stoke-on-Trent	Somerset
8 West Lothian	32 City of Derby	56 Reading
9 East Renfrewshire	33 City of Nottingham	57 Wokingham
10 Blackburn with	34 Telford and Wrekin	58 Windsor and Maidenhead
Darwen	35 City of Wolverhampton	59 Bracknell Forest
11 Knowsley	36 Walsall	60 Slough
12 St. Helens	37 Dudley	61 Camden
13 Wigan	38 Sandwell	62 Islington
14 Bolton	39 Birmingham	63 Hackney
15 Bury	40 Solihull	64 Hammersmith and Fulham
16 Rochdale	41 Coventry	65 Royal Borough of
17 Salford	42 City of Leicester	Kensington and Chelsea
18 Oldham	43 City of Peterborough	66 City of Westminster
19 Warrington	44 Milton Keynes	67 County of the City
20 Trafford	45 Luton	of London
21 Tameside	46 Merthyr Tidfil	68 Tower Hamlets
22 Stockport	47 Blaenau Gwent	69 Wandsworth
23 Manchester	48 Caerphilly	70 Lambeth
24 Halton	49 Torfaen	71 Southwark

© Infobase Publishing

power from Shetland in the late 15th century, Scandinavian and British politics would be intimately intertwined.

There is a long-standing tension in British and English history between identification with the culture and institutions of the Continent and the desire to assert a unique identity. This is felt most strongly by the English; the Welsh and particularly the Scots have often felt more comfortable with a European identity, as opposed to a British identity that often feels too English. The larger Continental institutions that have included all or a great part of Britain include the Roman Empire, the medieval Roman Catholic Church, and the European Union.

1

EARLY SETTLEMENTS, CELTS, AND ROMANS (PREHISTORY TO CA. 450 c.e.)

The earliest history of Britain is marked by its physical separation from the European continent, its settlement from Europe, its inhabitants developing from hunter-gatherers to farmers, and eventually the formation of political units larger than individual villages. These early inhabitants had some remarkable cultural achievements, including Stonehenge and other earth and stone circles.

Beginning in the first millennium B.C.E., Britain was increasingly influenced by the European continent, which brought Iron Age technology. The British were part of the cultural world of the Celts before many of them were forcibly incorporated into the Roman Empire. Although that empire had left Britain by the early fifth century C.E., the legacy of Christianity remained, a religion that would shape British culture and institutions to the 21st century.

The Early Britons

Human and prehuman remains have been found in Britain dating as far back as 250,000–300,000 years ago, but these earliest inhabitants seem to have left during the last ice age, which ended about 50,000 years ago. Britain was then resettled from Europe. At this time, it was physically attached to the continent; it only separated to form the island chain with which we are familiar about 11,000 years ago.

Not much is known about these early inhabitants of Britain. They were organized in small communities, and as the population increased they moved from hunting-gathering to agriculture in a way similar to that of many other peoples throughout the world. Britain in this early phase was very heavily forested, well suited to a hunter-gatherer economy. The beginnings of the Neolithic period, or New Stone Age, in the fifth millennium with farming cultures meant the clearing of some of the southern British forests, which started a process of deforestation that would go on for millennia. These Stone Age or Bronze Age peoples, who used flint or bronze implements rather than iron, exhibited different cultural traits, and there was no sign of a "British" identity. These Neolithic developments also meant a shift from the relatively egalitarian society of hunter-gatherers to a more stratified society based on class and gender hierarchies.

The most important physical remnants of the early Britons are the great stone or megalithic circles, notably Stonehenge on Salisbury Plain, which dates to about 3000 B.C.E.; and Avebury, built around the same time or a little earlier about 20 miles (32 kilometers) to the north. Avebury is actually larger than Stonehenge, but due to its greater erosion and the destruction of many of its stones in the medieval period, it is less impressive and not as well known. The efforts of modern archaeologists have revealed many other Neolithic constructions, both in stone and earthworks, in various parts of Britain and Ireland. More than 900 Stone Age circles, or *henges,* are known in the British Isles, and there were probably many more of which no trace survives. There are also surviving remnants of old wooden buildings, including some at Stonehenge, although these have all vanished from casual view. Some of the archaic structures, such as Stonehenge, were vast constructions requiring more than a million man-hours of labor—a remarkable commitment of resources given the general harshness of life in Stone Age society. Since most adults in the Neolithic period died in their 30s, this labor had to extend over generations. Some Stonehenge stones, weighing in the tons, were imported all the way from Wales, indicating trade or diplomatic relations and an amazing feat of organization, given the primitive technology available. Other, even larger rocks were transported from a closer area (the Stonehenge area itself is not particularly rocky, so importation was a necessity), but over land, an even more significant accomplishment.

Stonehenge has constructions and motifs in common with sites on continental Europe, along with the presence of some Continental goods. It used to be believed that the great circle had actually been built by people from the Mediterranean, particularly given the similarities to some circular monuments in the developed culture of Crete. However, modern students of Stonehenge and its sister circles believe them to have been within the capabilities of the British people themselves.

The ruins of Stonehenge continue to impress in their quiet majesty. (Library of Congress, Photochrom Collection)

Contrary to popular belief, there was no original connection between Stonehenge and the Druids, who came along much later. Construction began with earthworks, followed by the inclusion of wooden posts. By the mid-third millennium, vast stones were being placed in a circular design. The finished monument consisted of two concentric circles of stones surrounded by circular earthworks. Archaeologists and archaeo-astronomers continue to debate the relationship of various features of Stonehenge to events in the yearly astronomical cycle. There are indications of religious services such as the worship of deities—possibly to a sun god and an earth goddess whose marriage on the summer solstice the monument commemorates—although it is always risky to make assumptions about religion based solely on artifacts. The main avenue is oriented to the midsummer sun, and there are carvings on the stones associated with the earth goddess, such as the double-bladed axe. Sacrifices and burials of the dead were performed on the Stonehenge site and in the immediate area. The creation of a great ritual center attracting pilgrims and gifts from all over southern Britain and even the Continent may have been intended to mark the superiority of Stonehenge people over other groups in southern

Britain. The inner ring of blue stones from Wales may have been connected to beliefs that the blue stones had healing properties, and some archaeologists have theorized that Stonehenge in the later periods of its use may have been a healing center that even drew visitors from the European continent. Stonehenge declined as a center of activity in the second half of the second millennium B.C.E. as climatic changes to cooler and wetter conditions adversely affected British agriculture, leading to a population crash.

The Celts and the Iron Age

Britain from about the sixth century B.C.E. can be categorized as an Iron Age culture. Iron came relatively late to Britain compared to other parts of Europe, but the British were able to exploit their own iron mines. The smith had a high status in British Iron Age culture, even being represented among the gods. Iron ingots were used as currency, and the introduction of iron axes, combined with the need for fuel to smelt and forge iron, meant that deforestation continued more rapidly. Bronze continued to be used quite widely, as it was cheaper than iron.

In the Iron Age, Britain came to be dominated by a group of people known in modern times as the Celts, who are a difficult group to define. The term *Celt* was originally associated with peoples on the European continent, but there is little evidence of a common Celtic identity straddling the English Channel. While older historians viewed the changes associated with Celtic culture in Britain as an invasion by Celtic peoples from the European continent, more recently historians and archaeologists have found British people selectively adopting certain cultural characteristics of Celtic peoples on their own accord. The indigenous British aristocracy may have adopted Celtic ways as a means of distinguishing themselves from ordinary Britons. The spread of cultural artifacts and styles we now call Celtic constitutes a significant aspect of the long transition from Bronze Age to Iron Age Britain. However, this does not mean the people in Britain adopted a "Celtic" identity or even a "British" one. No ancient writer refers to the British as Celts, and there is some evidence that the "Celtic" languages of Britain—Gaelic, Cornish, and Welsh—had roots far predating the Celtic period. These languages, along with Breton and Irish, were only labeled *Celtic* in the 18th century. There is no indication that the ancient Britons thought of themselves as Celts, although there were substantial cultural, political, and trade connections with France, referred to in ancient times as Gaul and inhabited by Celts among other peoples. There is also no evidence of a "British" identity spanning the different peoples that lived in the island.

Iron Age Britain developed larger communities than there had been under the previous inhabitants, although there is no evidence of any island-wide organization or even anything on the scale of the later kingdoms of England and Scotland. Britain was divided into many territories of smaller or larger tribes, with fluctuating boundaries. Some of these tribes had a long-term influence on place-names—for example, the Cantiaci, after whom the county of Kent in the far southeast is named. These tribal groupings were very fluid and often only lasted for a few decades, a century, or just the life span of a powerful leader.

There were strong class divisions among the Britons, with a warrior aristocracy, some of whom may have been recent immigrants from the Continent, ruling over a peasantry that made up the majority of the population. Early Britain had a warlike culture, and many of the artifacts that survive are related to war. A common form of settlement was the hill fort, built on top of a hill to dominate surrounding territories. Britons used chariots in battle, a form of warfare obsolete in the Mediterranean and even Gaul but still formidable in the more primitive British setting. British armies also included cavalry, mounted on ponies, and infantry. One custom for which British warriors became well known was painting themselves blue, using a substance known as woad, before going into battle. The reason for this is not clear, but it may have had something to do with the display of individual valor. Upper-class British men also made a point of displaying personal courage through hunting, although of course much hunting was carried out primarily for meat.

The spear, which economized on the use of metal, was a popular Celtic weapon. This spearhead from the Thames Valley area is decorated with bronze inlays. (© British Museum/Art Resource, NY)

Our knowledge of Iron Age British religion is fragmentary due to the lack of written sources. The British were polytheists, worshipping a variety of local goddesses and gods and some whose cults covered a larger area. They venerated animals associated with the gods, particularly horses and pigs, and plants, particularly oak and mistletoe. They sacrificed animals, and sometimes humans, to their gods and goddesses. An important feature of Iron Age British religion and culture was Druidism, something the British shared with the Celts of Gaul but not of Ireland. Some classical Greek and Roman writers claimed that Druidism originated in Britain and that Druids from Gaul received training in Britain. The Druids were a class of men who seem to have had certain exemptions from taxation and military service. Being a Druid required skill and training. Druids memorized an extensive orally transmitted poetic literature and had knowledge of herbs, medicinal plants, divining techniques, and religious ritual. The Druids, many of whom inherited their profession, were political and intellectual leaders. They settled disputes between British communities or, alternatively, participated in battle by calling down curses on the enemy. Druids employed circles in their rituals and did use Stonehenge and other ancient stone constructions as ritual centers, but they preferred natural settings in the woods or at wells.

There were growing economic connections between the British and the classical Mediterranean world in the Iron Age. Britain's metal resources—including tin and copper (the components of bronze), as well as gold—attracted traders. The earliest link between Britain and the Mediterranean economy was the Cornish tin trade, mainly through Phoenician traders based in Spain and ultimately in Carthage. The Greeks followed the Phoenicians, and the Greek word for tin was derived from the Celtic word for Britain. Britain also became known for its pearls. One Greek navigator, Pytheas of Massilia, circumnavigated Britain in the fourth century, revealing to the Mediterranean peoples that Britain was an island.

When Britons first appeared in the written as opposed to the archaeological record it was not their own written record but that of the Mediterranean peoples—the Greeks and the Romans.

The Coming of the Romans

The first important exact date in British history is 55 B.C.E., the date of the first invasion of Britain by the Romans. Although Roman forces quickly withdrew, their coming initiated a period in which British

PYTHEAS OF MASSILIA

Pytheas of Massilia (Marseille), a Greek navigator, was the first person recorded to have circumnavigated Britain, establishing for the Mediterranean peoples that it was an island. His circumnavigation, part of a voyage of exploration to northern Europe and the Baltic, took place around 325 B.C.E. Pytheas wrote an account of his travels on the seas of northern Europe, including visits to Scandinavia and the Baltic Sea. Although his original account has been lost, quotations from it are found in other ancient writings, such as those by the Greek geographer Strabo and the Roman natural historian Pliny the Elder. Some theorize that Pytheas sailed as far as Iceland, which he called Thule, the land at the end of the world. Others argue that Thule was one of the northern British Isles such as Shetland. He is also the first writer recorded as using a form of the word *Britain* (*Britannike*), which derives from early Celtic, the same root as the Welsh word *Prydein,* referring to the island.

Celtic society was radically transformed, first by Roman contact and then, through much of the island, by actual Roman rule. It was also a time when the available evidence for British history explodes, due to the Roman habit of writing histories and commemorating events through stone inscriptions.

The Roman Empire in 55 B.C.E. was dramatically expanding in both western Europe and the Mediterranean. Competing Roman generals and politicians sought fame and wealth through conquest of weaker peoples. Britain became subject to the attention of the greatest of all Roman generals, Julius Caesar (100–44 B.C.E.), who had conquered Gaul in 58 and become proconsul of the province. Given its cultural, political, and economic links with Gaul, Britain was a convenient refuge for some of Caesar's Gaulish enemies, many of whom were identified as Belgae and formed a new ruling class in southern Britain. The mineral and agricultural wealth of Britain also made it a tempting prize. Keenly aware of his own prestige and the glory that extending Roman rule to the edge of the known world would add to his legend, Caesar saw Britain as a logical follow-up to his earlier conquests.

Caesar's first expedition was not very successful, although it was intended more as a reconnaissance in force than as an expedition of conquest. It was difficult to ferry the troops across the English Channel,

7

JULIUS CAESAR ON BRITAIN

In his *Commentaries on the Gallic War*, the Roman politician and general Julius Caesar was the first writer to give a full description of Britain and the British, although his perspective is that of a would-be conqueror rather than a historian:

> *The interior portion of Britain is inhabited by those of whom they say that it is handed down by tradition that they were born in the island itself: the maritime portion by those who had passed over from the country of the Belgae for the purpose of plunder and making war; almost all of whom are called by the names of those states from which being sprung they went thither, and having waged war, continued there and began to cultivate the lands. The number of the people is countless, and their buildings exceedingly numerous, for the most part very like those of the Gauls: the number of cattle is great. They use either brass or iron rings, determined at a certain weight, as their money. Tin is produced in the midland regions; in the maritime, iron; but the quantity of it is small: they employ brass, which is imported. There, as in Gaul, is timber of every description, except beech and fir. They do not regard it lawful to eat the hare, and the cock, and the goose; they, however, breed them for amusement and pleasure. The climate is more temperate than in Gaul, the cold being less severe.*

Source: Julius Caesar, *Caesar's Commentaries on the Gallic and Civil Wars*. Translated by W.A. McDevitte and W. S. Bohn (New York: Harper and Row, 1870), 111–112.

given Roman ignorance of the "Narrow Seas" between Britain and continental Europe. However, the knowledge gained on the preliminary expedition was applied to another, larger expedition with five legions the next year. During that expedition, Caesar was confronted by a coalition of British tribes under the leadership of Cassivellaunus, king of the Catuvellauni. Due to the superiority of the Roman army and Caesar's masterly use of the divisions between the British tribes and their fear of Catuvellaunic expansion, he defeated the Britons. However, rather than adding Britain as a new Roman province, he was forced to leave within a couple of months to face new problems in Gaul.

The situation following Caesar's departure from Britain was similar to that of many other areas in the preliminary stages of the imposition of Roman rule during this time. However, there was no immediate

Roman follow-up because of a long series of civil wars leading to the transformation of the Roman Republic into the Roman Empire, in addition to greater concern with other areas closer to home and the belief of the early Julio-Claudian emperors that the empire was already too big and should not expand farther. Yet Caesar's departure did not mean the end of Roman influence in Britain, as many tribes had made some sort of submission, given hostages, and promised to pay tribute. Even though the obligations of British tribes to pay tribute to Rome were generally ignored by both sides, both trade and diplomatic relationships flourished. Roman and British contact was mostly concentrated among the peoples of the southern and eastern coasts, such as the Atrebates, Trinovantes, and Catuvellauni, with far fewer contacts inland.

Following a common historical pattern, Britain's close relations with the large Roman Empire led to greater concentrations of political authority among the British tribes. The tribes competed with each other for control over the trade with the empire, and some leaders tried to use Roman support against other British kings. Some chiefs sent ambassadors to Rome or journeyed to Rome themselves. There was a great deal of disruption among British Celts as mainland Celtic groups fleeing Roman control arrived on the island, bringing more advanced Continental military technology and greater familiarity with Roman ways.

The British aristocratic lifestyle became increasingly Romanized. This can be seen even gastronomically, as Britain imported wine and other items of Mediterranean cuisine such as olive oil or the fish sauce known as *garum,* a Roman delicacy. Britons paid for the luxury items with grain, metals, and slaves. Coastal rulers who controlled the trade with Rome became increasingly wealthy, and their wealth helped them against both the aristocracy of their own peoples and rival chiefs. Coins issued by some Celtic rulers showed Roman influence and were probably made by Roman die cutters. Although coins were in use in the pre-Roman period—some with Latin inscriptions—by the first century, coinage was widespread in Britain south of the River Trent.

The Roman Conquest

The Roman conquest of Britain began in 43 C.E. under Emperor Claudius (10 B.C.E.–54 C.E., r. 41–54 C.E.). No longer the republic of Caesar's day, Rome had become an empire in 27 B.C.E. and was ruled by one man, who usually tried to monopolize military glory. Claudius, an emperor with a rather undistinguished past, sought to build a reputation by adding new territory to the empire, traditionally regarded as the highest achievement of a Roman general. Increased Roman knowledge of and contacts with Britain made an actual conquest much more feasible than it had been a century before in Caesar's time. Although the expedition was led by experienced Roman generals, the emperor was always presented as its leader; the capture of one important British center was even delayed until the emperor could get there. In addition to Claudius's glory, there were structural reasons for Rome to be interested in control over Britain. British meddling in Gaul was contributing to unrest there, and Roman authorities feared that a military command along the Atlantic coast facing Britain would be large enough and close enough to Rome to give its general imperial ambitions. A group of legions across the English Channel would be less of a threat to the emperor than troops in Gaul, who could reach Rome by land.

At that time, the Britons were still fighting from chariots, a style of warfare that had been abandoned by Mediterranean cultures centuries ago and was ineffective against the Roman legions. After the first defeats, many British chiefs, hoping to keep their dominant positions under the new order rather than engaging in a doomed struggle against it, surrendered to the Romans without a fight.

One of the major changes wrought by the Romans was the extirpation of the Druids, the Britons' religious and intellectual class. The Romans had already been campaigning against Druids in Gaul, partly because the Druids practiced human sacrifice and partly because they offered a nucleus for possible Celtic resistance to Rome. Given the importance of the British Druids, who provided much of the leadership for anti-Roman forces, the Romans considered it necessary to suppress Druidism in Britain as well. In 54 C.E. the Romans passed a decree banning British Druidism, and in 61 C.E. Roman forces under Suetonius Paulinus massacred Druids on the Isle of Anglesy as part of a campaign to pacify Wales, a remote area where traditional British culture and Druidism remained strong and anti-Roman. Descendants of the surviving Druids seem mostly to have merged into the general population. As a sign of the extent of the suppression of Druidism in Britain, there are no references to Druids in later Roman Britain. There was some Roman destruction at Stonehenge, which they were the first in a long line to misidentify as a Druidic temple, although much of it was too massive for the Romans to really do anything about it.

Druidism and other native beliefs were replaced among the elite, the people the Romans cared about winning over, by Roman cults, particularly the cult of the emperor, which served to bind all areas of

SUETONIUS ON CLAUDIUS IN BRITAIN

For many Romans, Britain was simply too remote for its addition to the empire to make much of an impression. The biographer of the first 12 Caesars, Suetonius (ca. 69–ca. 122 C.E.), dismisses the conquest in a single paragraph in his biography of Claudius, part of his *Lives of the Twelve Caesars:*

> *He made but one campaign and that of little importance. When the Senate voted him the triumphal regalia, thinking the honor beneath the imperial dignity and desiring the glory of a legitimate triumph, he chose Britain as the best place for gaining it, a land that had been attempted by no one since the Deified Julius and was just at that time in a state of rebellion because of the refusal to return certain deserters. On the voyage there from Ostia he was nearly cast away twice in furious north-westerns, off Liguria and near the Stoechades islands. Therefore he made the journey from Massilia all the way to Gesoriacum by land, crossed from there, and without any battle or bloodshed received the submission of a part of the island [44 C.E.], returned to Rome within six months after leaving the city, and celebrated a triumph of great splendor. To witness the sight he allowed not only the governors of the provinces to come to Rome, but even some of the exiles; and among the tokens of his victory he set a naval crown on the gable of the Palace beside the civic crown, as a sign that he had crossed and, as it were, subdued the Ocean. His wife Messalina followed his chariot in a carriage, as did also those who had won the triumphal regalia in the same war; the rest marched on foot in fringed togas, except Marcus Crassus Frugi, who rode a caparisoned horse and wore a tunic embroidered with palms, because he was receiving the honor for the second time.*

Source: Suetonius, *Suetonius*. 2 vols. Translated by J. C. Rolfe (London: William Heinemann, 1920), 2:35.

the empire together. A huge temple of the deified Claudius was built in Colchester shortly after the conquest to serve as a rallying point for pro-Roman Britons. The Romans, however, had no desire to eliminate the worship of British gods. In many places they simply built new shrines dedicated to the same gods on the site of old British shrines, both to placate the gods and to provide places for British and Roman subjects of the empire to honor their deities.

The Romans also introduced many new gods, including the official Roman gods—Jupiter, Mars, Mercury, Minerva, and others. The organs of the Roman state were permeated by official religion. A legion, for example, was expected to sacrifice to Jupiter the Supreme Ruler, Jupiter the Victor, Mars the Father, Mars the Victor, the goddess Victoria, the emperor's guardian spirit, and many others as part of its official duties. All human activities required the favor of the relevant gods.

In addition to the official gods, myriad gods were brought to the new province from all parts of the empire by immigrants and the Roman army. These included eastern gods such as the Persian Mithras and the Graecophonecian Heracles of Tyre; Continental Celtic gods such as Baudihillia and Fridiagabis, brought to Britain by soldiers from the Netherlands; and gods who seem to have originated during the time of the empire itself, such as the northern goddess Brigantia. The Roman army of the empire was an extremely ethnically mixed force, and the Romans liked to station troops in areas far away from where they were recruited. More gods were worshipped in Britain in Roman times than at any time before or since. British and Roman gods were frequently combined or equated. The Roman military worshipped combinations of Roman and Celtic deities, such as the god of war Mars Camulos. The Celtic goddess of the hot springs at Aquae, Sulis (today's Bath) was renamed Minerva Sulis.

Away from the centers of Roman civilization, British peasants and slaves probably continued worshipping British gods in the traditional way, although without the benefit of Druids or human sacrifice. Some Celtic customs seem to have been abandoned in the period, such as the burial of the dead with weapons as opposed to household goods, but there is no evidence this change had anything to do with the Roman occupation.

One reason for the Romans to conquer Britain was the desire to exploit its agricultural and mineral wealth. In addition to agricultural goods, Britain was an important source of minerals, particularly tin and lead, which for the ancients were necessary to refine silver. The Romans did not greatly change British agriculture, although they introduced several new crops, such as the cherry and the wine grape. However, British wine was not very successful in competition with the empire's established wine regions in warmer climates.

Roman civilization occupied a very different role in the lowlands than in the highlands. The productive lowlands saw extensive colonization and the Romanization of the British elite. The Roman presence in the highlands was largely restricted to military outposts. The highland

Tribal Groupings of Great Britain in the First Century C.E.

| 0 | 500 miles |
| 0 | 500 km |

N

The Minch

Moray Firth

Pictish tribes

North Sea

Firth of Fourth

Damnoni Glasgow • Edinburgh

Otadini

Newstead ■

Selgovae

Dalswinton ■

Novantae Nether Denton ■

Carlisle ■ Corbridge ■

North Channel

Solway Firth

Carvetii

Brigantes

Stanwick •

■ York

Irish Sea

Parisi

Ribchester ■ • Leeds

Manchester •

Setantii

Anglesey Liverpool •

Lincoln •

Gangani *Deceangli* ■ Chester Newton-on-Trent

Coritani

Old Sleaford •

The Wash

Trent R.

Wroxeter ■

Cardigan Bay *Ordovices*

Wall ■ Leicester ■ Longthorpe ■

Iceni

Cornovii

Dobunni

Ouse R.

Catuvellauni

Trinovantes

St. Albans •

St. George's Channel

Demetae

Sliures Usk ■

Gloucester •

London

■ ■ Colchester

Caerleon ■

Cirencester •

Richborough ■

Bristol Channel

Thames R.

Atrebates Canterbury • ■

Belgae

Ilchester • Winchester •

Cantiaci

North Tawton ■ *Durotriges* Fishbourne • Selsey •

Nanstallon ■ *Dumnonii* Exeter •

Regni

English Channel

— Approximate boundary of Roman Empire, ca. first century C.E.

■ Major Roman fort

© Infobase Publishing

13

Celts, particularly the Silures of southeast Wales, gave the Romans their toughest opposition.

Many Britons, both those who had fought the Romans and those who had supported them, resented the arrogance and grasping demands of Roman officials and Roman colonists. The brutality of Roman rule led to the largest revolt in the history of Britannia shortly after the initial conquest: Boudicca's rebellion in 60 C.E. Boudicca was the widow of the king of the Iceni in eastern Britain, who had been allied with Rome. Leaving two daughters and no son, the king had bequeathed half his kingdom to the emperor in hope that this would satisfy the Romans. In the Roman attempt to take over the whole kingdom, Boudicca was flogged, and according to the ancient historian Tacitus, her daughters were raped by Roman soldiers (Tacitus *Annals*, Book XIV). Her subsequent rebellion was the greatest challenge to Roman rule in Britain. The rebellion at first seemed successful, particularly since the main Roman army at the time was battling the rebellious Silures on the island of Anglesey off the west coast of Britain. Boudicca's forces attacked and burned the Roman provincial capital, Camulodunum, the old Catuvellaunian capital, massacring its inhabitants. The rebels also burned London, although the population was evacuated. However, they were not able to face a full Roman army. The rebellion was crushed when 10,000 Roman troops slaughtered 80,000 Britons in the Battle of Watling Street, and Boudicca committed suicide rather than become a prisoner of Rome. The rebellion resulted in the transfer of Roman provincial administration to London.

Boudicca's defeat was followed by harsh repression of the rebels, but subsequent Roman governors worked to win the support of the British aristocracy. Many British leaders received Roman citizenship, took Roman names, and adopted aspects of the Roman upper-class lifestyle such as Roman dress and the Latin language. This Romanization, however, was restricted to the upper classes. The lower classes were little affected by Roman influence, even compared to people living in the Roman Empire on the Continent. While many parts of the western Roman Empire continued to speak Latin dialects such as French or Spanish even after the fall of Rome in the fifth century, this was not true in Britain, where Latin never became a common tongue.

The Romans never conquered the entire island of Britain. To most Romans, the north seemed too poor and mountainous to be worth the trouble of taking and holding. There was a long series of attempts to find a stable and defensible area for the northern frontier. The most radical policy was that of C. Julius Agricola (40–93), the governor of

Britannia in the late 70s. Much more is known about Agricola than about most Roman provincial governors anywhere because he was one of the few Roman officials to be the subject of a biography. The biography was written by his son-in-law, the great Roman historian Cornelius Tacitus (ca. 56–ca. 117), an admirer of his father-in-law, whom Tacitus regarded as the embodiment of old-fashioned Roman virtue. Agricola planned to conquer all of Britain, and possibly Ireland as well. He carried out successful campaigns in southern Scotland, but the combination of trouble elsewhere in the empire and skepticism about the cost of conquering and occupying the whole island led to the abandonment of his plans. The frontier was eventually established at Hadrian's Wall, named after the Roman emperor Hadrian (r. 117–138). The wall ran from the fortress of Segedunum on the river Tyne (the site of the modern community of Wallsend) to the Solway Firth, south of the modern border between England and Scotland. Roman influence extended well beyond the border, however. The Romans traded with and indirectly influenced what became Scotland, and some of the people who lived there even served in the Roman army.

The position of governor of Britain was initially a military one resting on command of the three legions stationed in the province. It was usually given to a commander with experience along the imperial frontier in northern Europe. The army itself was increasingly drawn from native Britons, who were rewarded with Roman citizenship on retirement. Britain's relative poverty can be seen in the undistinguished backgrounds of its procurators, the chief tax gatherers.

The incorporation of Britain as a frontier province of the Roman Empire was mostly successful. The Romans introduced much of the infrastructure of civilization, such as roads and cities, to the island. The Roman Empire was based on considerable local autonomy and self-government of its cities, which had administrative responsibility for their surrounding territories. The first British cities, including London, were Roman foundations, and Roman place-names persisted long after the empire's fall. The common place-name component -chester, as in Manchester, is a derivative of the Latin word castra, meaning a military encampment. Cities were the centers for the diffusion of Roman culture to the British elite. Urban life in Roman Britain included some of the amenities of Mediterranean life such as public baths, games, and wine. Roman cities were usually built on the site of old tribal centers, with a mixed population of Romans and Britons and a temple dedicated to the emperor to foster the imperial cult and loyalty to Rome among the natives. Many cities were originally colonies of Roman veterans.

TACITUS ON THE BATTLE OF MONS GRAUPIUS

I n his biography *Agricola,* Cornelius Tacitus described the Battle of Mons Graupius (84 C.E.) on the Moray Firth, Scotland, between Romans led by Agricola and an alliance of Britons from different tribes led by Calgacus:

> *The action began with distant fighting. The Britons with equal steadiness and skill used their huge swords and small shields to avoid or to parry the missiles of our soldiers, while they themselves poured on us a dense shower of darts, till Agricola encouraged three Batavian and two Tungrian cohorts to bring matters to the decision of close fighting with swords. Such tactics were familiar to these veteran soldiers, but were embarrassing to an enemy armed with small bucklers and unwieldy weapons. The swords of the Britons are not pointed, and do not allow them to close with the foe, or to fight in the open field. No sooner did the Batavians begin to close with the enemy, to strike them with their shields, to disfigure their faces, and overthrowing the force on the plain to advance their line up the hill, than the other auxiliary cohorts joined with eager rivalry in cutting down all the nearest of the foe. Many were left behind half dead, some even unwounded, in the hurry of victory. Meantime the enemy's cavalry had fled, and the charioteers had mingled in the engagement of the infantry. But although these at first spread panic, they were soon impeded by the close array of our ranks and by the inequalities of the ground.*

The most important town in Roman Britain was London, which quickly became the capital of Britannia and the nodal point of the Roman road system: In Britannia, all roads led to London. London was the most Romanized town in Britain and one of the largest Roman cities in the generally backward Roman northwest.

The cities were the basis for the Romanization of lowland Britain, but eventually Roman art and the material trappings of Roman provincial life spread to the country villas of the British aristocracy, many of whom remained rurally based. By the second century the British elite was largely Romanized and incorporated into the empire's governing class, although due to Britain's remoteness and relatively small population, they did not enter the Roman senate the way Gaulish aristocrats did.

The battle had anything but the appearance of a cavalry action, for men and horses were carried along in confusion together, while chariots, destitute of guidance, and terrified horses without drivers, dashed as panic urged them, sideways, or in direct collision against the ranks.

Those of the Britons who, having as yet taken no part in the engagement, occupied the hill-tops, and who without fear for themselves sat idly disdaining the smallness of our numbers, had begun gradually to descend and to hem in the rear of the victorious army, when Agricola, who feared this very moment, opposed their advance with four squadrons of cavalry held in reserve by him for any sudden emergencies of battle. Their repulse and rout was as severe as their onset had been furious. Thus the enemy's design recoiled on himself, and the cavalry, which by the general's order had wheeled round from the van of the contending armies, attacked his rear. Then, indeed, the open plain presented an awful and hideous spectacle. Our men pursued, wounded, made prisoners of the fugitives only to slaughter them when others fell in their way. And now the enemy, as prompted by their various dispositions, fled in whole battalions with arms in their hands before a few pursuers, while some, who were unarmed, actually rushed to the front and gave themselves up to death. Everywhere there lay scattered arms, corpses, and mangled limbs, and the earth reeked with blood.

Source: Tacitus. *The Agricola and Germany of Tacitus and the Dialogue on Oratory*. Translated by Alfred John Church and William Jackson Broadribb. Revised edition (London: Macmillan, 1877), 36.

Britain in the Later Empire

By the second century, Roman Britain had moved from the initial phase of conquest, when the principal threats to Roman rule were rebellious Britons, to relative peace with an assimilated British aristocracy and a quiescent peasantry. Britain was only slightly affected by the move beginning in the late second century toward a more militarized empire, with frequent civil wars between claimants to the imperial throne and greater pressure from the outside, primarily from Germanic tribes. Its remote position and the fact that most Germanic tribes lacked naval power kept Britain isolated from outside pressure for a longer time than other western provinces.

The concentration of a large number of Roman troops in Britain under a single command made it a base for ambitious generals to launch a try for the imperial throne. The first of these, in 196, was Clodius Albinus (ca. 150–197), who launched the first recorded invasion of Europe from Britain. This was a problem for the inhabitants of the Roman province in Britain. In order to win the throne, it was necessary for a Roman leader to move all his troops to the Continent, opening up Britain to invasions by the northern tribes beyond the Roman borders, known to the Romans as Picts. Following an attack by northerners who had received word of Albinus's defeat, the British situation was considered serious enough that the emperor himself, the grim Septimius Severus (r. 193–211), came to this remote corner of the empire in 208 to lead the expedition against the northern tribesmen. The period also saw the province's division into two new provinces, mostly following the division between highlands and lowlands, in order to break up the concentration of troops and remove the temptation for Britain-based generals to try for the imperial throne. This division was followed by a long period of internal and external peace lasting for most of the third century.

Although Roman Britain was not threatened with full-scale invasion in the third century, there was an increasing problem with land and sea raids from the Picts of the north and sea raids from the Irish. Across the North Sea a new threat emerged of a Germanic people, the Saxons. The Roman response was the creation of a larger fleet and a system of naval bases along the coast called the Saxon shore, supervised by an official called the count of the Saxon shore. Toward the end of the third century, there was a brief period when Britain was the headquarters of an independent empire under the leadership of the Roman fleet commander, who turned his command into a protection racket for pirates.

In the late third and early fourth century, the Roman government attempted to deal with the problem of ambitious local commanders by further dividing the provinces to create smaller troop concentrations. Britain was divided into five small provinces. This was followed by another period of relative peace until the Irish, Picts, and Saxons started coordinating their operations in 365. Unlike previous invasions, the armies now actually penetrated into the southeast, the heart of Roman Britain, in force. However, they were eventually driven out by Roman troops from the Continent. This incident was followed by two occasions when aspirants for the imperial throne stripped Britain of troops, reopening the land to invasions from the north.

The late empire was also a time of economic decline, which after the early fourth century was hitting marginal areas like Britain particularly hard. There was less use of coinage and less participation in interregional trade. The third and fourth centuries saw power move from

Roman cities into the hands of great landowners. This was reflected in Britain in the rise of the so-called villa economy. Villas were large houses with varying degrees of economic prosperity and fields that were worked by tenant farmers. Many British aristocrats combined villa and city living.

In 410, members of Britain's ruling class, coping with some problem we do not know about, sent representatives asking the Western Roman emperor Honorius (r. 384–423) for help. The emperor, preoccupied with problems closer to home (Rome was sacked by the Visigoths that year), told them to take care of it themselves. This date is often considered the effective end of Roman rule in Britain.

Britain beyond the Wall

Historical sources on Britain north of Hadrian's Wall, which remained independent of Rome, are much sparser than for the Roman-ruled areas. The people spoke languages of the Celtic group and were more reliant on livestock than the residents of the more fertile lands of the south in the Roman province. They were also much less urbanized. After a brief extension northward under Emperor Antoninus Pius (r. 86–161) in the second century, the Romans adopted a defensive strategy toward the frontier. The campaigns of Septimius Severus in the early third century did little to change the basic relationship between the Roman province and its neighbors. By the late third century, Roman writers were referring to the people on the other side of the frontier as *Picts*, a term meaning "painted people" and possibly referring to Pictish use either of body painting or tattooing. Celtic-speaking peoples referred to the Picts as *Cruithne*, and the official Roman name was *Caledones*. Like other peoples adjacent to Roman frontiers, the Picts were transformed by contact with the Roman economy. Being close to Rome generally seems to have increased a society's wealth and inequality as the elite sought to control trade with the wealthier Roman provinces. We know little about Pictish social and political organization, but sometime after the Roman withdrawal they came to be organized as a kingdom. The Pictish kingdom subsequently had to share Scotland with the Irish invaders who settled in Britain and came to be known as the Scots.

Christianity in Britain

An even more important process than the decline and fall of the Roman Empire was the rise and spread of Christianity. There is no evidence of when the first Christian arrived in Britain, but the earliest archaeological evidence of British Christianity dates from around 200. (Later Christian Britons filled the gap between Jesus and the earliest British Christians with legends like the biblical character Joseph of Arimathea visiting Britain after Christ's death or an early British king, Lucius, adopting Christianity.) It would make sense for Britain, in the far northwest, to be one of the last places in the empire that a religion originating in the eastern Mediterranean would reach.

The church in Britain grew slowly. There is little record of persecution, probably because the British church was too small and weak for the Roman government to bother with. There is archaeological evidence of small churches and villas with rooms specifically dedicated to Christian worship by the fourth century. The British church was sufficiently organized to send bishops to a Gallic synod in 314. British Christians mostly escaped the last and most severe Roman persecution of Christianity, which took place under the Emperor Diocletian (r. 284–305) in the late third and early fourth centuries. Diocletian had divided the empire administratively into four parts, and the junior emperor who governed Britain and Gaul, Constantius I Chlorus (r. 293–305), was married to a Christian and kept the persecution out of his area.

As elsewhere in the empire, British Christianity was originally strongest in the cities. It began to attract rural landowners after Emperor Constantine the Great (r. 324—337) made it the official religion of the Roman Empire in the early fourth century, and it affected the rural lower classes last. Constantine, the son of Constantius, was actually first proclaimed emperor in 306 in the Romano-British city of Eboracum, later known as York. Constantine was treated as a British figure by medieval British historical writers for this reason.

Unlike every other religion of the Greco-Roman world, Christianity was theologically intolerant. However, while this is true on a theoretical level, in practice some people seem to have regarded themselves as Christians while making sacrifices to the old gods. The church eventually stamped out most of these practices, but it took several centuries. Paganism proved to be a tough plant in Britain, and there is evidence of new pagan temples being built as late as the 380s. Pagan cult centers remained in use into the fifth century, and a small-scale and localized practice of pagan cults by the rural population could have persisted for a long time. But the disruption of British life in the late fourth century by wars between Roman leaders and increased piracy meant that many pagan temples were sacked or abandoned, and others were deliberately destroyed by Christians. This is a very poorly documented period in

British history, and the rise of Christianity and decline and eventual end of British paganism is difficult to see in other than very broad outline.

The Church after Rome

The church survived the end of Roman power in Britain. British church-men continued to study classical writers, the Bible, and the major Latin Christian writers even after the Roman state left the island. There is no evidence of a hierarchy among the British bishops or an overall head of the church in Britain, although like bishops everywhere, the British bishops had councils and some form of loose association.

The most remarkable developments in British Christian history in the late fourth and early fifth centuries are the rise of vivid and influential Christian personalities and the beginnings of an evangelistic mission to the rest of the British Isles. Two of the most important personalities, and the most contrasting, were the heretic Pelagius (ca. 354–ca. 420) and the missionary Patricius (ca. 390–ca. 460).

The Pelagian heresy is the first movement in the history of ideas that can be identified with Britain. Pelagius himself is a mysterious figure; the details of his life, including the time and place of his birth and death, remain unknown. Even his ideas are mostly known to us from the writings of his enemies, notably the great North African bishop Augustine of Hippo (354–430). Pelagius was born and received his initial education in Britain, from which he went to seek his fortune and further education in Rome and the Middle East. Pelagianism is identified as the idea that salvation can be achieved by cooperating with God, usually by practicing some form of extreme self-denial or asceticism. Pelagius was convinced that the mainstream Christian belief that humans were innately sinful, and thus wholly reliant on God's grace for salvation, was breeding a dangerous moral laxity. He argued that God requires perfection, and that human beings do have the ability to be perfect. Pelagianism was rejected by the mainstream church as an infringement on the power of God and a denial of original sin. It was also denounced in an imperial decree in 418. Britain, outside the rapidly waning power of the Roman emperor, was the last place where the original Pelagians held out, causing dissension among the British bishops. There is a claim that Pelagianism was eventually suppressed in the 420s by the intervention of some of the orthodox bishops of Gaul, either sent by the pope or invited by orthodox Britons. Pelagian ideas continued to influence the West for about another century. As late as the mid-seventh century a pope accused the Irish church of Pelagianism. However, as the British church grew more isolated and its leadership less learned in the decades following the Roman withdrawal, these kinds of theological disputes became much less important.

Patricius is better known as St. Patrick, the apostle of Ireland. It is difficult to disentangle his life from the layers and layers of legend in which it is wrapped, much of which portrays him as a traditional Irish hero fighting monsters; driving snakes out of Ireland; and having contests with gods, magicians, and druids. Patricius's few surviving writings include no dates and refer to no verifiable historical events in this very obscure period of British history. Fortunately, he did write a short autobiography, which is the principal source for his life.

The name *Patricius* is Roman, and Patricius was a Christian Briton from the urban aristocracy who had survived the fall of Roman power in Britain. He was the son and grandson of priests, and his autobiography mentions this fact as if it were something normal. This is one piece of evidence that the British church had not adopted the doctrine of priestly celibacy that was being promoted in the Latin Mediterranean. The young Patricius was kidnapped by Irish pirates, taken to Ireland, and enslaved as a herdsman. While a slave, he underwent an intense spiritual experience and decided that God had commanded him to escape, which he managed to do with great difficulty. He vowed to spread the faith to the pagan Irish (there was probably already a Christian community in Ireland at this time, but pagans dominated). On his return to Britain, Patricius received religious training involving dogma and the Bible rather than higher education, and he was ordained as a priest and bishop. He returned to Ireland, probably in the 420s, and spread the Christian religion there, ordaining clergy and setting up monasteries and convents.

Christianity was also spread to the pagan Celts and Picts of the north by the semilegendary St. Ninian, the apostle of Scotland, a contemporary of Patricius about whose life even less is known than that of Pelagius or Patricius. In all likelihood, there was already some development of a Christian culture among the tribes of the north in direct contact with the Roman province. The son of British chieftains, Ninian was a Briton educated in Rome and, like many of the Christian missionaries of this time, a monk. His effort took place at the beginning of the conversion of the peoples of northern Britain, but this was a protracted process, most of which would be carried out not by Britons but by monastic missionaries from Ireland in the sixth century.

The British church was unusual among early medieval Western Christian churches, and certainly very different from the Irish church, in that monks and monasteries played only a minor role. The earliest firm references to British monasticism date from the mid-sixth century. The British episcopal-based church continued in the fifth and sixth centuries, with relatively little contact with Christianity outside the British Isles. The British church was not totally isolated, of course, and the British adopted the Roman system for assigning a date to Easter, a very contentious issue in the early church. Christianity gave the British a strong sense of identity in relation to the pagan peoples of northern Europe, an identity that in many ways took the place of a Roman identity that was no longer possible as the ties that had bound Britain to Rome fell away in the fifth century.

Britain after Rome

The period between the Roman withdrawal around 410 and the rise of the Anglo-Saxon kingdoms in the late sixth century is one of the shadowiest in British history. This period is currently referred to as sub-Roman.

The collapse of central Roman authority in Britain after 410 was preceded by years of weakening Roman military presence as usurpers took British armies to the Continent, and the central government withdrew troops from the remote island to use elsewhere closer to home. Landowners' loyalty to Rome was challenged by resentment of the taxation of their agricultural wealth and the loss of agricultural manpower to conscription. The Roman state was a parasite, draining men and wealth from the island while failing, or not even trying, to defend it from Picts, Irish, and Saxons. Into the gap stepped the local Celtic-Roman aristocracy.

Britain's upper class in many ways continued to identify itself as Roman, but the Roman Empire had become a hindrance in maintaining a Roman life. (Some links between Britain and the empire remained, and the Britons asked for support from the Western Roman Empire, then in its last throes, as late as the 440s, but they received none.) Romano-British landowners were in a better position to defend the island than Roman commanders and bureaucrats hoping to leave it for more civilized parts as quickly as possible. Southern Britain was also facing a fundamentally different type of outside threat than Roman continental Europe. It was dealing not with large armies or migrating peoples but with smaller groups coming from northern Britain or across the sea.

The British aristocracy, the one most recently incorporated into the empire of western Romans, seems to have maintained more of an inde-

23

pendent military tradition than Roman gentry elsewhere. The British pattern of independent landowners taking up defense against barbarians was unique in the empire. It is possible that the Pelagian idea of attaining salvation by one's own actions could have influenced people to political action as well, and also that Pelagians would have felt less loyalty to the orthodox empire. However, Pelagianism appears to have disappeared shortly after the Roman withdrawal.

There is little written evidence for the sub-Roman period. The British economy may have initially benefited from the Roman withdrawal as the tax burden shrank. However, the overall economy of post-Roman Britain seems to have slowly declined. Coins were no longer produced after the Roman withdrawal or even used much after the 430s. The coins that have been found from this period were minted on the Continent and treated by Britons as treasure rather than as a medium of exchange. Britain ran on a mixture of coins and an increasingly dominant barter economy, but it was not economically isolated as relations with the Mediterranean world continued. The tin trade and some other industrial production for export went on, and Mediterranean pottery has been found in archaeological sites from this period. There is evidence of the continuing importation of wine, olive oil, and other Mediterranean goods. However, continuing trends under the later empire, there was a general decline of urban life. Many Roman cities were abandoned, and there was an almost immediate switch from stone to the far cheaper wood as the main building material. In some places, the bulk of the city was abandoned, but a smaller population regrouped in the amphitheater, which was easily convertible into a fortress. This was not true everywhere. There were also other surviving cities where the empire's town councillors and their descendants maintained civic life, with a public treasury and the upkeep of waterworks. Another alternative was the revival of the hill forts of the Celtic period, largely abandoned by the Romans but now offering the attraction of defensibility.

Roman identity proved stubborn. Patricius, writing in the mid-fifth century decades after the withdrawal of Rome, continued to think of himself and his British countrymen as Roman. Although there was no Britain-wide institution taking the place of the Roman government other than the church, a British identity persisted. This was expressed in Latin with the word *cives,* or citizen, and in Celtic with various terms such as *combrogi,* or co-brothers. Britons saw themselves as a civilized and Christian people under constant threat from Irish, Pictish, and Saxon barbarians. There is little evidence of a revival of the Celtic tribal identities of pre-Roman Britain, and there was certainly no pan-Celtic identity—the Celtic Irish and Picts were as much the enemy of the Britons as were the Germanic Saxons (not to mention the wars between the Irish of Scotland, called the Scots, and the Picts). Patricius saw the Picts and Scots as evil and iniquitous, and he condemned a British king who enslaved Irish Christians for behaving like them. However, the disappearance of the Roman government and Britain's isolation from Mediterranean centers of culture eventually took its toll. As Britain became steadily less Roman in culture, Latin died out as a spoken language outside the church.

British identity was not reflected in political union or even the desire for such. Local territories became more politically important as the period saw a slow evolution from a dominant urban and landowning class through warlords whose power rested on effective force to dynastic kingship. For most of the sixth century, the British continued to hold most of the old Roman province, waging a slow, fighting retreat in the face of pressure from the Germanic Anglo-Saxons, while Anglo-Saxons and Britons also fought among themselves.

2

ANGLO-SAXONS, SCOTS, AND VIKINGS (CA. 450–CA. 850)

From the middle of the fifth to the end of the sixth century, a new culture established its domination over most of Britain outside Wales, the far southwest, and the north. These were the Anglo-Saxons, originally a group of Germanic peoples from the European continent. Around the same time, the Scots, originally a group of Irish immigrants, were settling in what became Scotland. These two cultures, both of which would adopt Christianity, became the foundation for what would be the dominant kingdoms of Britain—England and Scotland. The centuries after the Roman withdrawal were also marked by a distinct insular culture. This makes them different from both the prior Roman period and the period after the Norman conquest in 1066, when British culture was much more integrated into the European mainstream.

The peoples of Britain were then challenged by another invasion— that of the Scandinavians or Vikings. The Vikings would bring Britain into their world of raiding and trading and add to the cultural mix of Britain's peoples.

Anglo-Saxon Settlement and Expansion

The traditional date for the first settlement of the Anglo-Saxons in Britain is 449. According to legend, this was not an invasion but a response to an invitation by a Celtic ruler named Vortigern. If this story has any grain of truth, it is probably an example of the late Roman policy of encouraging Germanic groups to settle and defend the land they settled on against other Germanics. Legend also states that the first Anglo-Saxon leaders to arrive were named Hengist and Horsa. The Anglo-Saxons were originally concentrated in the eastern parts of

Britain, adjacent to the North Sea. The indigenous people, the Britons, lost control over much of eastern and southern Britain in the second half of the fifth century, but they retained extensive areas elsewhere in Britain until around 600.

Anglo-Saxon society and culture were less influenced by Rome and the Mediterranean than those of other Germanic peoples, such as the Franks of France or the Ostrogoths of Italy, because they were from northern Germany and Denmark rather than the southern regions that had prolonged contact with the Roman Empire. One Anglo-Saxon poem, "The Wanderer," refers to cities, meaning Roman cities, as the work of giants. The Anglo-Saxons were originally pagan in religion. The main group that originated on the North Sea coast of Europe was divided into Angles, Saxons, and Jutes, but some also came from other Germanic groups, as tribal affiliations were loose at this time.

Britain was one of the few areas of the former Western Roman Empire where Germanic speakers entirely displaced Roman or Romanized culture. The best evidence for this is language. Whereas France, Spain, and other areas speak Romance languages descended from Latin, English is largely a Germanic language. The Anglo-Saxon takeover led to the creation of a new British society, "England," spreading from the east and southeast of the island and closely integrated into a Germanic world. The greatest classic of Anglo-Saxon literature, the epic poem *Beowulf*, which was probably composed in Northumbria in the first half of the eighth century, sets its story of heroic monster killing not among Anglo-Saxons but among the equally Germanic Danes.

On a demographic level, many Britons, particularly women, were assimilated into the Anglo-Saxon people by marriage, enslavement, or adoption of Anglo-Saxon culture. Some of the earliest figures in Anglo-Saxon history are hard to place as either Anglo-Saxons or Britons. Cerdic (r. 519–534), the founder of the royal house of Wessex—which would later develop into the Kingdom of England—had a British name but is described by Anglo-Saxon writers centuries later as an Anglo-Saxon invader. The Anglo-Saxon takeover took two centuries, slowed by both British resistance and the limited numbers of Anglo-Saxons who could arrive by ship. The Anglo-Saxon invasions were more a matter of small groups of settlers than vast armies. Most battles in Britain during this period involved fewer than a thousand people on either side. Battles were also fought on a low matériel level; the archaeological evidence shows that the principal weapon of ordinary Anglo-Saxon warriors was the spear, as only the elite could afford enough metal to make a sword. Anglo-Saxon armies were mostly infantry, as few could afford expensive warhorses.

The early Anglo-Saxons were a warrior culture that valued men for their courage and skill in battle, as reflected in Anglo-Saxon literature. They were organized—particularly in the early stages when they entered Britain as mercenary soldiers or pirates—into bands of warriors who followed chieftains. One of the marks of a successful early Anglo-Saxon leader was his generosity to his warrior followers. Great leaders were called ring-givers, after the gold rings they gave their followers. The weapons of war—swords, spears, and shield—were highly valued, and the weapons of the elite were often richly decorated. Anglo-Saxon wills frequently mention weapons and refer to their history and previous owners.

The earliest Anglo-Saxon leaders saw themselves as leaders of peoples rather than as territorial rulers. The following of a successful war leader would increase as his military success and generosity attracted more and more warriors to his banner. Some of the most successful would take the title of king, but none were powerful enough to rule Britain or England as a whole.

Celtic culture remained strong in several areas of the old Roman province of Britannia. One was the far southwest, in Cornwall and the Isles of Scilly, where speakers of Cornish—fisherfolk and tin miners—retained cultural and some political independence. Another was the mountainous region of Wales. The term *Welsh* derives from an Anglo-Saxon word meaning "foreigner," and the Welsh principalities retained their independence and a distinct Celtic culture and literature. Their own term for themselves was *Brythoniaid*, "Britons," which was gradually replaced by *Cymry*, "the people." Despite the persistence of a common identity, Wales's poor internal communications meant that political authority remained fragmented. A British state in the north of Strathclyde lasted until the 11th century, when it was absorbed by the rising Scottish monarchy. Some Britons also fled to the far northwestern peninsula of modern France, which eventually became known as Brittany.

Anglo-Saxon Culture

The pagan religion of the early Anglo-Saxons was marked by a strong sense of fatalism and doom, but Anglo-Saxons also believed that humans could manipulate supernatural forces through spells and charms. They worshipped the same gods as other pagan Germanic peoples, and many of the royal houses boasted of descent from Woden, chief of the gods. The Anglo-Saxons were oriented not to an afterlife, although they may have believed in one, but to glory. The hero of *Beowulf* stated: "Each of us must experience an end to life in this world; let him who can achieve glory before he die, that will be best for the lifeless warrior afterward" (quoted in Whitelocke 1952, 27).

The Anglo-Saxons strongly valued family ties; the kinless man was an object of pity. If an Anglo-Saxon was killed, it was the duty of his or her family to attain either vengeance or a monetary payment, known as *wergild*, from the killer. *Wergilds* varied by social class and gender. Kinship practices differed from those of the Christian British. One example, which horrified Christians, was that the Anglo-Saxons allowed a man to marry his stepmother on his father's death. (This helped keep property in the family.) Anglo-Saxons were also able to divorce, a practice forbidden by the church. Even after the Anglo-Saxons became Christian, the church had little influence over their marriage practices.

As it stabilized, Anglo-Saxon society was divided into roughly three main social classes under the kings. At the top were the thanes, or as they were called in Kent, the earls. They held a specified quantity of land, usually five hides. The hide was a measure that varied by region, but it basically referred to the amount of land necessary to support a family. A single hide in the Midlands could cover 120 acres, while the same unit in Wessex was about half that.

The next class were the churls, a term that later denoted a rude countryman but in Anglo-Saxon times referred to an independent freeman who owned less than a thane did. The churl's wergild might be as little as one-sixth of the thane's. As Anglo-Saxon society developed, the position of churls deteriorated as they became more dependent on thanes.

Slaves comprised the third class. They had no wergilds, although if a slave was killed by a person other than the owner, compensation was owed as in other cases of the destruction of property. Slaves had certain rights to be supported, and the church generally promoted humane treatment of slaves and even their manumission. Some slaves were descendants of the indigenous Britons, while others were prisoners of war or persons forced to sell themselves into slavery out of hunger. Some crimes were punishable by enslavement, and the children of a slave were also slaves.

There were major cultural differences between the Britons and the Anglo-Saxons, particularly religious differences. British Christians despised Anglo-Saxon paganism; one of the very few British Christian writers whose works survive, the monk and historian Gildas (ca. 516–570), spoke of the sins of the Britons in inviting pagan mercenaries to the island, calling them "the ferocious Saxons (name not to be spoken) hated by man and God" (quoted in Snyder 1998, 249). The Anglo-Saxons reciprocated this dislike and added contempt for British weakness—the word for "Briton" eventually became the word for "slave."

Despite these prejudices and cultural differences, as Britain increasingly fragmented and memory of Roman unity faded, British and Anglo-Saxon values converged. British culture and society became more warrior-dominated, and eventually the Anglo-Saxons converted to Christianity. Anglo-Saxon art influenced British art, and Anglo-Saxon objects have been found in British graves from shortly after the first Anglo-Saxon landings.

The Irish in the North

The fall of Rome was also followed by great changes in the north beyond the Roman province. The Picts of the north faced challenges similar to those faced by the Britons. While the first Anglo-Saxons were settling in eastern Britain, a similar process of Irish settlement was taking place in Wales and the north. The Irish in Wales were eventually driven out or absorbed into the Welsh population, but the Irish of the north, known as Scots, would have a far greater impact. The kingdom of Dál Riata in the west of Scotland held land on both sides of the Irish Sea from the mid-sixth to the mid-seventh century. By the ninth century their settlements would form the kingdom of the *Scots,* a word that at that time meant "Irish." There was also the kingdom of Alt Clut, or Strathclyde, in the Clyde River valley, a British kingdom that survived Anglo-Saxon assaults and only finally disappeared by the 11th century.

There was a long history of conflict between the peoples of north Britain—Picts had raided northern British communities, and the Britons regarded the Picts with nearly as much loathing as they did the Anglo-Saxons—but there were also forces uniting these disparate peoples. Increasingly prominent among them was Christianity, a religion that would eventually include the Anglo-Saxons as well.

From Britannia to England

By the seventh century the Anglo-Saxons dominated lowland Britain, which was both more valuable than the highlands and easier to conquer. This meant they controlled the more economically prosperous areas, giving them a long-term advantage over the remaining Britons in the highlands of Wales and the north.

There were both continuities and discontinuities between the post-Roman period and the Anglo-Saxon arrival. The deurbanization that had begun in the late empire continued, and many Roman foundations were abandoned. However, others, including London, survived with reduced populations. There was continuity in rural England. Not much land seems to have gone out of cultivation. The written text, which had been valued highly in the urban culture of the Roman period, was replaced in importance by the more portable arts of the bard and the goldsmith, both of whom ultimately served the Anglo-Saxon or British warchief. Unfortunately, both the oral epic and the gold amulet were highly perishable, and not much of either survives.

The victory of the Anglo-Saxons marks the beginning of the history of the English people and language and the establishment of a unique culture in England and lowland Scotland differentiating itself from the speakers of Celtic languages in other parts of the British archipelago. The English are not purely, or even primarily, of Anglo-Saxon descent. Anglo-Saxons intermixed with Britons and subsequent immigrants, but Anglo-Saxon language, tradition, and history have been fundamental to the shaping of a distinctively English people.

The Anglo-Saxon period also saw the basic development of English agriculture, and the amount of land under cultivation and the number of settlements did not change much between the 11th and 19th centuries. Basic agricultural techniques such as the use of the heavy plow were also established by Anglo-Saxons.

The Conversion of the Anglo-Saxons

The most important event of the first centuries of Anglo-Saxon Britain was the conversion of the Anglo-Saxons to Christianity. Initially there seems to have been little interest on the part of the Christian Britons in converting the Anglo-Saxons. Some Britons were even reluctant to accept the Christianity of the Anglo-Saxons as genuine even after conversion. The religious dynamic in the first Anglo-Saxon century may have actually gone the other way, with Christian Britons converting to Anglo-Saxon paganism as part of their assimilation into the dominant Anglo-Saxon community.

The conversion of the northern Anglo-Saxons and many of the pagan Celtic peoples of the north was first taken up by the Irish, who had no particular grudge against the Anglo-Saxons. Anglo-Saxon England was merely one theater of the prodigious Irish missionary effort in the British archipelago and Europe during the sixth and seventh centuries. The traffic between Ireland and England was not one-way: There are records of Englishmen in Irish monasteries. Christianity spread from the great monastery of Iona, founded in the Hebrides by the great Irish monk and missionary Columba in 563. A Pictish king, Brude, was converted by Columba, and Iona also established numerous daughter houses as well as a position of providing spiritual guides to the kings of the Scots.

KING ARTHUR?

One of the most mysterious figures in British history is the legendary king named Arthur. Most historians agree that if there actually was a King Arthur, he was a leader of the British resistance to the Anglo-Saxons, which is how he appears in the earliest legends. The legend of Arthur may be based on someone for whom we have a little more evidence—an Ambrosius Aurelianus who was a successful leader against the Saxons in the fifth century and a man of Roman descent— but it is not even certain that Ambrosius existed. The earliest mention of Arthur is in passing in a Welsh poem, "Y Goddodin," supposedly dating from around 600, but the earliest surviving manuscript version is in a collection, the *Book of Aneirin,* dating from the 13th century, when the legend of Arthur was already firmly established. Merlin, the wizard, is also a legendary figure from the post-Roman period, although the stories associating the two come from later periods. Another legendary figure, Old King Cole, that "merry old soul" of the nursery rhyme, also seems to have been a post-Roman British king.

Tintagel in Cornwall is associated with the conception and birth of the legendary King Arthur. (Library of Congress, Photochrom Collection)

The second wave of conversion originated from the papacy in Rome and started in the southern part of the island, closest to the European continent. This was the first papal mission to a foreign land. Pope

Gregory the Great (ca. 540–604; pope, 590–604) had initially thought of going himself and then considered converting Anglo-Saxon slave boys in Italy to Christianity and sending them back to England. He ultimately rejected this plan on the grounds that it would take too long, and in 596 he sent Augustine (d. 604), a missionary of Greek origin and an experienced church leader.

In 597 Augustine landed in the small but relatively wealthy Anglo-Saxon kingdom of Kent in southeastern England. Kent was the area of England closest to Europe, and it had a long-standing relationship with the Frankish Christian kingdom of France. Augustine set up his mission in the chief Kentish city of Canterbury, revising Gregory's original plan that he make his headquarters in London; this had proved impossible because London was dominated by pagans. Augustine's choice had long-lasting historical consequences, as to this day the Church of England is headed by the archbishop of Canterbury. Augustine tried to enlist the cooperation of the leaders of the British church, who showed little interest in the mission. This may have been due to resentment of Augustine's pretensions to authority over all the bishops on the island. The British Christians of what would become Wales would long maintain their separation from the Roman mission.

Augustine succeeded in converting the king of Kent, Ethelbert (d. 616), whose wife Bertha was a daughter of the Christian French king Charibert. This set a precedent for the conversion of the English, which followed a top-down pattern. The key to the conversion of an Anglo-Saxon kingdom was the king, the queen, and the top nobles. A Christianized leadership would then support the missionary effort among the common people. Under a stubbornly pagan king, there was not much the missionaries could do other than wait for another king. Ethelbert was also the first Anglo-Saxon king to issue a written law code, with the help of Augustine. This was necessary because the church had no status in Anglo-Saxon custom and needed some form of institutional protection. Since the missionaries were foreigners with no families to protect them or take vengeance on those who would harm them, it was necessary for the king to declare himself their protector. Ethelbert's code differed from other European law codes of the period in that it was written in the vernacular language rather than Latin.

There was continuing contact between Augustine and Pope Gregory. Much of the correspondence between the two has been preserved, although given the difficulties of communication, Augustine was largely independent of papal supervision. There was discussion between them on issues such as pagan temples, which Gregory first thought should be destroyed but then decided should be reconsecrated as Christian sacred sites.

Christianity in its Roman form was particularly attractive to Anglo-Saxon rulers who wanted to strengthen links between their kingdoms and the more developed areas of the Continent. The conversion of Ethelbert occurred at a time of increasing political and economic ties between the Anglo-Saxon kingdoms and the Frankish monarchy of Gaul. There was some pagan resistance, particularly among the common people and in the extreme south, Sussex and the Isle of Wight. Some Anglo-Saxons were not converted until the middle of the eighth century, and some pagan customs held out for centuries. Christian Anglo-Saxon kings continued to trace their descent from the god Woden, and there was a constant struggle against such Anglo-Saxon customs as men marrying their widowed stepmothers in order to keep the property in the family. Conversion was not a steady process but saw many ups and downs, as when Ethelbert of Kent was succeeded by his pagan son.

The Irish and Roman missions met in Northumbria, the area north of the Humber River, an increasingly powerful kingdom in the early seventh century with an immensely checkered religious and political history. The kingdom had seen the succession of an Anglo-Saxon king, Edwin (616–632), converted by the Roman mission and defeated and killed by a British king, Cadwallon. After a brief interval of chaos, the next ruler was the Anglo-Saxon king Oswald (634–641), who had spent several years in Iona and was a pious follower of Irish Christianity. He was defeated and killed by a pagan Anglo-Saxon king of Mercia in central England, Penda, (d. 655) and was followed on the throne by his brother, Oswiu (641–654), also a Celtic Christian, under whom Anglo-Saxons trained by Irish missionaries started evangelizing the Midlands and Essex.

Although the Irish and Roman missions generally cooperated, there was a conflict between them centered on the issue of when to celebrate Easter. The differences between the two could cause all kinds of problems, as when some members of a family or community celebrated the Lenten fast while others of the same family or community celebrated the Easter feast at the same time. There were also minor issues such as differing tonsures: The Irish shaved the heads of clerics from ear to ear, leaving hair in the front and back, while the Romans shaved the entire head.

Northumbria settled the matter at the Synod of Whitby in 664. The convent of Whitby in East Yorkshire was an example of a unique institution in Anglo-Saxon Christianity. Founded in about 657, it combined a monastery of men and a nunnery of women under the overall control of the abbess. At the synod the Celtic side appealed to the alleged sanction of Saint John the apostle, always particularly reverenced by the Celts, and the tradition of the great Irish monk and missionary St. Columba in arguing for the Irish usages. The Romans, represented by one of the first Englishmen to go to Rome, argued for the Roman usages on the grounds that their authority was based on the universality of the Roman obedience and the primacy of Peter, doorkeeper of heaven and founder of the papacy. The victory of the Roman position in Northumbria, the central focus of Irish missionary effort among the Anglo-Saxons, was followed by its imposition on the whole of England by the archbishop of Canterbury. The English church became particularly devoted to the papacy, to which it credited its conversion. The British Christians of Wales, however, took more than a century to follow the English into the Roman customs, not falling into line until 768.

The Christian Church in Anglo-Saxon Britain

The period after Whitby was marked by a flowering of English Christianity and the first organization of an institution for all Anglo-Saxons, the English church. Much of this was due to the leadership of Archbishop Theodore of Tarsus (ca. 602–690), a Greek sent by Pope Vitalian (pope, 657–672) to be archbishop of Canterbury in 668, shortly after Whitby. Theodore was already an old man when he arrived in England, but he lived for another 20 years and was in good enough physical condition to undertake a tour of England shortly after his arrival.

Theodore slowly and carefully moved away from a system of a few big dioceses that were generally coextensive with a kingdom into a system of many smaller dioceses, each with a central town with good communications via rivers and Roman roads and well-defined borders. This was resisted by some of the English bishops of big dioceses, who feared the diminishment of their power and wealth, but Theodore was patient and successful. For example, he took advantage of a bishop's death and the resultant vacancy to split a diocese rather than try to do it under a sitting bishop. Theodore brought the bishops together in a series of synods that for the first time provided a meeting place for people from all the Anglo-Saxon lands. The first took place at Hertford, about 19 miles (31 km) north of London, in 673. The laws of the church put forward in the synods were the first legislation binding on all Anglo-Saxons. Theodore also tried to cut down on the mobility of clergy and monks and began to set up a system of parishes to bring Christianity and the power of the church into the villages.

The episcopate of the increasingly institutionalized English church originally included men from the Continent such as Romans and

Franks, but as it developed there was an increasing predominance of Anglo-Saxons. The Anglo-Saxon church's growing independence from outside forces, Irish or Roman, can be seen in the fact that it was now producing its own saints, albeit mostly from the upper classes. There was a growing cult of saints such as Cuthbert (d. 687), a monk and hermit who had an enormous following in the north of England. Christian literature in Anglo-Saxon also developed. One particularly moving Christian Anglo-Saxon poem was *The Dream of the Rood,* which recounts the Crucifixion from the point of view of the cross. Like many Germanic Christian works, it shows Christ as an epic hero.

Anglo-Saxon kings, queens, and nobles founded numerous monasteries, sometimes as charitable works and sometimes as places for their own retirement. (Some also retired to Rome to die in the holy city.) Monasticism in the Irish style, with its flamboyant individualism and asceticism, was slowly displaced by more moderate, anti-individualist Benedictine monasticism originating on the Continent and more closely identified with Rome. Benedictine monasticism had a greater emphasis on discipline and stability: Monks were forbidden to leave the monastery without the permission of the abbot, as opposed to the wanderings of the Irish. Whereas the Irish emphasized abstention from food, one monastery having a standard diet of herbs and water, Benedictines ate adequate although plain meals. They lived in large group rooms called dormitories as opposed to the individual cells of the Irish. This monastic style fit in well with the emphasis on stability characteristic of the English church after Theodore. The monks spread the Christian word to the people in the surrounding villages and provided the translations necessary for reaching the Anglo-Saxon–speaking people in the country.

The conversion led to the opening of England, until then a rather isolated culture, to a variety of foreign influences. One way this happened was pilgrimages. The first recorded Anglo-Saxon visitor to Rome was there in 653, and he was followed by thousands of others over the centuries. Since pilgrims traveled through France to get to Italy, pilgrimages also strengthened ties between France and Britain. Churchmen learned about the practices of other regions such as Gaul and Italy and came back to England eager to try them out. Glass windows in churches were introduced from the Continent in this way.

The Anglo-Saxons also joined the Irish in taking the Christian message abroad. The first target of Anglo-Saxon missionaries was Frisia, in the modern Low Countries, whose Germanic-speaking peoples had long-standing connections with England through trade. Anglo-Saxon missionaries also participated in the conversion of Germany.

The Northumbrian Renaissance and the
Flowering of Anglo-Saxon Christianity

The peak of intellectual culture among the Christian Anglo-Saxons occurred in the most unlikely of places. The Kingdom of Northumbria was an economically backward and primitive society, even compared to the rest of early medieval Europe. However, in the seventh and eighth centuries an astonishing flowering of culture and thought took place in the monasteries on this edge of Europe that had little effect on ordinary people or the secular world. Northumbrian monks benefited from the combination of Continental and Irish learning and from the labor resources of their houses. During this period, called the Northumbrian Renaissance, the region developed an accomplished Christian art, incorporating influences from Anglo-Saxon and Celtic art but also from foreign countries as far away as the Byzantine Empire, reflecting the increased openness of England to foreign influences that followed the conversion.

The foremost scholar of the Northumbrian Renaissance was Bede (672–735). He was a monk at Jarrow, a Northumbrian monastery

AN ENGLISH MISSIONARY:
ST. BONIFACE

The greatest representative of the English church on the Continent was the missionary Wynfrith, better known as St. Boniface (680–754). Wynfrith was born in the area where Wessex was expanding into the British territories of the West Country. He became a monk and began his efforts by assisting a Northumbrian missionary in an unsuccessful mission to the Frisians. Wynfrith then went to Rome to receive guidance from the pope. In Rome he received the name Boniface, meaning "doer of good." He made many missionary journeys into Germany, where he became known for converting large numbers of Germans and chopping down trees sacred to them, thus demonstrating the greater power of the Christian God he championed over the pagan gods who had failed to protect their sacred trees. Many English men and women later followed Boniface to Germany, where they exercised a strong influence on the development of the German church. Boniface also oversaw a reorganization of the Frankish church to bring it more firmly under papal control. He died a martyr, killed by angry pagans on another journey to Frisia. Boniface is the patron saint of Germany.

specifically founded as a stronghold of the Roman Christian tradition, although Irish influences remained strong in the region, particularly in the area of learning. Bede was the author of *Ecclesiastical History of the English People*, the principal source for the history of the early Anglo-Saxon people and Anglo-Saxon Christianity. The work is remarkable for its use of original documentation and critical evaluation of sources, although it also includes many miracle stories. Bede was a strong supporter of the Roman system of Easter dating, on which he wrote a technical treatise, but he paid tribute to the Irish missionaries. His writings were also important in the creation of a specifically English identity. *Ecclesiastical History* is organized around the concept of an English people transcending differences between the various Germanic tribes and the divisions of the Anglo-Saxon kingdoms, but opposed to the British, whom Bede disliked. This sense of an English identity preceded the formation of a united English state by centuries. Bede also wrote a number of lives of saints, including that of Cuthbert, and of abbots, with the object of providing role models for the monks of his monastery. Although he never left Northumbria and only left his monastery twice after professing as a monk, Bede was one of the most widely learned and versatile scholars of the Middle Ages, writing on nature, cosmography, and the Bible, as well as history. He was one of the few in the West capable of reading the Bible in Greek. Bede's writings continued to be highly popular throughout the Middle Ages, surviving in dozens of manuscripts. He was particularly influential as an early user of the system of dating events from the supposed date of the birth of Christ—the Christian Era.

One of the northern English figures Bede discusses in *Ecclesiastical History* is the herdsman Caedmon, the first poet in English whose work survives. Caedmon was a lay brother at the Abbey of Whitby, probably in the late seventh century. Bede describes Caedmon as divinely inspired to compose religious poetry (and only religious poetry) in a dream. The name *Caedmon* is of Celtic origin, although Bede insists that English was Caedmon's native tongue. There is little evidence for Caedmon outside Bede, and only one of his works survives, supposedly the first poem he ever composed, a nine-line hymn of praise to God the creator. It is one of the oldest surviving pieces of poetry in Anglo-Saxon or in any Germanic language.

Despite the importance of the renaissance there, Northumbria was not the only place where Christian culture reached a high point in the seventh and eighth centuries. Another area was also a frontier: the West Country, where the Anglo-Saxon kingdom of Wessex was encroaching on the British territories of Devon and Cornwall. Wessex, Northumbria, and the Kingdom of Mercia in central and southern England were the dominant Anglo-Saxon kingdoms of the time. Kent was still the headquarters of the archbishop of Canterbury but had become a political and religious backwater after Theodore.

The Reign of King Offa

King Offa (r. 757–796) of Mercia became one of the most powerful of Anglo-Saxon kings, referred to in later records by the title Rex Anglorum, or king of the English, although those documents dating from Offa's own time call him king of the Mercians. He built on the achievements of previous Mercian kings such as Aethelbald (r. 716–757), who had established control of London and the strategic center of England. Like many rulers in those dangerous times, Offa came to power after a civil war. Quickly consolidating power in Mercia, Offa extended his suzerainty to Sussex and Kent, and after a series of wars he established a loose overlordship over Wessex, marrying one of his daughters to its king. Although he was never able to dominate Northumbria as he did the southern kingdoms, Offa also established a marriage between another daughter and a king of Northumbria.

Offa corresponded as an equal with the great Frankish king Charlemagne (742–814; r. 768–814), although their relationship was often tense and enemies of Offa found hospitality at Charlemagne's court. His coinage reached a height in terms of artistic quality for Anglo-Saxon currency and exceeded that of contemporary Frankish rulers. It is

Offa was one of the few Anglo-Saxon rulers to mint gold coins. These coins closely imitate contemporary Islamic models, including Arabic lettering. (© British Museum/Art Resource, NY)

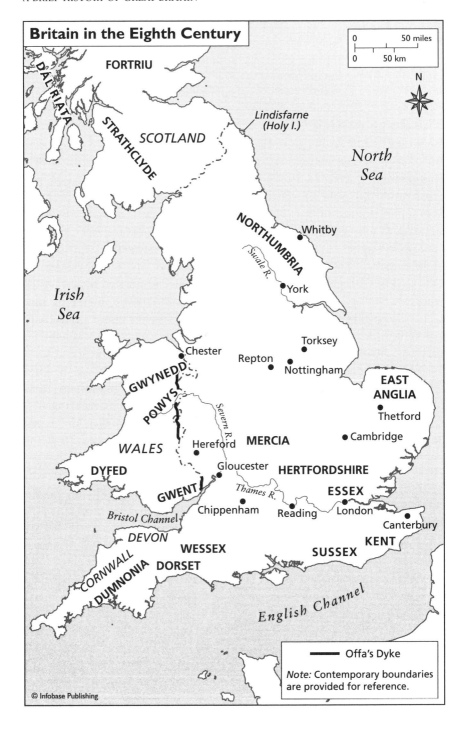

Britain in the Eighth Century

0 — 50 miles
0 — 50 km

N

FORTRIU

DALRIATA

STRATHCLYDE

SCOTLAND

Lindisfarne
(Holy I.)

North
Sea

NORTHUMBRIA

Whitby

Swale R.

York

Irish
Sea

Chester

Torksey

Repton

Nottingham

GWYNEDD

POWYS

EAST
ANGLIA

Thetford

Severn R.

Hereford

MERCIA

Cambridge

WALES

DYFED

Gloucester

HERTFORDSHIRE

GWENT

Thames R.

ESSEX

London

Bristol Channel

Chippenham

Reading

Canterbury

DEVON

WESSEX

KENT

CORNWALL

DUMNONIA

DORSET

SUSSEX

English Channel

—— Offa's Dyke

Note: Contemporary boundaries
are provided for reference.

© Infobase Publishing

remarkable for several reasons. Offa's is the only Anglo-Saxon coinage to depict a queen, his consort Cynethryth (d. after 798). He is also one of the few Anglo-Saxon rulers to mint surviving gold coins. The dominant currency of Anglo-Saxon England was the silver penny known as the *sceatta*, and Offa's gold coins were probably minted for foreign trade or tribute rather than circulation. They are modeled on the dinar minted by the Abbasid caliphs of Baghdad, the dominant economic power in western Eurasia at the time. One includes Arabic lettering, of whose significance the moneyer would have had no knowledge.

Offa's most enduring historical achievement was Offa's Dyke, a gigantic earthwork roughly establishing the border between England and Wales. He fought several wars with Welsh rulers, and the dyke may have been part of a shift to a defensive strategy or part of a negotiated settlement. It was a massive undertaking, the greatest public work of the entire Anglo-Saxon period, with a deep trench on the Welsh side next to a bank at some points reaching eight feet high on the Mercian. The dyke did not cover the entire border but extended for about 64 miles (103 kilometers). There are other defensive earthworks along the border, but their relationship to Offa's Dyke is unknown. Although today's border between Wales and England does not exactly follow the line of the dyke, it became a physical and cultural marker of the division between England and Wales. Offa died in 796; his England did not long survive him.

The Coming of the Scandinavians

Beginning in the late eighth century, the British Isles were one of the many areas in Europe hit by a new force, the Scandinavian peoples called Vikings. The term *Viking* denotes a profession or activity rather than an ethnic group; it essentially means "sea raider." The Scandinavians initially came in search of loot and slaves, both for personal exploitation and for sale in the active Mediterranean slave markets.

The Scandinavians were divided into three main groups: Swedes, Danes, and Norwegians. Danes and Norwegians were the most prominent in Britain. Danes led the invasion of England, while Norwegians led the invasions of Ireland and Scotland. The situation was complicated by the fact that England and Wales were also raided by Norwegians based in Ireland. While different groups of Vikings often competed, they were similar enough that the British peoples did not usually distinguish between them. The English collectively referred to the invaders

A ninth-century Viking ship (Werner Forman/Art Resource, NY)

as Danes whether they were Danes or Norwegians since the Danes were the initial leaders in attacks on southeastern England.

Part of the broad group of Germanic peoples, the Scandinavians had many cultural, religious, and linguistic similarities to the pagan Anglo-Saxons, although their languages were not initially mutually comprehensible. Their tradition of fishing in the North Sea and North Atlantic led to the development of good ships and seafaring skill. The so-called dragon ships, long and narrow, carried only about 30–60 men apiece, but the Scandinavians were able to exploit a principal military weakness of the British peoples and, indeed, Western Christian powers generally—their lack of sea power. The British, used to trade and invasion across the relatively narrow seas of the English Channel, the southern North Sea, and the Irish Sea, were shocked by the Scandinavians' ability to sail directly across the North Sea.

Although Scandinavians were the nucleus of the Viking bands, they were often joined by runaway slaves or outlaws from English or Celtic society. The Vikings were able to sail rivers as well as seas and use horses for transportation, although they preferred to fight on foot. Their mobility made it difficult to concentrate the forces of the Anglo-

THE ANGLO-SAXON CHRONICLE ON THE FIRST SCANDINAVIAN INVASIONS

*T*he *Anglo-Saxon Chronicle* was an account of Anglo-Saxon history kept in monasteries from the ninth century. It incorporated much earlier material and gave a Christian view of Anglo-Saxon history. The following passage associates the coming of the Scandinavians, described in religious terms as *heathens*, with dire consequences.

> *An. DCC.XCIII. In this year dire forewarnings came over the land of the Northumbrians, and miserably terrified the people: these were excessive whirlwinds and lightnings, and fiery dragons were seen flying in the air. A great famine soon followed these tokens; and a little after that, in the same year, on the vith of the Ides of January (Jan. 8th), the havoc of heathen men miserably destroyed God's church at Lindisfarne, through rapine and slaughter. . . .*

> *An. DCC.XCIV. In this year pope Adrian and king Offa died; and Jethelred, king of the Northumbrians, was slain by his own people, on the xiiitth of the Kal. of May (Apr. 19th); and bishop Ceolwulf and bishop Eadbald departed from the land; and Ecgferth succeeded to the kingdom of the Mercians, and died the same year. And Eadberht succeeded to the kingdom in Kent, whose other name was Praen. And the aldorman Aethelheard died on the Kal. of August (Aug. 1st). And the heathens ravaged among the Northumbrians, and plundered Ecgferth's monastery at Donemuth (Wearmouth); and there one of their leaders was slain, and also some of their ships were wrecked by a tempest, and many of them were there drowned, and some came to shore alive, and they were forthwith slain at the mouth of the river.*

Source: *The Anglo-Saxon Chronicle According to the Several Original Authorities.* 2 vols. Edited and translated by Benjamin Thorpe (London: Longman, 1861), 2:48–49.

Saxon kingdoms against them. Anglo-Saxon and other British military forces were mostly independent farmers serving as soldiers part-time, and they were not as committed or as skillful as the Scandinavian professional warriors.

The Scandinavian impact on Britain took place in three phases. At the end of the eighth century, it began with smash-and-grab Viking raids by single ships or small groups of ships. Viking attacks were made by fairly small bands of a thousand warriors at the most. The most noteworthy of these early raids, often treated as the beginning of the Viking phase in British history, was the savage attack on the monastery of Lindisfarne, on the coast of Northumbria, by three Viking ships in 793. Then, beginning in the mid-ninth century, the Scandinavians formed larger groups for bigger projects; a fleet of 350 ships arrived on the Thames near London in 851. They developed permanent bases, began to winter over in England, and sometimes even formed small kingdoms. The last phase was the invasion by military forces of Scandinavian kings, both Danish and Norwegian. This led to an entanglement of Scandinavian and British politics that lasted until the late 11th century in England and into the 15th century in Scotland.

The first recorded encounter between Scandinavians and English took place around 790, when a small group of Scandinavians who had landed in Dorset killed the royal emissaries sent to find out who they were. The Viking attacks, like those of the early Anglo-Saxons, initially focused on eastern and northern Britain, the areas closest to the North Sea. They sacked and temporarily ruled London and Canterbury, even killing an archbishop of Canterbury as well as several Anglo-Saxon kings. They had their greatest effects in the north. The Scandinavian invasions marked the end of the Northumbrian Renaissance, as well as the kingdom of Northumbria. Northumbria became a land of constant warfare between Britons, Scots, Danes, Norwegians, and Anglo-Saxons. Many scholars from Northumbria and elsewhere in the British Isles fled to the court of Charlemagne in Aachen, contributing to the revival of learning known as the Carolingian Renaissance.

Having resisted conversion to Christianity, the Vikings sacked and looted monasteries and churches; killed and enslaved monks and priests; and killed, raped, and enslaved nuns. Monasteries were particularly attractive targets to early Viking raiders since they were usually unfortified and full of precious things that had been donated by kings, queens, and other wealthy and pious Christians. They also contained populations that could be enslaved or ransomed, as well as saints' relics, which could be sold for large sums. Vikings raided famous monasteries, including Iona, which they first attacked in 795 and returned to on several occasions thereafter, in addition to Lindisfarne. These raids were particularly shocking to the British Christians as they usually respected the property and personnel of the church and the saints in their wars with each other. Since the surviving sources on the Scandinavian invasions are almost entirely monastic in origin, they place a heavy emphasis on the devastation the Vikings wrought. In many areas the Viking attacks meant the destruction of monastic life, and British monasticism would later have to be restarted virtually from scratch. But despite their love of sacking sacred treasuries, the Vikings had no interest in persecuting Christians. Some bishops and archbishops were willing to work with Scandinavian leaders, who after all were not much more uncivilized than the Anglo-Saxon and British monarchs with whom the church was already working. At the end of the Viking occupation of an area, church estates were generally better off than secular estates.

Despite their alienness and violence, the Scandinavians could be incorporated into the existing political system through alliances. There were alliances between groups of Britons and Vikings against the Anglo-Saxon kingdoms, and Anglo-Saxons also collaborated with the invaders when it suited their purposes.

In England, Scandinavians from Denmark settled mostly in the north and northwest, the area of the old kingdom of Northumbria. However, the areas of the British Isles where Scandinavian culture would have the most long-term impact were the western and northern islands—including the Shetlands, Hebrides, and the Isle of Man—which were settled by Scandinavians from Norway. The Viking-founded lordship of Man, centered on the Isle of Man and including the Hebrides, was an independent power under the distant overlordship of the Norwegian kings until 1266, when the Scots took it over. Orkney and Shetland remained under Norway until the 15th century. The areas taken over were originally in the form of large estates, but the disruptions of the various wars between the Anglo-Saxons and the Scandinavians and different groups of Scandinavians led to fragmentation and the emergence of a freer peasantry.

The Vikings had the least impact in Wales, a relatively poor country with little to attract looters and whose mountain fastnesses were difficult for Scandinavian bands to attack. The principal Viking assaults on Wales did not come directly from Scandinavia but from the Scandinavian communities of eastern Ireland and the smaller British islands. Scandinavian mercenaries also served the Welsh kings, and Scandinavian traders bought slaves and grain from the Welsh. Although there is some evidence for the formation of small communities in Wales, there were no Welsh Scandinavian kingdoms as there were in England, Scotland, and Ireland.

The Scandinavian impact on England and lowland Scotland was particularly marked on language. Since both English and the Scandinavian tongues were part of the Germanic family of languages, the English adopted Scandinavian loanwords much more easily than did Celtic peoples, such as the Welsh. English was the language used to communicate between people speaking different Germanic tongues, and so over time English simplified its grammar, with less use of gender and case endings than other Germanic or European languages.

Alfred of Wessex and the Anglo-Saxon Recovery

The English recovery from the Viking invasions was led by King Alfred of Wessex (849–899). Alfred was the youngest brother of the Anglo-Saxon royal family of Wessex; he inherited the throne in 871 after all his brothers died. Alfred himself saw many ups and downs over his career. At one point his power was reduced to rule of a small island. However, he fought an able guerrilla campaign and eventually managed to expel the Scandinavians from Wessex. His unification of much of southern and western England was facilitated both by his leadership of the struggle against the Vikings and by the fact that the Scandinavians had killed off all the other Anglo-Saxon royal families and disrupted the relatively stable multi-kingdom structure of early Anglo-Saxon England.

Alfred's achievements have made him the only monarch in English history given the title of *the Great*. He reorganized the army of Wessex to keep it in the field longer and set up a system of defended cities or burghs, eventually referred to as *boroughs* from the Germanic term for a fortified place. Alfred's plan required the local landowners to build and maintain the fortifications under strong central direction. His reign saw the beginning of the system of shires around boroughs, often based on a preexisting settlement. Roman walls were restored in some areas, and new walls built in others. Ideally, everyone was close enough to a burgh to have someplace to go when under attack. This led to increased royal support of markets as well. Alfred issued charters granting economic privileges to towns, such as the right to hold markets on specified occasions. Cities continued to be small. London was by far the largest with a population of about 10,000, while others were mostly between 2,000 and 3,000. Alfred also built a navy to defend Wessex.

Alfred was eventually accepted as king of the English, although he was not the ruler of all the land later to be known as England. He was the first king of the English as a people, as opposed to kings of particular English kingdoms, but his enlarged Wessex coexisted with an area of Danish settlement and rule in the northeast known as the Danelaw, covering the old kingdom of Northumbria in the north, east Anglia, and part of central England, where Danish customs held sway. In order for peace and mutual acceptance to occur between Danes and English, it was necessary for the Danish leader Guthrum (d. ca. 890) and his leading men to convert to Christianity. After Alfred's forces defeated Guthrum's in the battle of Ethandun (present-day Edington) in 878, they agreed on the bounds of their respective territories in the Treaty of Wedmore in 878 or 879. Guthrum agreed to become a Christian, and Alfred served as his godfather.

Alfred was a pious man who had gone on a pilgrimage to Rome as a boy and viewed kingship in a Christian context. He lamented the passing of the golden age of English Christianity. Alfred's efforts to attract scholars from Britain and the European continent to his court—such as the monk Grimbald and the Welsh monk Asser, who wrote the king's biography—and his own scholarship and translations of early Christian writings into Anglo-Saxon were attempts to revive the Christian culture of pre-Viking England. He also sponsored the translation of Bede's *Ecclesiastical History* and other works into Anglo-Saxon, and he promulgated a code of law. Alfred's reign saw the beginnings of *The Anglo-Saxon Chronicle,* a record of current events kept in Anglo-Saxon; eventually the chronicle would be kept at monasteries. The extensive use of the written vernacular language for scholarly and religious purposes in Alfred's England had very little parallel elsewhere in Europe, where Latin was the language of writing.

Alfred also attempted to restore English monasticism, but his newly founded monasteries were not very successful, possibly because the country, devastated by decades of raids and wars, was unable to support large religious houses. Alfred's patronage of men of letters also helped create his personal legend. Works speaking of Alfred's greatness were produced at his court by people who worked for him. Alfred's efforts, the political unification of the Anglo-Saxons, and the awareness of differences between Anglo-Saxons and Scandinavians would all contribute to the creation of a common Anglo-Saxon, or English, identity. Alfred's heirs worked out the political implications of the new English unity. However, the Anglo-Saxons located north of the old kingdom of Northumbria in present-day Scotland were separated by the Danelaw from the main body of Anglo-Saxons who were united under Alfred. The northern Anglo-Saxons were gradually and permanently drawn into the Kingdom of Scotland. In both England and Scotland, native resistance to Scandinavian invaders eventually forced territorial compromise; the integration of Scandinavian settlers and native populations; and stronger, centralized kingdoms.

3

SCOTLAND, ENGLAND, AND WALES (CA. 850-1272)

Out of the chaos of the Scandinavian invasions in the late first millennium came the political entities that would dominate British history into the early 18th century: the kingdoms of England and Scotland. In the 10th and 11th centuries the kingdoms and societies located between the English king in the south and the Scottish king in the north were squeezed out of existence. Only Wales and some of the islands remained outside the jurisdiction of the new monarchies. This process continued into the late 13th century, as the Scottish monarchs pushed back successfully against Scandinavian rule in the archipelago while the English rulers took over Wales. The new monarchies also moved out of the cultural and political orbit of Scandinavia and into that of the cultures across the English Channel, the most important being France.

England moved into France's political and cultural orbit when it was conquered by the duke of Normandy, a region of France, in 1066. The resulting entanglement of England and France would last for nearly five centuries and strongly affect the history of both countries.

The Founding of Scotland

Scotland was home to many peoples, including the Picts of the northeast, the Irish Scots in the west, the Britons of the old Kingdom of Strathclyde in the southwest, the Anglo-Saxons of north Northumbria, and some Scandinavians in the far north and on the islands. Geography made ethnic fragmentation inevitable as hill masses separated the main lowland areas and islands composed much of Scotland's land surface. Islands and coastal areas that survived by fishing looked outward to the sea rather than inward to the rest of Scotland. It took some time for the Scots to form a united state and identity. The key moment was the formation of the united Scottish-Pictish kingdom of Alba under Scandinavian pressure. The traditional date for the founding of the kingdom is 843, and the traditional founder is Kenneth MacAlpin (r. ca. 843–858), a Scottish king, although contemporary Irish records refer to him as "King of the Picts."

The Scottish element dominated Alba. Pictish identity faded, and by the late ninth century the name *Pict* had disappeared from the records. Scandinavian and English pressure drove the Strathclydians and north Northumbrian Saxons into the arms of the kings of Alba. Strathclyde gradually fades from the scattered records of early medieval Scottish history. The last known king of Strathclyde was Owen the Bald, who died in the early 11th century, although Strathclyde itself may have survived for a few more decades. The Scottish monarchy as finally formed had few central institutions, and the king wielded little power in many areas. Power was exercised in the periphery largely independent of the monarchy, and some regional leaders actually referred to themselves as kings.

The Scottish monarchy sought to preserve its independence from its neighbors to the south. The Scots supported the Scandinavians in the north of England as a buffer between themselves and the English Wessex kingdom. The English were not the only foreign kingdom the Scots had to deal with, though. Ties between the northern islands and Norway persisted for centuries. Much of the north and west retained its Norwegian connections and effective independence from Scotland until Norway ceded the western islands to Scotland in 1266. Large lordships under the king of Scotland were formed in the north in the 11th century to police the military frontier. These northern lords could grow powerful enough to challenge the throne itself, particularly as Scotland lacked a clear law of succession. The 11th-century border lord Macbeth (d. 1057) took and held the throne (1040–57), only to be driven out by Malcolm Canmore (ca. 1031–93), a rival claimant with English support. The Canmore dynasty subsequently moved to stricter hereditary succession and ruled Scotland until 1286.

Wales and Its Princes

While centralization was growing in England and Scotland, Wales, with its poverty and poor internal communications, remained politically fragmented. The main centers of power were the kingdoms of Gwynedd in the north, Powys in the center, and Deheubarth (formerly Dyfed) in the south. Political unity in Wales depended not on the building of institutions but on the short-term ascendancy of individual princes who faced not only Welsh rivals but Scandinavian raiders and expansionist Anglo-Saxons. The two most prominent makers of a unified Wales were a study in contrast: Hywel Dda ap Cadell (880–950) and Gruffydd ap Llywelyn (ca. 1007–63).

Hywel "the Good" was the founder of Deheubarth and ruler of all Wales except for the far southeast from 942 to 950. He was remembered in Welsh tradition as a wise, peaceful, and pious ruler who created a code of laws for Wales—the Laws of Hywel Dda—although subsequent Welsh writers probably exaggerated the extent to which Hywel was personally responsible for the laws. The sense of Welsh unity as it would develop over centuries when Welsh rulers were often at each other's throats would owe much to Welsh law. Hywel, a frequent visitor to the English court, generally remained at peace with the Anglo-Saxons and may have accepted the overlordship of the English king Athelstan (r. 924–939). He was one of the few Welsh rulers to have coins minted in his own name, although they were actually minted outside Wales in the English city of Chester. However, he failed to establish a unified kingdom, and after his death Wales quickly fell into chaos with renewed English and Scandinavian attacks.

Gruffydd ap Llywelyn, who ruled all of Wales from 1055 to his death in 1063, was the opposite of Hywel Dda: He was a ruthless and brutal warlord who fought Welsh rivals and Anglo-Saxons with equal zeal, even raiding into England and burning the English city of Hereford. He met his death not in battle but through assassination by Welsh rivals who cut off his head and sent it to the English leader Harold II Godwinson (ca. 1022–66). Both the disunity of Wales and the growing power of the English state contributed to the failure of Gruffydd ap Llywelyn to do for Wales what had been accomplished in Scotland and England: the creation of a stable kingship.

The Anglo-Saxon Kingdom of England

King Edward the Elder (ca. 870–924; r. 899–924) and Aethelflaeda (ca. 872–919), the son and daughter, respectively, of King Alfred of Wessex, advanced Alfred's goal of creating a unified England. Aethelflaeda married the Anglo-Saxon ruler of Mercia in central England, and after his death in 911 she ruled the territory under the title Lady of the Mercians, in alliance with her brother. After Aethelflaeda's death, Edward brought Mercia under his direct rule. The Kingdom of England is traditionally considered to have been founded in 927 when Edward's son Athelstan

(d. 939) subjugated the Danish and English parts of Northumbria. Northumbria remained a nominal kingdom under Scandinavian rulers, though under overall English lordship, until 954.

Small, relatively isolated England was ahead of other European kingdoms in developing centralized institutions. It had a national army, the *fyrd*, commanded by the king, and the English kings were unique in Europe in possessing a monopoly on coinage. The English silver penny was of a high standard. There was a centralized tax, the danegeld, so called because it was first raised to pay off Danish armies. The English monarchy also developed a procedure called the *writ*, a letter from the king carrying the force of a command. This theoretically put the entire kingdom under the king's authority, a marked contrast to the weak feudal kingships of the European continent or the loosely associated Kingdom of Scotland. The Anglo-Saxon government of England also differed from its continental contemporaries in that the language of government was the same language people spoke in everyday life, Anglo-Saxon, rather than Latin.

The Anglo-Saxon kings took a strong interest in the church, which repaid them with loyalty. The new rulers rebuilt English monasticism

ERIC I BLOODAXE AND THE END OF VIKING ENGLAND

The last Viking king of Northumbria was the colorfully named Erik Bloodaxe. Eric was the son of King Harald I Fairhair of Norway (ca. 854–ca. 936) and may have earned the name *Bloodaxe* for murdering his brothers and rivals for the throne. In 934 or 935 he was driven from Norway by his surviving brother, Haakon (who may have survived by being fostered at the court of King Athelstan of England). Erik was made king of Northumbria in 948, ruling from the old Viking capital of Jorvik (York) with the obligation of defending northern England from the Scots, Irish, and other Vikings. For reasons that are unclear, he lost the throne after a year but was then restored in 952. Eric fought for Northumbria against the Viking dynasty based in Ireland and was killed in battle, probably against Irish Vikings, who may have been supported by King Eadred of Wessex, in 954. After Eric's death, Northumbria was absorbed into the Anglo-Saxon kingdom, so 954 is sometimes viewed as the end of the Viking age in English history.

after the disaster of the Viking invasions. Following the Continental example, the new monasteries emphasized an elaborate schedule of services. English monasticism never regained the intellectual vitality it had before the Viking invasions, but many monks established reputations for sanctity. Both abbots and bishops were royal appointees. A ritual of coronation and anointing was imported from the Continent to emphasize the sacredness of kings and kingship. The legitimacy of kingship was based largely on tradition: The king was the realm's owner, protecting its people and leading them in war. The clergy emphasized the king's justice and his protection of the church. Royal succession was based on the monarch's selecting an heir within the royal family. This led to problems when he nominated more than one successor at different points in his reign, or when he failed to nominate a successor at all.

Anglo-Saxons believed the king should have a witenagemot, or council, whose members were called witan. These leading nobles and churchmen had little independent power as a group, except sometimes in disputed successions. Despite the mythology of some later historians seeking the roots of the English parliament in the Anglo-Saxon period, the witan did not gather in a formal assembly with legal rights but advised the king when he sought their counsel. The country was relatively prosperous in the late Anglo-Saxon period, partly due to the Scandinavian raids tapering off, partly due to improvements in the climate. The people were divided into thanes (nobles), freemen, and slaves, whose numbers seem to have diminished in the late Anglo-Saxon period as the distinction between slaves and the larger category of the unfree was breaking down. Freemen were expected to have lords; the "lordless man" was an outlaw.

Administratively, England was divided into shires with royally appointed *shire-reeves,* or sheriffs. Shires were further divided into units called *hundreds.* The most powerful nobles were the ealdormen, who eventually became known by the Scandinavian term *earls.* The earls were originally royal officials assigned big, contiguous blocks of English territory, particularly in the north. The position became increasingly hereditary, and by the end of the Anglo-Saxon kingdom, the earls of the house of Godwin, who ruled Wessex in south-central England, were more powerful than the king himself. One of them, Harold II Godwinson, even seized the throne in 1066, becoming the last Anglo-Saxon king of England.

By the late 10th century the English kings were strong enough to claim hegemony over Great Britain. In 973, in a token acceptance of his position, eight British, Welsh, and Anglo-Scandinavian kings, including the king of Scotland, rowed a boat carrying the king of England. The frontier of English settlement expanded, particularly at the expense of the Welsh.

The conversion of Denmark and Norway to Christianity in the late 10th and early 11th centuries diminished the cultural distance between Scandinavians and the English, and their contacts were less hostile in the 11th century than in earlier periods. Scandinavian attacks on England persisted throughout the 11th century, but the survival of the English state was no longer endangered. Opportunistic Scandinavian raiders took advantage of weak kings, and strong Scandinavian kings attempted to seize the English throne. The most successful of these was the Danish king Canute (995–1035), king of England from 1016 to his death in 1035. Canute was invited to rule by witan who feared a disputed succession more than Scandinavian rule. Rather than incorporating England into Denmark or settling it with Danes, Canute ruled England as an English king through English nobles and English bishops and following English law and customs. His reign saw a partial blending of English and Scandinavian culture; Scandinavian poets and soldiers served English kings and nobles, and thus emerges a North Sea aristocracy with interests and connections in different kingdoms.

In the 11th century the English connection to Scandinavia was complemented by increased contact with the Continent, particularly Normandy, along the northern coast of France, and Flanders, a region now divided between Belgium and France. It was important to have good relations with them both to prevent them from providing bases for Scandinavian raiders and for the health of the English wool trade, the most important English export trade. These connections were strengthened by royal intermarriage and the fact that the next-to-last English king of England, Edward the Confessor (ca. 1003–1066), spent much of his youth in exile at French courts. Edward was the son of King Aethelred II (ca. 966–1016)—who had lost the support of the witan and was replaced by Danish king Canute—and Emma of Normandy (ca. 985–1052). When Edward became king of England in 1042, he returned with Norman warriors and churchmen, the beginning of the Norman presence that would overwhelm England after Edward's death. The court of the Confessor (so called due to his reputation for personal holiness) was quite cosmopolitan, a meeting place of the Romance, Celtic, Germanic, and Scandinavian worlds.

The Norman Kingdom of England

The most famous date in English history is 1066, the year Duke William of Normandy (1027–87) conquered the Anglo-Saxon kingdom of England. The duchy of Normandy, in northern France, was originally ceded to a Scandinavian Viking ruler in the early 10th century by the king of France to protect against other raiders. The ships that brought William over to England, as depicted in the famous Bayeux Tapestry, were Viking longships in design. However, by the late 11th century the Normans were entirely French in identity.

William's victory was precipitated by the death of Edward the Confessor in early January 1066. Edward had left no children, and the witan proclaimed Harold II Godwinson, from the powerful Anglo-Saxon family of Godwin, to be king. William, however, claimed that Edward had recognized him as the successor and that Harold had accepted this claim. Complicating the situation was the king of Norway, Harald Sigurdson (1015–66; also known as Hardrada, or "hard ruler"), who also invaded England in an attempt to seize the throne in alliance with Harald's brother Tostig Godwinson (ca. 1026–66). (Another claimant was Edgar the Atheling, a descendant of the English royal house. Although Edgar had a strong hereditary claim, he was a boy in 1066, and English leaders at the time did not view him as qualified to take on the kingdom and defend it from his rivals.) The Norwegians won one battle at Fulford (September 20, 1066) and lost the second at Stamford Bridge (September 25), where both Harald and Tostig were killed. However, the campaign against Harald and Tostig seriously weakened the English forces for their confrontation with William.

The decisive battle between the English and the Normans took place on October 14, 1066, at Hastings in Sussex. Harold, along with most of the fighting aristocracy of Anglo-Saxon England, was killed in battle, and William was crowned king. The Battle of Hastings was a victory of Continental military technology, particularly the mounted warrior, against the old-fashioned, infantry-dominated army of the Anglo-Saxon kingdom. The actual conquest was a more protracted process than a single battle. English earls who had initially supported William rebelled against him; English resistance continued in various regions, particularly the highlands of the west and north; and Danish and Scottish invasions tried the new regime. However, William's own military skill and his control of the vital south and southeast enabled him to surmount these challenges. William was also a leader of immense brutality whose massacres and devastation in the north while putting down the rebellion of the northern Anglo-Saxon earls Edwin and Morcar after 1071 left a mark on the region for a century. After years of warfare, William finally crushed the resistance of the Anglo-Saxon nobility in 1075; the few surviving male Anglo-Saxon aristocrats went into exile.

William presented himself both as the legitimate heir of Edward the Confessor and as the conqueror of England. During his reign the prestige of the monarchy continued. Many English governmental institutions, such as writs, royal control over coinage, and national taxation, remained, helping to foster the high degree of centralization characteristic of the Norman-English monarchy. The organization of the kingdom into shires also remained, and the title *earl* remained the highest secular honor and responsibility that could be given to a subject. The name *Edward* was one of the few Anglo-Saxon names to survive the conquest, and it would later be adopted by the French-descended kings themselves. On the other hand, William fostered the image of himself as a conqueror and the ultimate owner of all the land in the kingdom. The conquest was followed by a massive redistribution of land, the greatest in all English history, and power along with it. The richest single landowner was the king, who by the end of the century owned about 18 percent of the land.

The Norman triumph was followed by the importation of a new ruling class rather than widespread settlement. The English ruling class was replaced by Norman, Breton, and French nobility. This process was facilitated by the high death toll of the Anglo-Saxon nobility in 1066 and during the following rebellions, and by the subsequent exile of the remaining leaders. Anglo-Saxon widows were married to the newly arrived French nobles.

William took inventory of his kingdom in the Domesday survey ordered in 1085 and recorded in the Domesday Book completed before his death in 1087. The Domesday Book was a written description or inventory of all the productive land in the kingdom; it named about 13,400 places. Although its coverage was not quite complete, it was the most all-inclusive and precise document produced by any medieval government, and it remains an enormously important source for historians. However, it was less useful to the English government in subsequent decades as its information quickly grew out of date.

The conquest tied England to the French cultural sphere and essentially severed the Scandinavian connection. The last attempt of a Scandinavian monarch to rule England was by King Svein Esrithson of Denmark (r. 1046–74), who invaded England in 1069, but despite early successes it came to nothing. For centuries afterward, the English elite was mostly French in descent, French in culture, and avidly engaged in

French politics. Many English kings saw themselves first and foremost as French barons and were lords of extensive territories in France. When the Angevin Henry II ascended to the throne of England in 1154, he added the French territories of Anjou and Aquitaine to Normandy. England was deeply involved in French politics for centuries and open to French cultural tendencies—in language, religion, architecture, literature, and many other areas. This political and cultural orientation to Europe was accompanied by an economic orientation. The dominant English export was now wool for the clothiers of Flanders, who valued fine English wool above the wool of Flanders itself. The wool trade had roots in the Anglo-Saxon era but expanded after the conquest. Flemish payment for wool in silver helped England maintain a high-quality currency, with little of the debasement of precious metal common in most European countries. Wool continued to be the most important English export until the Industrial Revolution of the 18th century.

The Norman Kings of England

William the Conqueror was succeeded as king of England by his second son, William II Rufus (ca. 1056–1100; r. 1087–1100). The Duchy of Normandy went to his eldest son, Robert II Curthose (ca. 1051–1134), putting those Norman landowners with estates in both England and Normandy in a difficult position should conflict arise between the two brothers. William Rufus, so nicknamed for his red beard and flamboyant personality, had several disagreements with the church over the extent of royal control over it and his habit of taking church revenues for his own. Since most histories were written by churchmen, the king gained a bad reputation for violence, irreligion, and sodomy. However, as a military and political leader William Rufus was quite successful. He turned back an invasion of the north by Malcolm III of Scotland (Malcolm Canmore, r. 1058–93) and forced the Scottish king's submission. Taking advantage of his brother Robert's determination to join the First Crusade, he took possession of Normandy in return for a loan to finance Robert's expedition. Much of William's success in expensive wars was owed to his treasurer, Ranulf Flambard (1060–1128), a man of obscure origins whom William promoted to bishop of Durham.

William Rufus died in a hunting accident in 1100. There were rumors that the arrow that killed him had been shot deliberately, although rumors were inevitable in such incidents, and most modern historians believe that it was indeed an accident. Robert, the next in the strict line of succession, was still off crusading when William died, so his ambitious younger brother, Henry I (r. 1100–35), seized the opportunity and succeeded William Rufus to the throne. After Robert returned and challenged him, Henry defeated his brother at the Battle of Tinchebrai in 1106, reuniting kingdom and duchy. Robert spent the rest of his life in captivity, although he was allowed the amenities appropriate to his noble status.

After some early disagreements over royal versus episcopal authority, Henry adopted a more conciliatory approach to the church. He also founded institutions of centralized justice and finance, such as the exchequer, introduced around 1110 to handle royal accounts. Henry focused a great deal of effort on expansion in France. He retained good relations with the Scottish kings to whom he was related by marriage and asserted Anglo-Norman power in Wales. His marriage to Matilda (1080–1118), a descendant of the Scottish and Anglo-Saxon royal families, may have helped to reconcile the Anglo-Saxon leaders who still remained important in the localities to Norman rule.

Henry's only legitimate son, William (1103–20), died in a shipwreck, and when Henry died in 1135, the succession was disputed between his only legitimate daughter, Matilda (1102–67), and his nephew, Stephen of Blois (ca. 1096–1154). The subsequent wars severely tested the framework the Norman kings had built.

Feudal England under the Normans

The Norman regime was based on different principles than that of the Anglo-Saxons. William the Conqueror and his heirs wanted to prevent the development of large, semi-independent territorial lordships such as the Anglo-Saxon or Scottish earldoms or the Duchy of Normandy itself. Rather than giving away huge blocks of territory, the Norman kings dispersed the lands of the great feudal lords in smaller parcels. Building on Anglo-Saxon centralism, they imposed a very tight feudal structure where all lords swore allegiance to the king and all land was held feudally—that is, in return for services, usually military services. The aristocracy was small: About half the income from the country went to around 200 barons, the rest to the king and the church. The most powerful landowners in England were also landowners in Normandy, which caused difficulties for them when the kingdom and the duchy were in different hands. The king also owned land outright in every part of the kingdom, giving him a presence throughout his realm that the medieval monarchs of France, Scotland, or elsewhere lacked.

The feudal system rested on a new military technology of castles and mounted knights. The Normans put up hundreds of castles all over

England, and these became the new nobility's military strongholds. Unlike Anglo-Saxon earthwork burghs, which covered an area averaging 25 acres (10 hectares), these fortified places covered only about a couple of acres (.8 hectares), and were designed to hold only the lord, his family, and his troops. Unlike the wooden halls of the Anglo-Saxon and Scandinavian nobility, the castles contained wooden towers, usually located on mottes—artificial hills built with the forced labor of English peasants and surrounded by a wooden palisade, sometimes a ditch or moat, and an earthwork bank. Castles could be bases for royal authority or for predators and brigands when the king was weak. The stone castle was a later innovation and much more expensive. The White Tower, which William the Conqueror built in London in 1078 to control and overawe his new capital city, was one of the few early Norman stone castles. The largest stone building built in England for secular purposes since the Romans, it became the nucleus for the building complex known as the Tower of London.

Horsemanship became one of the most important qualities of the male aristocrat, since lords had to support their horsemen in battle by fighting from horseback themselves. A nobleman who could not ride was fit only to be a priest. In fact, the aristocratic class of the new England was primarily one of knights—cavalrymen who wore a coat of chain mail, helmet, shield, lance, and sword and rode warhorses.

The Normans also ended the relatively complex Anglo-Saxon class structure in favor of a two-class system of the free and the unfree, although the unfree were not considered slaves—they had some rights and were not bought and sold as chattels. The boundary between the lord and the ordinary freeman was initially quite fuzzy, and the nobility of Norman England was not protected by the unique set of legal rights that would clearly distinguish the English nobility of the later Middle Ages

This seal, used to authenticate documents, shows a knight in armor. It belonged to a 13th-century noble named Robert Fitzwalter. (© British Museum/Art Resource, NY)

and the early modern period from ordinary people. They were more leading freemen than distinguished by a defined higher status. In the lower classes, there was movement in both directions as slaves moved upward into the status of serf and free Anglo-Saxon peasants moved downward. All peasants, but particularly the unfree, owed produce and labor dues to the lord of the manor. Lords also maintained private courts, a practice unknown in Anglo-Saxon England.

Latin quickly displaced Anglo-Saxon as the language of government in the first few years after the conquest. The aristocracy mostly spoke French but had some fluency in English by the early 12th century, accentuated by the marriage of Norman and French incomers to Englishwomen. Some of the new language eventually worked its way down to the lower classes, where English was steadily marginalized as a written language, and traditional English names such as Aethelred were replaced by French-influenced ones like William. However, French always remained an aristocratic language. Unlike Latin, Anglo-Saxon, or Scandinavian, it had little impact on place-names.

The decentralized nature of feudal power proved disastrous during the civil wars ignited by the succession dispute between William the Conqueror's grandchildren, Stephen and Matilda. Local warlords, operating from castles, were able to extort peasants and other non-nobles, and the destructiveness of war laid a heavy burden on the English people. Many lords who led their followers into either army seem to have been more motivated by the desire to loot and to increase their holdings at the expense of the rival faction than by any real loyalty to either Stephen or Matilda. The king of Scots, David I (r. 1124–53), fought on the side of Matilda and her son, the future Henry II, partially because he was a major English feudatory as earl of Huntingdon and as such was expected to pick a side.

Feudal lords, not the king, began England's longest foreign involvement when Richard FitzGilbert de Clare, earl of Pembroke (1130–76)—one of the Marcher Barons who held the English lands bordering Wales—allied with an exiled Irish ruler, Dermot Macmurrough of Leinster (1110–71). Clare, who later became known as Strongbow, took his troops to Ireland in 1170, following a path already taken by English mercenaries, married Macmurrough's daughter, and carved a principality for himself in Ireland. He and other English nobles were followed by King Henry II (1133–89; r. 1154–89) the next year. Henry was less interested in Ireland for its own sake than in preventing English nobles like Strongbow from establishing independent power bases there. Henry's army was the greatest ever seen in Ireland and won the submission of most Irish rulers. English control over Ireland would wax and wane for the rest of the medieval period.

The Church in Feudal England

The Norman Conquest changed the church as well as the state. The higher levels of the church—archbishops, bishops, and abbots—were almost entirely Normanized in the first few years after the conquest. Numerous monasteries saw tension between the old English monks and new monks from the Continent, but in the long run the English lost. New ideas and new books from the Continent came to revive the church intellectually. Many new Norman or French abbots were shocked at the meager libraries of the English monasteries, which had never really recovered from the Viking attacks.

The new English church was graced by its greatest intellectual since Bede: Anselm, archbishop of Canterbury from 1093 to 1109, a philosopher, statesman, and saint. Anselm's conflicts with William Rufus and Henry I were part of a Europe-wide struggle over investiture, the right of secular rulers to invest bishops with the ring and the staff, the symbols of episcopal power. Although the conflict was sometimes bitter, it never reached the heights in England that it did in the Holy Roman Empire, where the Investiture Controversy actually led to civil war. In the end, the settlement, which theoretically allowed the staff of clerics attached to a bishop's cathedral—the chapter—to freely elect their bishop, was compromised as the king retained a great deal of control over a nominally independent church, even commanding the election of particular individuals as bishops.

Discontinuities of personnel between the pre- and postconquest churches masked institutional continuities. Norman-appointed archbishops of Canterbury based their cases for Canterbury's primacy over Britain on English precedents. Norman-dominated monasteries found or forged grants from English kings to establish their rights over property. Although some Normans pointedly spurned the Anglo-Saxon saints, many of them continued to be venerated, and where a successful cult of an Anglo-Saxon saint existed, the Norman-dominated church kept it going.

The church was also feudalized with the imposition of military obligations and tighter organization under a series of strong archbishops of Canterbury. The requirement that bishops and abbots furnish troops to the king was a novelty that initially aroused great horror. Bishops and abbots even served as military commanders on occasion. Alternatively, religious landowners fulfilled their obligations by praying for the soul

ANSELM AND THE ONTOLOGICAL ARGUMENT

Anselm of Bec, archbishop of Canterbury from 1093 to 1109, is best known in the history of philosophy for his famous ontological argument for the existence of God. In his *Proslogion,* Anselm defined *God* as that which nothing better could be conceived of as existing. If God did not exist, something better—that is, a God who existed—could be conceived of, and therefore God must exist. Although most philosophers today do not think the ontological argument is valid (whether or not they believe the existence of God can be proved), it influenced theology for centuries.

of the person who had donated the land or endowed the monastery and his or her family.

Those affiliated with the church, however loosely, were referred to as the clergy, and they had legal privileges and exemptions that limited the king's power over them. This issue led to the greatest conflict between church and state in medieval England: the Becket affair. Thomas Becket (ca. 1118–70) was a chancellor and friend of the first king of the Angevin dynasty, Henry II, who appointed Becket archbishop of Canterbury in 1162. Henry wanted to transfer jurisdiction over criminal clergy to secular courts, as church courts were often reluctant to convict guilty clergymen. Becket refused, and a long struggle involving the pope and the king of France ended with Becket's murder in Canterbury Cathedral in 1170. The murderers were knights carrying out what they thought was the king's will, although Henry never gave a formal order. Becket was widely recognized as a saint and martyr across Europe, and Henry did penance for his part in the murder in 1174, being publicly flogged by monks at Canterbury. Becket's shrine at Canterbury became a major pilgrimage site not just for English people but for Europeans, and criminal clergy continued to enjoy lenient ecclesiastical jurisdiction.

The Towns of Feudal England

Norman England participated in the general revival of European urban life in the 11th and 12th centuries. The 1087 Domesday Book listed 112 boroughs, or towns; most of the largest were built on old Roman sites. Even when these towns had lost population or been deserted after the withdrawal of the Roman Empire and the subsequent decline of the English economy from its Roman height, their walls made them natural sites for reurbanization. The largest towns were also bishop's seats. The English mercantile class survived the Norman Conquest, and the urban world continued to grow. More than 125 new towns were built in England in the 150 years following the conquest.

Medieval English towns were small by modern standards, or even compared to the great medieval cities of the East. London was clearly the largest city. Although there is no hard record of the total population of medieval London at any point in its history, and estimates by modern scholars vary widely, one common estimate is that the capital had a population of about 18,000 in 1100 (Inwood 1998, 113). Townspeople were a mixture of French and English. The Norman Conquest also led to the introduction of the first Jewish population in England since the Romans. The Jewish immigrants were French speakers from the Norman capital Rouen, and the medieval Jewish population of England remained Francophone.

Jews originally settled in London. Beginning around the middle of the 12th century, they established small communities in other urban centers. The Jewish community was useful to the kings as moneylenders, and Jewish moneylenders also lent to private individuals. The law of the church forbade Christians from lending money at interest, so the Jews filled this economic need. However, Jews were increasingly targets of Christian anti-Semitism, some based on the Christian myth that the Jewish community was responsible for Christ's crucifixion and some on the Christian debtor's resentment of Jewish creditors.

Towns were part of the feudal system. What legally constituted a town, the possession of a charter, was in the hands of either the feudal lord of the territory or the king. Each town was put under a particular legal regime at the establishment of its charter; often, one legal regime was simply copied from town to town. A town's rights included the right to hold markets, the right to have its own courts, and the right to sell land freely in a less legally complicated way than land held by a feudal lord. Towns were strongly associated with personal freedom: An unfree peasant or villain who lived in a town for a year and a day became free—hence the saying "town air makes free." A lord could also free a town's citizens from paying the toll on his roads or bridges, and thus the most desirable lord for a town was the king, who could do this for the entire country.

The king was by far the most important lord of towns in England. Nearly all the large towns, including London and about 40 percent

ENGLAND AND THE ORIGINS OF THE BLOOD LIBEL

The blood libel, the myth that Jews sacrifice Christian babies—in some versions in order to make matzos—became a central trope of Christian anti-Semitism for centuries. Its first recorded appearance is in medieval England, although there may have been unrecorded instances earlier or elsewhere. The blood libel first appeared in 1144, during Easter week, which was always a bad time for Jews in Christian societies as preachers whipped up anger over the Jewish "betrayal" of Christ. A monk charged the Jewish community of Norwich with having killed a Christian child, William, who had mysteriously disappeared. The monk claimed that the Jews practiced human sacrifice every year, as an ancient prophecy claimed that they would never gain their freedom or return to Israel without the shedding of human blood. In this case, the anti-Jewish movement was quashed by royal judges. William of Norwich became recognized as a saint, and the blood libel was prominent in future pogroms in England and elsewhere.

of towns overall, were directly under the king. Towns in England never attained the self-governing independence characteristic of many European towns, particularly in Germany and Italy. London, whose particular weight in the kingdom was widely recognized and whose wealth gave it a certain amount of leverage, achieved some measure of independence in 1141 when King Stephen, then a captive of Matilda, recognized a commune in the city, a stronghold of his supporters. A commune in the Middle Ages was a group of leading citizens who took on the responsibility for town governance. For the first time London had an elected mayor.

The Feudal Scottish Kingdom

Much less is known about Scottish medieval history than about that of England. The less-sophisticated Scottish administration did not produce the masses of records that the English did, and many Scottish records were destroyed in wars and disasters.

The Scottish monarchy underwent many changes similar to England's in feudalization and even the arrival of Norman warriors, but Scotland was not conquered, and the Scottish monarchy retained control over the changes. Norman kings inherited the Anglo-Saxon monarchs' claims to British overlordship, and after the conquest many Anglo-Saxons regarded the Scottish monarchy, intermarried with the English one, as a leading Anglo-Saxon institution. The Anglo-Saxon claimant Edgar the Atheling (ca. 1051–ca. 1126) was received in the Scottish court following the Norman Conquest. Malcolm III of Scotland (r. 1058–93) married Edgar's sister Margaret (ca. 1045–93) and supported rebels against William the Conqueror. William eventually forced Malcolm to become his vassal, but this status was difficult to enforce.

Queen Margaret was a remarkable woman whose piety was such that she was canonized in 1251. She was a great patron of the Scottish church, building churches and taking an active role in promoting reforms such as stricter observance of church law. She was also known for acts of piety and humility such as fasting, frequent attendance at Mass, and feeding the poor and orphans. Margaret sponsored the influence of English and Continental culture in Scotland. Her sons received either English names or names derived from the ancient world rather than the traditional Celtic names of the Scottish royal Canmore dynasty. Margaret and Malcolm's daughter Edith or Matilda (ca. 1080–1118) married King Henry I of England, William the Conqueror's son, linking the new Norman dynasty to the old Anglo-Saxon line.

Later Scottish kings sponsored Norman immigration from England or directly from France to build up a nobility familiar with the latest French and English military and administrative technology. The new nobles, with no roots in the land, owed immediate loyalty to the king. The most important Scottish king of the Middle Ages, Malcolm and Margaret's son David I (ca. 1080–1153; r. 1124–53), had spent many years at the English court and possessed territories and vassals in England. David brought many of his Anglo-Norman liege men with him when he succeeded, giving them control over vast territories in the south of the country. He also set up a network of castles throughout parts of the country to serve as royal strongpoints under the control of appointed sheriffs, a title and office derived from the English example, with modification for Scottish circumstances. David was the first Scottish king recorded as minting coins and the first to grant charters to cities or burghs. An Anglo-Scottish nobility with holdings and family connections on both sides of the border developed in the 12th and 13th centuries.

Generally speaking, strong kings of England tried to impose their will on the Scottish kings. Henry II forced William the Lion (ca. 1142–1214; r. 1165–1214) to swear homage to him after William joined a rebellion of English barons against the monarchy in the Treaty of Falaise in 1174. Henry occupied strongpoints in Scotland, including Edinburgh, and kept interfering in Scottish politics. However, Scotland was seldom a high priority for the English kings. Henry's son Richard I (1157–99; r. 1189–99) essentially sold the Scots their independence back for 10,000 silver marks in 1189 to raise money to go on a crusade.

The Scottish church in the early 12th century still lacked a settled diocesan organization. Bishops existed but did not have defined territorial sees. This made Scotland particularly vulnerable in the late 11th century, when the papacy was imposing a great wave of reform and standardization over the European church. One obvious instrument of reform from the papal point of view was the English church hierarchy. Both the archbishop of Canterbury, who could still claim a superiority over the British church as a whole based on Pope Gregory the Great's charge to Augustine in the sixth century, and the archbishop of York, who outranked any Scottish bishop since the Scots did not have archbishops at this time, could claim to direct the Scottish church. This had been made explicit by William the Conqueror, in whose church the archbishop of Canterbury was recognized as primate of all Britain and the archbishop of York as primate of all regions from the Humber to the utmost limits of Scotland.

The central issue was who would consecrate the Scottish bishops. The papacy was a strong supporter of York's claims, believing that York offered the best hope for Scottish reform. The popes sent streams of bulls to the Scottish bishops telling them they were subject to York. However, during the Becket affair the York archbishop was a firm supporter of Henry II. This caused the pope to recognize the independence of the Scottish church, subject only to himself. An 1192 bull declared that Scotland was a special daughter of the see of Rome, subject directly to the pope with no intermediary. By this time the Scottish church had a much more settled diocesan organization with defined territories and synods.

During these struggles, Scotland developed a national cult of St. Andrew, the apostle credited with the conversion of Scotland in Christian legend. The bishop of St. Andrew's, a community built around Andrew's shrine, was known as the bishop of Scotland and often took the leading role in Scottish church affairs, although at most he was first among equals in relation to other Scottish bishops. St. Andrew's was the capital of Scotland as much as any place was, as Scottish kings had to travel extensively to maintain control over their subjects.

Scottish kings' control over the west and north of their kingdom was weak but increasing. The king of Norway, never able to exert much control over the Hebrides, ceded them to the king of Scotland in 1266, but the Hebrides and the northern islands remained separate from the rest of the kingdom in culture and politics for centuries.

Feudal Wales

Although it never reached the level of centralization of Scotland, let alone England, Wales in the 13th century was also transformed by the impact of feudalism. The Anglo-Norman Marcher Barons—feudal lords established on the "Marches," or frontiers, between England and Wales—had more independence than other feudal lords and were expected to defend the kingdom from the Welsh and seek to expand at Welsh expense. The Marcher Barons took an aggressive stance, introducing the new techniques of cavalry warfare based on the mounted knight and fortification, while the area of Wales under the rule of Welsh princes shrank. Welsh rulers did homage to English kings, intermarried with the Anglo-Norman nobility, and even allied with the English against Welsh rivals. Nor was Wales merely a passive receiver of European feudal culture; it was also the source of one of the most important elements of feudal art and literature. The Welsh mythology concerning the legendary British hero King Arthur would spread as far as Iceland, Italy, and Russia and find an enthusiastic audience within and beyond the feudal nobility.

The political and military challenge to Wales was taken up by the princes of Gwynedd in north Wales. In the 13th century two Gwynedd princes, Llewelyn the Great (ca. 1173–1240) and Llewelyn ap Gryffud (ca. 1223–82), brought Wales to its peak of unification since the 11th century, for the first time controlling the entire country. In 1267 England recognized Llewelyn ap Gruffyd by the new title of Prince of Wales, bringing Welsh independence to a new height. The crash would not be long in coming.

The Angevins and the Magna Carta

In England, the succession crisis after the death of Henry I was eventually settled in a compromise. The war between Stephen (r. 1135–54) and Matilda lasted from 1139 to 1153, a period called the Anarchy. It only ended when Stephen recognized Matilda's son Henry as his heir in the Treaty of Wallingford. The treaty was facilitated by the recent death of Stephen's son Eustace, giving him little reason to continue the war. Under the treaty's terms, Stephen was allowed to keep the throne for his life, after which it would go to Henry.

In addition to being king of England and duke of Normandy, Henry II (1133–89; r. 1154–89) was count of Anjou—hence the word *Angevin* to describe the dynasty—in his own right and ruler of Aquitaine by right of his wife, Eleanor (1122–1204). An alternative designation of Henry's dynasty is Plantagenet, after his father, Geoffrey Plantagenet. In addition to being king, Henry was the most powerful of French barons, and much of his and his son Richard I's time, resources, and energy would be devoted to their French holdings. However, rebuilding the institutions of royal government in England after the destruction wrought by the civil war in Stephen's reign was also a priority. Henry's reign was particularly important in the development of English law and judicial procedures. He established a system whereby royal judges—called *justices in eyre*—traveled circuits covering the entire kingdom and worked in cooperation with local juries—a partnership that would lie at the heart of English justice for centuries. The law worked out by the royal justices in Henry's reign—the common law—would build on Anglo-Saxon and Norman precedents to become one of the world's great legal systems. Richard lacked Henry's administrative abilities and showed little interest in England during his reign, but his outstanding abilities as a warrior and crusader added to the prestige and power of the English throne.

The centralization and fiscal extortion practiced by the early Angevin dynasty led to resentment on the part of the aristocracy. This came to a head under Richard's brother and successor, King John (r. 1199–1216). John was a highly intelligent man but untrustworthy and cruel, evoking little loyalty. Significantly, he was unsuccessful in his most important wars, those with the rising power of western Europe, the king of France, Philip II Augustus (r. 1180–1223). John lost Normandy and much of the inheritance of Henry II in France, with disastrous consequences for his prestige in England. This loss had long-term consequences as well, ending the time when English kings were predominantly French magnates. John spent more time in England than any king since the conquest, setting the pattern for future English rulers.

John also had major problems with the papacy, then at the height of its power under the formidable Innocent III (ca. 1160–1216; pope, 1198–1216). Innocent and John quarreled over the right to appoint bishops. Eventually the king surrendered to the pope, making the kingdom a papal fief.

For all these reasons, John needed money. His ruthlessness in squeezing money from his barons, including the confiscation of baronial lands and the promotion of gangsterish favorites, aroused massive resistance. Exploiting the rights of wardship, a legal claim the king had to be the guardian of minor children of deceased nobles, he married off the daughters of nobles to rich merchants for money, an insult to noble families. Following the catastrophic defeat of the forces allied to John at the battle of Bouvines (July 27, 1214) in the war with Philip II that had begun in Normandy in 1202, there was a baronial revolt. John was forced to sign the Magna Carta—the great charter—in 1215. The Magna Carta was designed to stop the king's abuses and safeguard the baronage's feudal rights. It established tight aristocratic control over the central government through the requirement that new taxes could only be imposed with the consent of a great council of the baronage. The Magna Carta guaranteed both rights of interest to the baronage, such as restrictions on wardship, and rights of all freemen in the kingdom, such as trial by peers. However, most men in the kingdom were not freemen but serfs. There was nothing democratic in the Magna Carta: A committee of 25 barons would oversee its enforcement, with the right of revolt if the king failed to observe the charter. The establishment of the idea that the king could be limited by some form of agreement with his subjects was more important than the actual limitations.

John hoped that these concessions would unite the country behind another attempt to recover the French possessions. Disappointed, he later revoked the Magna Carta with the permission of the pope, who claimed the right to free him of his oath, after their reconciliation. This led to another civil war, with the participation of Louis, the son of the king of France—who hoped to become king of England—along with the English barons. The war ended when John died and his nine-year-old son, Henry III, became king. The new regency government reissued a slightly modified version of the charter minus the baronial committee and the right of revolt to gain baronial support against the French. This measure was successful, and the French prince left England shortly thereafter. England was now in the hands of a child.

Henry III and the Origin of Parliament

Henry III (1207–72; r. 1216–72) was very unlike his father. He was very pious, not cruel or ruthless, but rather feckless. His unsuccessful attempts to recover the lost French provinces required much money and led to resentment by the barons. There were two disastrous attempts at conquering France during his reign. In the eventual Treaty

Built in the Gothic style by Henry III, Westminster Abbey has been a center for English and British royal rituals for centuries. (Library of Congress, National Photo Company Collection)

of Paris in 1258, Henry acknowledged the loss of his provinces and became the vassal of the French king for the remaining English territories in southern France.

Many English leaders thought the king was too much under the thumb of the pope. Under Henry there was a massive influx of Italian churchmen holding English benefices, at a time when the papacy was increasingly thought to be too concerned with politics and finance rather than spiritual things. Henry was also extravagant with his friends and a great builder and patron of the arts, all of which cost money.

Parliaments began as great councils convoked through writs to various magnates and prelates, as called for in the Magna Carta. There was no sharp dividing line when great councils became parliaments. Great councils were used to raise taxes, both in particular areas and nationwide. The move from great councils to parliaments was precipitated by a crisis in 1258. Out of the desire to provide a crown for his second son, Edmund (1245–96), and to oblige the papacy, Henry had become involved in a war in Sicily by agreeing to guarantee the papal debts incurred there. When those debts became exorbitant, the king announced that he would not pay them, leading the pope to threaten him with excommunication—an effective threat to a pious man like Henry. A group of barons who included Simon de Montfort, earl of Leicester (1208–65), demanded that Henry agree to reforms and get the pope to back down before the money was granted. The Sicilian adventure collapsed quickly, but the council of barons set forth an ambitious program to make the king merely the head of a system of baronial councils that would actually rule the realm. This form of government worked for a while, forcing Henry to the humiliation of having to rearrange his personal household to conform to what the barons wanted, but it was eventually brought down by divisions within the baronage and its own weaknesses and ambiguities. Questions about the length of terms on committees and how people were to be replaced had been left unaddressed. In 1261 the pope absolved King Henry of his obligation to keep the provisions and declared them and the baronial government dissolved.

The dissolution of the baronial government was followed by the rebellion of Simon de Montfort. Montfort was actually a Frenchman married to the king's sister Eleanor and godfather to the king's eldest son, Edward. He and Henry had had a long-standing quarrel over Eleanor's dowry, and Montfort thought Henry a fool. After capturing the king and his heir, Prince Edward, at the battle of Lewes in 1264, Montfort established a much tighter and more baronial government for England, with himself at its head. Concerned about baronial opposition, he tried to broaden the social base of his regime by setting up a system of regular parliaments incorporating elected burgesses and knights as well as the barons, and he began to claim that parliaments should exercise authority beyond that of the king. This was when the word *parliament* came into general use.

Edward escaped from captivity and defeated and killed Montfort at the battle of Evesham in 1265. Henry faded into the background, and Edward was the effective ruler of the country for the rest of Henry's reign until he succeeded to the throne at Henry's death in 1272.

4

BRITAIN IN THE
LATE MIDDLE AGES
(1272–1529)

The period of the late Middle Ages in Britain was a testing time for the British social and political order, marked by war, civil discord, plague, and economic crisis. The island's surviving rulers, the kings of England and Scotland, fought a series of bloody wars, which ensured the separate identity of Scotland for centuries to come, but at a cost of many deaths. Both countries were affected by the worldwide calamity of the Black Death. The English government faced both peasant and aristocratic violence, while the Scottish monarchy was brought to a point of humiliation as two of its rulers were murdered. However, Britain also shared in the Renaissance movement, with exciting new cultural developments and a key invention of the 15th century—the printing press.

The Reign of Edward I

In Edward I (1239–1307; r. 1272–1307), England got its most competent king since William the Conqueror. A fine general, superb military organizer, and farsighted statesman, Edward was the first king of England since the conquest with an English name, a product of his father Henry's devotion to the cult of Edward the Confessor but also an indication of the growing sense of English identity among the aristocracy. The warlike Edward had an insatiable need for money and used parliaments as a means of raising it. Getting a group of community leaders together to accept a tax increase was actually easier than just trying to do it through royal fiat. At this time it was up to the king's discretion who was invited to a parliament. No one possessed a legal right to be summoned, although the greater lords nearly always were since without them a parliament would have little authority. One of the parliaments' functions was to prevent the king from alienating his great barons, as had happened to John and Henry III. Edward sometimes followed Simon de Montfort's precedent in sending summons to the knights or burgesses of a given area to select representatives—that is, the commons—as well as summons to the barons and prelates—usually the bishops and about 30 of the major abbots. The barons and prelates later became the House of Lords. The commons were not usually summoned in Edward I's reign, however, and those parliaments that did include representatives of the commons were not considered as possessing more authority than those that did not.

In addition to raising taxes, parliaments were occasions for grievances and petitions to be heard and specific wrongs to be remedied. They were not, however, institutions for carrying on the realm's day-to-day government, which continued to be done by the king, his advisers, and his bureaucracy. Hearing petitions took up most of a parliament's time. In theory, any petition submitted to a parliament was supposed to be answered during that parliament. Since petitions often referred to legal disputes, a parliament was in many ways a court of last resort. It was usually referred to as a court—the High Court of Parliament. As a court of law, it was sacrosanct. No one could come to it carrying arms, and those who attended it could not be hindered in their comings and goings, nor could their property be seized or harmed in their absence.

Edward's greed led him to attack a vulnerable target: England's Jewish population. In 1290 a series of measures aimed at gaining tighter royal control over Jewish wealth culminated in the expulsion of the Jews from England, the first such expulsion from a medieval European kingdom. Jews would not be allowed to live openly in England again until the mid-17th century. Some may have fled to Scotland, creating a Jewish community in that kingdom, but the history of Jews in Scotland before the modern era is very obscure, and the community would have been tiny. In their absence in England, Edward was able to turn to alternative sources of credit, such as the rising Italian banking houses. Lombard Street in London, for centuries thereafter the center of English banking, was originally named after the financiers from the Italian region of Lombardy who did business there.

Wales under English Rule

Like most medieval and early modern rulers, Edward principally desired money in order to wage war. He was concerned with preserving England's deteriorating position in France, where the demands of

73

the French king that he pay homage for Gascony, the last remaining English possession in France, was a constant source of friction between the two kingdoms. However, Edward's reign was most notable for the expansion of English power within Britain itself. It had the greatest effect in Wales, then under the Gwynedd prince Llewelyn ap Gruffud. Taking advantage of divisions in the house of Gwynedd, and bringing together some of the largest armies yet seen in Britain, Edward smashed Gwynedd's power in two campaigns in 1276–77 and 1282. Llewelyn himself was murdered, and his head was sent to Edward in an eerie echo of the fate of Gruffud ap Llewelyn in the 11th century.

To cement English rule in Wales, Edward built some of the largest and most formidable stone castles to be found anywhere. He also created English colonies in Wales where Welsh people were forbidden to live or to trade. Wales was administratively reorganized, and while some of it was shared out among Edward's followers or left in the hands of Welsh collaborators, much was put under direct royal control. By bringing Wales under English law, Edward's Statute of Rhuddlan (1284) ended the history of independent Wales. Its future was as a dominion of the English Crown.

The Anglo-Scottish Wars

The subjugation of Wales was only the beginning of Edward's program of expansion. Two years later, he seized the opportunity to realize an ancient English dream, the union of England and Scotland, when the adept Scottish king Alexander III (1241–86; r. 1249–86) died and his granddaughter, the infant Margaret of Norway (d. 1290), was left as heir to the throne. Margaret's mother had married Norway's Erik II (r. 1280–99), and therefore Edward negotiated the Treaty of Brigham with Erik, which called for the marriage of Margaret to Edward's son, Edward of Caernarvon (1284–1327), who would later reign in England as Edward II. The Scottish assembly approved the arrangement, but four years after her grandfather, young Margaret herself died. Thus ended Scotland's Canmore dynasty and began a series of conflicts between the two remaining British states, the kingdoms of England and Scotland.

Without a direct heir, there were several Scottish nobles descended from the royal house who could make a claim on the throne. Scottish leaders who feared civil war were willing to turn to the only possible person with the power and legal position to adjudicate the dispute: Edward I. In addition to the old English claim of overlordship over Scotland, Edward had the intelligence to make a decision that would

74

hold up legally and politically, as well as the power to make his decisions stick. Unfortunately, he also had his own agenda.

The main competitors for the throne were John Balliol (ca. 1249–1314) and Robert Bruce (ca. 1215–95), both descendants of King David I. After exhaustive hearings, Edward decided on Balliol, who became king in 1291 after swearing fealty to Edward and acknowledging him "superior and direct lord of the Kingdom of Scotland." The conflict began because Edward and the Scots had fundamentally different concepts of what Balliol's acknowledgment meant. The Scots were thinking of a loose political association to be used in situations of disputed succession or other major problems Scotland could not handle on its own. Edward was thinking of full legal and feudal superiority and demanded as early as 1291 that the Scottish nobles acknowledge his supremacy. After declaring Balliol's right to the Scottish throne, Edward treated the new king as a vassal and entertained appeals from the Scottish courts. Even worse, he required Balliol to send troops to fight in Edward's wars in France, which had nothing to do with Scotland.

Scottish leaders were unhappy at the prospect of losing their independence, and Balliol, seen as Edward's puppet, faced a full-fledged baronial revolt. The barons actually allied with the king of France against Edward and Balliol, who changed sides, renouncing his homage to Edward in April 1296. This military and political challenge to Edward's overlordship as well as his dreams of victory in France could not be ignored. On May 28, 1296, Edward invaded Scotland.

At first Edward was overwhelmingly successful. Balliol was forced to resign the crown and sent into exile in England and eventually France, although Scottish rebels continued to invoke his authority. No new king was named; instead, an English nobleman was installed as governor. Edward even took the Stone of Destiny—traditionally used for the coronation of Scottish kings—back to England with him, where it would remain for the next 700 years. Despite his initial success, however, Edward found it was much easier to conquer Scotland than to hold it. Much of the land was remote, poor, inaccessible, and unable to support an occupying army.

Due to their harsh rule and the contempt they displayed for the Scots, the English became very unpopular among both the Scottish nobility and ordinary people. There was a series of risings, the most important under the petty noblemen William Wallace (ca. 1272–1305) in the south and Andrew Moray (d. 1297) in the north. The rebels scored some victories against the English troops left to garrison Scotland. After a victory against the English forces led by John de Warenne, earl of

Surrey, at Stirling on September 11, 1297, Wallace and Moray declared the liberation of their country. However, Moray, perhaps wounded in the battle, died shortly afterward, and Wallace was unable to stand up against a full English army led by Edward, who crushed the Scots in one of the great victories of English archers at the Battle of Falkirk on July 22, 1298. Wallace fled to the Continent, where he attempted to find allies.

Edward lacked the resources to follow up his victory at Falkirk and failed to restore English rule outside the southeast, as much of the country fell into the hands of local Scottish nobles. With the surrender in 1304 of the Comyns, one of the leading families of Scots who claimed the throne, and the capture of Wallace, who had returned to Scotland the following year, things began to look better for the English. In London, Wallace received a painful and elaborate execution as a traitor, cementing his role as a Scottish national martyr.

However, the following year Robert the Bruce (1274–1329), the grandson of the original Bruce claimant, went into open rebellion. Edward's crushing of the Balliol faction and Bruce's own murder of the head of his rivals, the Comyns, in 1306 gave him a clear shot at the crown. There was also optimism that the terrifying Edward, the "Hammer of the Scots," was not going to survive for much longer, and indeed he died in 1307. His son and successor, Edward II (1284–1327; r. 1307–27), was not nearly as effective. Bruce managed to establish himself as king of Scotland with the great victory of Bannockburn in 1314. He was allied to leaders in the Scottish church from whom he received a declaration in 1308 supporting his rights to the throne. This was followed by another, more famous declaration in 1320. The Declaration of Arbroath, the foundation of Scottish nationalism, was addressed to the pope and stated that the cause of Scotland was separate from Bruce's claim to the throne, although the two were allied. Bruce, who had served Edward I early in his career, was to be recognized as king only as long as he supported Scottish independence from England: "Yet if he should give up what he has begun, seeking to make us or our kingdom subject to the King of England or to the English, we would strive at once to drive him out as our enemy and a subverter of his own right and ours, and we would make some other man who was able to defend us our king; for as long as a hundred of us remain alive, we will never on any conditions be subject to the lordship of the English. For we fight not for glory, nor riches, nor honours, but for freedom alone, which no good man gives up except with his life" (quoted in *Records of the Parliaments of Scotland to 1707*).

THE HEART OF ROBERT THE BRUCE (1274–1329)

I t was a common custom in the Middle Ages for the heart of a person of distinction to be embalmed and buried separately from the body. Robert the Bruce had cherished the ambition of going on a crusade but died before he was able to do so. He asked that his heart be carried to Jerusalem and buried in the Holy Sepulchre. The Scottish noble entrusted with the king's heart, Sir James Douglas (1286–1330)—the "Black Douglas," one of Bruce's most important lieutenants—died on the way to Jerusalem, fighting the Muslims in Spain. Legend has it that Douglas threw Bruce's heart at the enemy. The heart was recovered and brought back to Scotland, where, sealed in a lead casket, it was buried in Melrose Abbey.

The war between Scotland and England dragged on, but peace was eventually achieved in 1328. The Treaty of Edinburgh was a clear-cut victory for the Scots, as the English recognized that Scotland was a completely separate kingdom, free of any subjection to England. (The treaty was actually written in French, the common language of the English and Scottish aristocracy.) Bruce did not have much of a chance to enjoy peace, though, as he died the following year. He was succeeded by his son, David II (1324–71; r. 1329–71).

The Reign of Edward III

Edward III (1312–77; r. 1327–77) came to the English throne under a cloud due to the misfortunes of his father, Edward II. The fact that England shared in the great northern European famine from 1315 added to Edward II's unpopularity, as did his infatuations with ambitious male favorites such as Piers Gaveston (ca. 1284–1312) and Hugh Despencer (1223–65). Both Gaveston and Despencer were killed by English noblemen who feared their influence on the king. Edward's wife, Isabella of France (1295–1358), turned on him with French backing, and he was imprisoned and then murdered in 1327 (although there is some evidence suggesting he survived and fled the country). Isabella and her lover, Roger Mortimer (1287–1330), after making peace with the Scots in 1328, settled down to loot the country until they were overthrown by a baronial faction backing the young Edward III in 1330.

Edward III's long reign was marked by the disaster of the Black Death, the beginnings of the Hundred Years' War between England and France, and the rise of Parliament as a governing institution. In some ways the handsome and chivalrous Edward was the model of a medieval king, and his power over his kingdom was not significantly challenged. But unlike his grandfather, he had little in the way of permanent achievement.

The Growth of Parliaments

The English parliament grew increasingly complex and differentiated in the time after Edward I. Edward II's ineffectiveness and Edward III's interest in foreign wars rather than administration created a gap in the kingdom's government that Parliament partially filled. Increased taxation also led to the strengthening of Parliament as a tax-approving institution. In the early 14th century, attendance at Parliament began to be seen not simply as a matter of the king issuing an invitation. Instead, members of certain families, so-called peers of Parliament, asserted that they possessed a hereditary right to be summoned. The difference between peers and ordinary knights led to increased legal and social stratification within the landed class and a growing separation between the different elements of Parliament. Originally, parliaments had included representatives from the lower clergy, but they now met at their own convocations, a sort of parliament for the English church. There was also a gradual division between those holding baronies from the king—bishops, abbots, and peers—and others that eventually developed into the division between the House of Lords and House of Commons. After 1327, the representatives of the counties and boroughs, or towns, began to be invited to every parliament, rather than only occasionally. However, the lords continued to dominate politically, while the commons were expected to petition rather than be the actual decision makers.

The Scottish parliament grew in a similar fashion, although its growth is not as well documented or as dramatic as the English. It began as a council of the king's advisers, supplemented by the leading nobles, bishops, and other leaders of the realm. These full parliaments could advise the king, and on some occasions magnates could even publicly speak against the king's policies. Like its English contemporary, the Scottish parliament made laws, ratified treaties, and settled legal disputes. Although kings summoned parliaments, they were not dependent on kings to meet: Parliaments met and had an active role in the governance of the realm during royal minorities or when a king was held captive.

The Hundred Years' War

Edward III initially devoted his foreign policy to attacks on Scotland, where at first he was much more successful than his father or Mortimer. In the long run, however, Edward aggravated the Scottish problem. Edward's hostility to both Scotland and France helped lead to an alliance between the two countries that would become a prominent feature of western European politics for centuries. Edward responded to his enemies' alliance by working with the leadership of the Flemish cities and intriguing against the count of Flanders, vassal of the French king.

In addition to the conflicts over Scotland and Flanders, there were several other issues contributing to increased hostility between England and France. The French monarchy was aggressively asserting its sovereignty over the English possessions in southwestern France that remained from the wars between the English kings and the French in the 13th century. The requirement that the English king pay homage to the French for Gascony continued to poison relations between the two countries, as the French king had declared land confiscated when there were difficulties with England. The immediate cause of the Hundred Years' War between England and France was the rival French and English claims to the French throne when the direct line of the French ruling family, the Capetians, failed. The last French king of the direct line of the Capetians, Charles IV, died in 1328. The Salic law, which declared invalid all claims from the female line, including Edward's, was rediscovered by French jurists with the intention of keeping the English out. Edward had a claim derived from his mother, Isabella, the daughter of the Capetian king Philip IV.

The Hundred Years' War lasted from 1337 to 1453, although the conflict was not constant and there were long periods of inactivity. It differed from the previous wars between England and France in that the English defined themselves as English. Unlike the previous wars of the English Plantagenets and the French Capetians, the Hundred Years' War was not a struggle between two French magnates, one of whom happened to be king of England, but between two nations. In 1362 the English parliament, which was quite important in Edward's reign due to the necessity for money and organized consent for his wars, switched its official language from French to English. Even though the English armies in France included many French soldiers, they were referred to collectively as "the English."

The enmity that developed between the two nations was particularly bitter on the French side due to the savagery of English warfare in France. One of the basic tactics of warfare used by the English was the *chevauchée,* essentially large-scale devastation through burning and pillaging that was meant to deny agricultural resources to the French and spread fear of the English. The devastation wrought by the English in southwestern France remains part of French historical memory to this day.

The French brought their alliance with Scotland into play, carrying the war to northern England. Scottish activity was mostly limited to raiding; when the Scots tried to invade in force in 1346, they were resoundingly defeated and their king, David II, taken prisoner. This provoked a breakdown in Scottish government, as it took 11 years for the king to be ransomed. It also took Scotland out of the war.

The first few decades of the war saw mostly English victories, but France's size prohibited its complete absorption as English territory. Given the French monarchy's greater resources and prestige, then the greatest in Europe, this was a remarkable achievement, but in the long run the English lacked the resources to conquer France.

The Black Death

British society was fundamentally changed by the Black Death, a plague that first hit England in 1348, a year after its arrival in Europe, and spread rapidly throughout the British archipelago. The disease was named after the black pustules it raised on the bodies of its victims. It first struck through the southern ports in direct contact with the Continent. By 1349 the plague covered the entire British Isles, the northern isles of Scotland, and the western part of Ireland. It killed about 35–45 percent of the English population in its first assault and was particularly devastating in cities due to overcrowding and poor sanitation. The plague was not a onetime occurrence but recurred with diminishing intensity into the 17th century. These recurrences made it difficult for the population to recover.

Depopulation brought economic benefits to those who survived, however. One striking testimony to the large population of England relative to its resources at the time is that most vacancies on the land caused by the plague's first wave filled immediately. Tenants were also in a favorable position to bargain on rents, as there was more land available than people to work it. Marriage rates rose after the plague since more people took spouses as part of the process of establishing themselves on the land. Yet subsequent plagues created vacancies that could not be filled. Living conditions improved for the survivors as the smaller agricultural workforce was able to concentrate on more productive land. Peasant diet improved greatly after the plague as more marginal land was devoted to raising livestock and meat became more common. There was more beer as barley and oats were used for brewing rather than human consumption.

The more favorable situation for peasants and laborers was a disaster for landowners, who were forced to pay higher wages as the labor pool shrank. Landowners, who dominated England's parliament, used the law as a weapon in the economic struggle. In 1351 Parliament enacted the Statute of Laborers in an attempt to control wages. It required all able-bodied men and women without land to serve anyone who offered them work at the rates prevalent in 1347, before the plague arrived in Britain, and prohibited any employer from offering higher wages than that. The statute also forbade peasants from breaking a contract and inflicted harsh penalties on those who dared to leave their land. Local authorities, the justices of the peace drawn from the landowning classes, were to confiscate excess wages. The statute was enforced for several years after passage, and though it did not succeed in the goal of keeping wages to pre-plague levels, it did keep wages from going as high as they would have without it. The statute helped sharpen and embitter class conflict in the rural areas, eventually leading to the great Peasants' Revolt of 1381.

In the long run, landlords realized that enhancing personal freedom was an effective way to keep workers on the land. The late Middle Ages saw the end of serfdom as an institution in most of England. Unfree tenants—bondmen, villeins, and day laborers who were subject to the lord of the manor—often simply migrated from their home manors and took up free tenures on newly available land in other parts of the country.

The plague wreaked great damage in Wales as well, killing about a third of the population. The old kinship-based Welsh society began to dissolve with the deaths and with the Welsh people's increased social and geographical mobility after the plague had ended. The new availability of land due to depopulation also promoted the immigration of English people and other non-Welsh into Wales. Towns and villages were abandoned for sheep farming, and land was sold for cash, allowing a rising gentry class, the *uchelwyr,* to buy land and build estates. The Welsh economy declined for the rest of the century.

The plague was introduced to Scotland in 1349 through contact with English soldiers on the border. The Scots originally called it "the death of the English" and identified it as divine punishment for England, a view they quickly revised as it penetrated their country. The effects of the plague on Scotland were similar to those in England but less intense, probably because the disease spread more slowly in the less densely populated country. Perhaps a quarter of the population died, with the poor the most vulnerable. Scottish chroniclers described the plague less emotionally than English or European witnesses, indicating that the disease was less disruptive in Scotland. However, it had some of the same effects as it did in England, encouraging the shift of lands from grain to raising stock and benefiting tenants against landlords. One difference was that the Scottish parliament was not oriented to passing laws like the English, and there was no Scottish Statute of Laborers. Scottish peasants did not rebel against their lords. The need for workers in England after the plague drew some Scots south of the border, either as farmers or as soldiers in the Hundred Years' War. The increased availability of land in the fertile lowlands also halted the immigration of lowland speakers of Scots, a Scottish dialect of English, to the Scottish highlands, widening the divisions between highland Gaelic-speaking and lowland Scots-speaking Scotland.

Internal Conflicts in England

The violence and devastation of the Hundred Years' War and the Black Death had devastating effects on English society. For the century between the death of Edward III in 1377 and the accession of the House of Tudor to the English throne in 1485, the country was racked by class conflicts; national conflicts between English and Welsh; the struggles of aristocratic factions; and the rise of a new religious movement, Lollardry. However, the period also saw important cultural transformations, including the rise of the printing press and the revival of English as a literary language.

The Peasants' Revolt of 1381

The Peasants' Revolt of 1381 was ultimately a response to the Black Death and the Hundred Years' War. The Statute of Laborers, the attempt of England's landowning rulers to keep peasants' wages down in the wake of the labor shortage caused by the plague, sharpened peasant resentment, as did attempts to introduce a poll tax to pay for the war with France. The rebellion began in areas of southeastern England exposed to raids from French vessels, leading to peasant anger at the royal government's failure to fulfill its responsibilities in guarding the coast. A peasant army marched on London and actually took the city, killing Archbishop of Canterbury Simon Sudbury (ca. 1316–1381).

This illustration of the 14th-century French historian Jean Froissart gives an idealized picture of the Peasants' Revolt. The reality was less picturesque. (HIP/Art Resource, NY)

Sudbury was also lord chancellor, the head of the English legal system and the top government official after the king, and the rebels considered him responsible for the poll tax. Many foreigners resident in London, mostly Flemings and Italians, were also killed.

The rising was not republican or antiroyalist, but rebels called for better counsel to be given to the young king, Richard II (r. 1377–99), Edward III's son. They demanded the end of serfdom, a ceiling on rents, and the abolition of the legal privileges of nobility and gentry. While parleying with the king outside London, the revolt's leader, Wat Tyler, was stabbed to death by the city's lord mayor, William Walworth, and one of the king's esquires, Ralph de Standish. The revolt broke up shortly after that.

There were subsequent peasant rebellions into the 15th and 16th centuries, but they were not as widespread or successful. Richard II (1367–1400; r. 1377–99) faced more successful opposition from aristocratic politicians, led by Henry Bolingbroke (1366–1413). Bolingbroke overthrew Richard and took power as King Henry IV (r. 1399–1413). The doubt this introduced into the succession would have calamitous consequences in the 15th century, leading to the Wars of the Roses (1455–85).

Rebellion in Wales

England also faced difficulties with the principality of Wales. Formally a dominion of the English Crown, Wales had become a land marked by massive discrimination in favor of English settlers and against Welsh inhabitants. Welsh national feeling did not disappear with the English conquest. The French, perhaps hoping to repeat their successful Scottish policy, backed Welsh adventurers in attempts to take Wales from the English, but they were never able to devote sufficient resources to Wales to accomplish this. The English government took the possibility of a French-backed Welsh revolt seriously enough, however, to have the last heir of the royal house of Gwynedd, then a captain in the French service, assassinated in 1378. The most important Welsh rebellion began in 1400 and lasted until 1409. In the absence of a claimant to Welsh royalty, it was led by the squire Owain Glyndwyr (who appears as Owen Glendower in William Shakespeare's *Henry IV*). Despite French aid and some ambitious plans to divide England among rebellious English nobles, Glyndwyr (ca. 1354–1416; r. 1400–ca. 1416) was overthrown when Prince Henry, the future Henry V, devoted sufficient resources to his defeat. Glyndwyr also faced opposition from other Welshmen who saw collaboration with the English ruler as the best way of maintaining their privileges. The defeat of the rising was followed by the de facto integration of much of the Welsh gentry into the English ruling class, paving the way for the accession of a Welsh dynasty, the Tudors (or Tydders), at the end of the 15th century.

Henry V

The reign of Henry V (1387–1422; r. 1413–22) is an interlude of domestic peace and stability between the troubles of the reign of his father, Henry IV (1366–1413; r. 1399–1413), and the far greater troubles of the reign of his son, Henry VI (1421–71; r. 1422–61, 1470–71). Drawing on his unchallenged control over England, Henry V brought the English the closest they would ever come to the conquest of France. He became a national hero, as portrayed in William Shakespeare's patriotic play *Henry V*. Henry was a great military leader although a brutal and somewhat psychopathic man, even by the standards of late medieval warfare.

One important advantage for the English in the Hundred Years' War was the longbow, a weapon restricted to Britain due to the scarcity of yew trees, whose wood was necessary for its construction. Long training was necessary to use it effectively, and the English and Scottish kings tried to encourage longbow training by issuing decrees forbidding the practice of other sports.

The high point of English power in France followed the victory of English longbowmen over French knights at the Battle of Agincourt in 1415. French knights charged straight ahead into devastating longbow fire from the greatly outnumbered English army, and 6,000 Frenchmen died in a few minutes. Following the battle, the French king, Charles VI (1368–1422), recognized Henry V as his heir, cutting out his own son, the dauphin Charles. English monarchs would retain the official title King of France until the 18th century. Henry spent his subsequent career in France until his early death in 1422, and some English people worried that England would become a satellite kingdom of a monarchy headquartered in Paris.

Magnate Wars

The greatest of the internal British struggles of the 15th century was the Wars of the Roses (1455–85) in England. The conflict is named after the white rose and the red, emblems of the rival houses of Lancaster and York, which were contending for the throne of England. However, the real force driving the conflict was not dynastic rivalry but the emergence of powerful nobles known as magnates, whose wealth, much of it gained in the French wars, enabled them to build personal armies paid in cash, as opposed to the smaller feudal forces characteristic of the earlier Middle Ages. The contest for the throne became mixed up with noble feuds or regional struggles for predominance, such as that between the Percy and the Neville families in the north.

The problem was compounded by the extraordinary weakness of royal leadership under Henry VI, arguably the most incompetent king in English history. Henry's reign saw both the final loss of France in 1453 and protracted civil war leading to his abdication in 1461. Henry himself was murdered, probably at the command of the Yorkish king Edward IV (1442–83; r. 1461–70, 1471–83) after a brief interlude in 1470 in which Henry, now almost completely senile, was put back on the throne as a puppet of Edward's enemies. This interlude is known as the Readeption of Henry VI. The Wars of the Roses would culminate in the crowning of Henry VII in 1485.

Fifteenth-century Scotland faced struggles similar to those of England. Scottish magnates were increasingly calling on large followings who shared their clan names; the clan system was prevalent in the highlands, but similar practices could be found in the Scottish lowlands, particularly on the border with England, where surname groups, such as the Montgomerys, wielded more power than the Scottish state. An epic struggle between the Scottish royal house and the Black Douglases ended in the victory of the former and the annihilation of the latter at the Battle of Arkinholm in 1455. Despite the murder of two Scottish kings, the Scottish throne never fell to quite as low a level as did that of England under Henry VI. The Scottish monarchs were never reduced to puppets of their nobles. While English rulers were driven from all of France except the Norman town of Calais, Scotland was still expanding. The last remaining Scandinavian possessions in the archipelago, the islands of Orkney and the Shetlands, passed from Norway to Scotland in 1472 as part of the dowry of Princess Margaret of Norway, thus bringing an end to the long Scandinavian involvement in the British Isles.

John Wycliffe and the Lollards

Throughout medieval history, England and Scotland had been noteworthy for their Catholic orthodoxy. What few heretics were found in Britain were often immigrants from Continental areas with established heretical movements. In the 14th century England produced its own heresy: the Lollard, or Wycliffite, movement founded by John Wycliffe (ca. 1330–1384). Twenty-six different ways of spelling his name appear in medieval manuscripts. Wycliffe, an Oxford professor, was troubled by the papacy's corruption and politicization. To solve the problem of papal authority's decreased legitimacy, he located ultimate religious authority in the Bible rather than in the institutional church. His followers later produced the first vernacular English translation of the entire Bible. Biblicism led Wycliffe to question other aspects of traditional doctrine, such as transubstantiation—the belief that the bread and wine of Mass actually transform into the body and blood of Christ—and the pope's supremacy, both doctrines developed with little biblical support. Wycliffe argued that the body and blood are present spiritually but not actually, and Wycliffites eventually went so far as to claim that the pope was the Antichrist.

Wycliffe was forced out of Oxford, but, protected by noble patrons, he was allowed to retire to the cure of a parish church, where he produced a stream of books and pamphlets. The spread of his ideas ultimately led most English leaders to see him as a threat to the social and religious order, particularly after the Peasants' Revolt of 1381, which had some Wycliffite involvement. Most nobles interested in Wycliffe returned to Catholic orthodoxy after the revolt.

Initially Wycliffe's followers—derogatorily called Lollards, or mumblers—were allowed to move freely in some parts of England, protected by a network of sympathetic gentry. Opposition to the movement strengthened and intensified, however, eventually driving it underground. Some bishops organized persecution of the Wycliffites in their dioceses, but the Inquisition was never established in England, where the kings saw it as a threat to their authority. Wycliffe's ideas were also pushed back on the intellectual front as distinguished scholars produced intellectual refutations, although these did not have much effect on Wycliffe's ordinary uneducated followers. Eventually the term *Lollard* was attached to anyone critical of the official church, and it lost any strict doctrinal meaning. Lollardry was driven into the lower, but not the lowest, classes. Like other heretical groups, the Lollards also attracted a disproportionate number of women, seeking more freedom than allowed to them in established society; the Lollards may even have ordained women priests. By 1450 the movement was clearly diminishing in strength and numbers, but there was a Lollard revival in the last decade of the 15th century, when the Lollards were still a very small—and widely despised—religious minority, concentrated in some areas of the country where they did have influence. Urban and small-town artisans such as weavers continued to meet in secret Lollard circles until the 16th century.

The Lollard movement also reached Scotland. Lollard heretics were occasionally burned in the early 15th century, and anti-Lollard legislation was passed in 1425. The archbishop of Glasgow denounced 30 heretics to the king in 1494, and an Ayrshire notary named Murdoch Nisbet translated a Lollard English version of the New Testament into Scots in the early 16th century.

The Rebirth of English Literature

The internal and external conflicts of the 14th century were accompanied by a great cultural revival in England—the revival of English as a literary language. After the Norman Conquest of England in 1066, English had virtually disappeared as a written language as literature was written in French or Latin. English always remained the spoken language of ordinary people, however, and its vocabulary was enriched by French and Latin words. By the 14th century, English—now Middle English as contrasted with the Old English of the Anglo-Saxons—reappeared as a language of literature and poetry in the works of a striking group of contemporaries: Geoffrey Chaucer (ca. 1343–1400), William Langland (ca. 1332–ca. 1386), John Gower (ca. 1330–1408), and the anonymous *Pearl* poet.

Chaucer, by profession a government clerk and diplomat, was the most important of these poets. He is best known for *The Canterbury Tales,* an unfinished group of poems recounting the stories told by a group of pilgrims on the way to Thomas Becket's shrine at Canterbury. The pilgrims, male and female, are members of different social classes and professions, and their stories give vivid pictures of medieval culture. Among Chaucer's other works are *Troilus and Criseyd* (ca. 1380–87), recounting a legend of lovers in the Trojan War; and *The Legend of Good Women* (ca. 1386–88), which he claimed he had written as penance for his many works that showed women in an unflattering light.

John Gower, whom his friend Chaucer called "moral Gower," was a more serious poet. He wrote verses in English, French, and Latin. His most important poem is one written in English, *Confessio Amantis,* or *Lover's Confession,* probably completed in 1390. It tells the story of a lover wounded by Cupid's arrow. Cupid's mother, the goddess Venus, instructs the lover to confess to her priest, Genius, who tells many tales of lovers arranged under the headings of the seven deadly sins. The stories emphasize the importance of constant and mature love, which Gower refers to as "honest love." Gower drew heavily from the ancient Roman poet Ovid as well as other classical writers, the Bible, and medieval sources for his anecdotes. At the poem's conclusion, Cupid removes the arrow from the lover, now too old for love. *Confessio Amantis* was one of the most popular long poems in English during the later Middle Ages, surviving in 49 manuscripts and even being translated into Portuguese and Spanish. Translation into other languages was extremely rare for English writings in the Middle Ages.

Far less is known of William Langland and the *Pearl* poet. Langland is known for one poem: *The Vision of Piers Plowman,* an allegorical vision concerned with the corruption of contemporary society and the difficulty of leading a truly Christian life. The author scourges the corruption of the clergy, but his knowledge of religion indicates that he may well have been a cleric himself.

While Chaucer, Gower, and Langland were all concerned with their contemporary society, the *Pearl* poet was more backward-looking. His

THOMAS MALORY AND LE MORTE D'ARTHUR

The 15th century saw the production of one of the most influential works of English literature, Sir Thomas Malory's *Le Morte d'Arthur* (*The Death of Arthur*). Published by William Caxton in 1485, *Le Morte d'Arthur* is a compilation of the legends of King Arthur that defined the basic Arthurian canon for centuries. The legend of Arthur had been told in increasingly elaborate versions for centuries by French, English, and German authors, but the version of the tales of the legendary round table that people know today is Malory's.

Malory (ca. 1405–71) was himself a fascinating character, rather different from the common perception of a writer. He was a tough, unscrupulous man who flourished in the anarchic England of the Wars of the Roses. He was charged with burglary, rape, and sheep stealing, and escaped from jail twice, once by fighting his way out. Most of *Le Morte d'Arthur* was probably written in prison.

or her vocabulary was also more Germanic, less influenced by words of French or Latin origin. The work of Chaucer, Gower, and Langland survives in numerous manuscripts, but the *Pearl* poet is known from only one. Along with the religious allegorical vision *Pearl,* the manuscript includes three other poems, of which by far the best known is the Arthurian romance *Sir Gawain and the Green Knight,* and the *Pearl* poet is sometimes referred to as the *Gawain* poet. The poems demonstrate an astonishing technical facility.

English literature also benefited from introduction of the printing press in 1476 by William Caxton (ca. 1422–1493). Caxton had learned the new technology of printing on the Continent and was eager to bring it to England. He printed chivalric tales and poems for aristocratic customers, including an edition of Chaucer's *Canterbury Tales.*

Scotland in the Reign of the Stewards

After a long and eventful reign, including a period of exile in France and several years spent as a prisoner of the English, David II died in 1371 without a legitimate son. The crown passed to a descendant of a daughter of Robert Bruce, Robert the Steward (r. 1371–90). The

Steward—or, as it was later known, Stuart—dynasty would be the last dynasty of Scottish monarchs.

The consequences of the Scottish wars of independence included the creation of a long-standing tradition of anti-English Scottish nationalism. In many ways the extensive Scots literature on the wars became the Scottish national epic, with William Wallace and Robert the Bruce the Scottish national heroes. Scotland and England also moved politically and culturally further apart as the old class of Anglo-Scots nobility with holdings on both sides of the border disappeared. In place of the relationship with England, the Scots built a new and much closer relationship with France. The alliance between Scotland and France is known in Scottish history as the Auld Alliance.

The Anglo-Scottish border became an increasingly militarized society, where localized war involving murders, ambushes, and cattle raids was carried on between English and Scottish lords into the 16th century. The stories of these conflicts are recounted in the so-called border ballads. Both English and Scottish kings found the borders difficult to control, and Scottish and English rebels and dissidents often sought help from the other country.

James IV (1473–1513; r. 1488–1513) is often considered the most successful of the Stuart kings of Scotland, although his reign ended in disaster. His father, James III (ca. 1451–88; r. 1460–88) had not been a successful king and had had a long conflict with his brother Alexander, duke of Albany, who allied with the English. In 1482 James III lost the town of Berwick-upon-Tweed, which had been changing hands between England and Scotland for centuries. Richard of Gloucester, the future Richard III of England, took the town for the last time. (Curiously, although administered by England, Berwick was never formally incorporated into the kingdom.) The future James IV actually joined a rebellion against his father, provoked by James III's increasingly fruitless attempts to ally with England and what was viewed as his partiality for his second son, also named James. James III died in or was killed shortly after his defeat by the rebels in the Battle of Sauchieburn on June 11, 1488. Charges of complicity in his father's death would thereafter haunt James IV.

James IV was a hardworking king who took a passionate interest in justice and in new technological developments. It was during his reign that printing came to Scotland in 1507. Most early Scottish printing was devoted to religious subjects, and part of the agenda of the king and his most important councillor, Bishop William Elphinstone (1431–1514), was to preserve specifically Scottish customs in print to prevent

Holyrood Palace in Edinburgh was first built by James IV as a seat for the Scottish monarchy. In the following centuries, parts of it were destroyed and rebuilt. (Library of Congress, National Photo Company Collection)

the encroachment of English uses. The reign also saw the founding of a new university, Kings College in Aberdeen, and the founding of a college of surgeons in 1505.

Like other early modern rulers, the king tried to maintain powerful military forces. He was at peace with the traditional enemy, England, for most of his reign but did not allow his army to decay. James's parliament passed laws forbidding the playing of golf or football to encourage the king's subjects to practice with the bow. The king was also interested in artillery and maintained a formidable weapons shop in Edinburgh Castle. On the seas, James built huge ships, including the *Michael*, built in 1511 and the largest ship in Europe at the time.

The reign of James IV saw a golden age of Scottish literature, particularly poetry. Poets of the time include Robert Henryson (ca. 1424–ca. 1506), William Dunbar (ca. 1460–ca. 1520), and Gavin Douglas (ca. 1474–1522), sometimes referred to collectively as the *makars*, or makers. They were influenced by the English poet Geoffrey Chaucer and by French poetry as well as Scottish traditions and the new spirit of the Renaissance. Henryson's best-known works include *Morall Fabillis of Esope the Phrygian*, a recounting of several of Aesop's fables in nearly

3,000 lines. Dunbar wrote many poems, of which one of the most famous is *Lament for the Makars,* a tribute to earlier Scottish poets. Douglas, a bishop, was best known for his translation of the ancient Roman poet Virgil's epic *Aeneid* into Scots.

The Early Tudors

The House of York proved unable to hold the English throne. The ultimate winner of the Wars of the Roses was Henry Tudor, Henry VII (1457–1509; r. 1485–1509), who was of Welsh, English, and French descent and whose claim derived from John of Gaunt. Having spent most of his youth in European exile, he came to power after defeating the last Yorkist king, Richard III (r. 1483–85), at the Battle of Bosworth Field on August 22, 1485. Henry was shaped by his long experience of exile, during most of which no one thought of him as a serious contender for the throne; indeed, it took a long series of crimes and political blunders by Richard, whose noble followers betrayed him on the battlefield itself, to make Henry king. Even afterward, Henry faced challenges from the pretenders Lambert Simnel and Perkin Warbeck, two men from obscure backgrounds who claimed to be Yorkist heirs and were backed by exiled Yorkists, discontented nobles, Irish lords, and, in Warbeck's case, James III of Scotland. Henry defeated Simnel at the Battle of Stoke Field in 1487, although he spared the pretender, whom he considered a child manipulated by others. Simnel received a job in the royal kitchens. Warbeck, captured in 1497, received no such mercy and was executed in 1499.

As a king, Henry was known for his love of money and lack of interest in military glory. His successful foreign policy was based on staying friends with everyone, renouncing ambitions on the Continent, and even avoiding the perpetual temptation of English kings to meddle in Scotland. After the Warbeck troubles, the king followed a conciliatory policy with his northern neighbor, signing the Treaty of Perpetual Peace in 1502. The peace was reinforced the next year by the marriage of Henry's daughter Margaret (1489–1541) to James IV, a marriage that after a century would bring a Scottish dynasty to the English throne.

Henry VII reasserted domestic royal power, which had weakened in the 15th century. He inaugurated a long and eventually successful struggle against "over-mighty" subjects—those magnates who employed private armies and gangs of followers in livery. He also began to change the English relationship with Wales. On his landing from France, Henry had appealed for Welsh support with promises to

AN ENGLISH COURT OFFICIAL: THE GROOM OF THE STOOL

Medieval and early modern monarchy was personal monarchy, and few officials demonstrated this more than the groom of the stool, an official with responsibility for the monarch's excrement. The groom attended royal eliminations, and on the monarch's death, received his or her chamber pots and commodes. The groom also assisted the monarch in personal aspects of life, such as dressing and eating. The groom first appears with Henry VII's founding of the Privy Chamber around 1495. The Privy Chamber, of which the groom was the head, attended the monarch in his private rooms. The groom was of low status under Henry VII, but under his son and successor, the far more social Henry VIII, the groom of the stool became one of the most powerful officials at court. The office was not abolished until 1837 at the accession of Queen Victoria.

redress their grievances. His succession to the crown was seen by some Welsh bards as fulfilling the ancient prophecy that someday the Welsh, the descendants of the inhabitants of Britain before the coming of the Anglo-Saxons, would once again rule the country. As king, Henry eased but did not eliminate discrimination against the Welsh. He employed Welshmen in his administration; named his eldest son Arthur, after the legendary British king and Welsh hero (Arthur never succeeded to the throne as he died before his father); and created a council for Wales.

Henry was unusually interested in financial transactions, inspecting books and receiving cash, highly unusual behavior in a medieval or early modern king. He did not increase taxes, which would have involved calling Parliament, but rigorously enforced customary dues. He set up a more efficient system of handling the king's guardianship of the wards of feudal tenants who had died leaving children who were still minors. He also made extensive use of forced loans, requiring wealthy Englishmen to lend money to the king. These loans were referred to euphemistically as *benevolences*. Henry's avarice was unpopular and considered unkingly. There was a popular story that he repented his greediness on his deathbed. Henry actually died leaving a surplus in the treasury, which was almost unheard-of. In addition to spending the surplus in a hurry, the old king's only surviving son, Henry VIII

(1491–1547; r. 1509–47), judicially murdered two of his father's tax collectors at the beginning of his reign, courting popularity.

At the beginning of his reign, Henry VIII seemed to restore strength and glamour to the English monarchy. He shunned his father's policy of peace and hoped to reestablish English power in France in alliance with Holy Roman Emperor Charles V, whose aunt, Catherine of Aragon (1485–1536), was Henry's queen. (Catherine had previously been married to Henry's brother Arthur and married Henry after Arthur died.) Henry's military efforts in northern France were unsuccessful, but his early reign saw a decisive English victory over Scotland at the battle of Flodden in 1513. Henry's brother-in-law, James IV of Scotland—following the Auld Alliance, which obligated him to fight as a French ally— took advantage of the English army's absence to invade England with the largest army Scotland had ever assembled. The fact that this carefully assembled army, led by the king himself, was crushingly defeated not by the main English army, off in France, but by a hastily put together English force led by local noblemen crushingly demonstrated Scotland's military inferiority. The death of James IV along with nine Scottish earls and 14 lords of Parliament was one of the great disasters of Scottish history, and it eliminated Scotland as a threat to England for more than a century. Catherine, regent for King Henry while he was with his army in France, sent James's bloody coat to France as a gift to her husband.

Meanwhile, Henry was increasingly worried about Catherine's failure to deliver a son who would solidify the Tudor claim on the throne of England. This failure would lead to the greatest transformation in early modern British history.

5

THE MAKING OF PROTESTANT BRITAIN (1529-1689)

The history of Britain from the early 16th to the late 17th century was dominated by two processes. One was the cultural, religious, and political transformation of both England and Scotland from Catholicism to Protestantism. The other was the joining of the two nations under a single dynasty ruling the entire British archipelago—the "kingdom of Great Britain," when James VI of Scotland became James I of England after the death of the last Tudor queen, Elizabeth I. These two phenomena were closely related. The Reformation ended a time of relative cultural isolation between England and Scotland, inaugurating a period when their history would be closely intertwined. Although the establishment of Protestantism in both countries was complete by the beginning of the 17th century, the political implications of the new religion and the complex relationship of England, Scotland, and Ireland was worked out, often violently, over the course of that century.

The Reformation in England and Wales

Many of the modern differences between England and Scotland can be traced to the different processes by which they adopted the Protestant Reformation. England's Reformation was driven more by decisions made by the central government, while Scotland's began later and was largely carried out by convinced Protestants outside and sometimes against the government.

The most important monarch in the story of the English Reformation was Henry VIII (1491–1547; r. 1509–47). Henry's Reformation began not with an interest in Protestant doctrines, to which he was resolutely opposed, but by difficulties with the Catholic Church, in particular those surrounding his hopes for a divorce from his first wife, Catherine of Aragon (1485–1536), to marry his lover, Anne Boleyn (ca. 1507–36). Henry was particularly worried because Catherine had failed to give birth to the male heir who would cement the Tudor claim to the English throne. Frustrated in his attempts to win a divorce, Henry eventually removed the English church from the pope's jurisdiction and put it under his own headship in the Act of Supremacy of 1534. Henry further dissolved monasteries and other religious institutions, selling much of their land and adding their wealth to the royal coffers. Although Henry's Reformation was not fully Protestant, it did require people to deny beliefs and institutions that had been accepted dogma for many generations, such as papal supremacy, priestly celibacy, monasteries, saints' days, masses for the dead, and relics. Widespread opposition was expressed in one major rising in the north in 1536, the Pilgrimage of Grace, which was defeated by royal forces. Generally speaking, the early Reformation was strongest in the south and east, weakest in the north and west.

Anne Boleyn became one of the most hated women in England, as many English women identified with the cause of Queen Catherine, seeing the Spanish queen as a wronged but faithful wife as well as a champion of the traditional religion of England. Anne, too, failed to produce a son and heir for Henry, although like Catherine she did have a daughter, Elizabeth, who would eventually ascend the throne. Anne was executed on trumped-up charges of adultery in 1536.

There was a vast increase in the activity of the central government associated with the Reformation. The Reformation did not openly violate established ideas of the rule of law, nor was it simply carried out by royal decree. At every stage, new laws were passed in Parliament. The Reformation is often dated from 1529, when the parliament that became known as the Reformation Parliament first met, and their legislation culminated in the Act of Supremacy. Henry occasionally had trouble with his parliaments, but he was usually able to control them, particularly since he had independent financial resources. The legislation was usually enforced with regard to legal procedure, including the rights of the accused, and some persons who publicly opposed the Reformation were able to get away with it by manipulating the laws. However, local authorities and a small but enthusiastic minority of convinced English Protestants saw to it that the measures were implemented.

The Reformation in Wales was bound up with Henry VIII's insistence on lowering or abolishing the legal distinctions between England and Wales. In 1536 Parliament passed an Act of Union abolishing the special status of Wales and legal discrimination between the Welsh and the English. The special privileges of the residents of the Welsh Marches dating back to the Middle Ages, such as exemption from some royal taxation, were also abolished, and the whole area was divided into shires based on the English model. For the first time, Wales was represented in the English parliament. The government attempted to impose the Reformation on Wales, but the poverty of much of the country made the task difficult, as did the necessity of producing Protestant religious materials in Welsh.

The dissolution of the Catholic monasteries and the confiscation of their lands was an enormous windfall for the monarchy, most of which was spent on Henry's court and wars in France and Scotland. The noble and gentry families who bought the lands were a powerful obstacle to any reestablishment of Catholicism, which might threaten their right of ownership. The greater number of independent landowners created by the dissolution would eventually challenge both the great magnates and the Crown.

Henry was succeeded by his much more Protestant son, Edward VI (1537–53; r. 1547–53), the product of his union with his third wife, Jane Seymour (1509–37). Edward's brief reign was followed by that of Henry and Catherine of Aragon's Catholic daughter Mary (1516–58; r. 1553–58), who in turn was followed by Henry's daughter by Anne Boleyn, Elizabeth (1533–1603; r. 1558–1603), a moderate Protestant. Each changed the church to suit him- or herself. These rapid changes created a number of martyrs willing to die for their religion, but among the population at large it encouraged passivity as people followed the government's successive leads. The removal of England from the universal church also marked a growing separation of England from Europe. The last bit of land England held in France, the Norman city of Calais, was lost to the French in 1558 under Mary.

The Scottish Reformation

There was even less heresy before the Reformation in Scotland than in England. The principal leader of the Reformation in Scotland was John Knox (1513–72), a disciple of the great Continental Protestant leader John Calvin (1509–64). Knox had spent some time in England as a chaplain to Edward VI and a great deal of time on the European continent. He was inspired by Calvin's city of Geneva in modern Switzerland, which he called a perfect school of Christ. Calvin and Knox wanted a Christianity austere in worship and emphasizing obedience to a strict moral code. Calvinists saw the true church as a small gathering of the "elect" whom God had chosen for salvation, rather than as a gathering of the whole community. Knox was a man of great boldness and little tact whose emphasis on church discipline and rigid doctrine became hallmarks of Scottish Protestantism. To the very end of the 1550s, a Protestant party among the Scottish aristocracy saw the possibility of an alliance with England's new Protestant queen, Elizabeth.

In the 1550s Scotland was ruled by the regent Mary of Guise (1515–60), a French Catholic noblewoman and the widow of King James V (ca. 1512–42; r. 1513–42), in the name of the young Mary, Queen of Scots (1542–87; r. 1542–67). Mary herself was in France as wife of the French dauphin, Francis (1544–60). Francis's death in 1560 led to Mary's return to Scotland. Mary was a good Catholic but fundamentally uninterested in recatholicizing Scotland, both because she was not particularly ideological and because she was uninterested in Scotland. She was more interested in the English throne, to which she had a fairly good claim as the great-granddaughter of Henry VII. Accusations that she had participated in the murder of her second husband, Henry Stuart, Lord Darnley (1545–67), another descendant of Henry VII whom she had married to strengthen her claim to the English succession, followed her throughout her reign. Her later marriage to James Hepburn, earl of Bothwell (1534–70), a man of great abilities but very bad personal reputation who was probably involved in Darnley's murder, further diminished her reputation as a woman and a ruler. It precipitated a massive revolt organized by Protestant lords and resulted in Mary's expulsion from the kingdom. Mary's illegitimate half brother, James, earl of Moray (1531–70), a strong Protestant, became regent after Mary was driven from the kingdom into England. There she became involved with English plotters against Elizabeth and was executed in 1587 in an act that shocked many people across Europe.

Scottish Protestant reformers attacked the structure and practices of the old church much more zealously than the English. The movement contained a strong Presbyterian element. Presbyterians believed in erecting a new church organization without bishops, based on the equality of parish ministers and rule by synods and committees. Their movement was called *Presbyterianism* after the Greek New Testament word for "priest." Presbyterians were much stronger in Scotland than in England, and after a struggle that lasted more than a century, they got their way.

The combination of Mary's opposition to Protestantism with her refusal simply to crush it led Scottish reformers to develop a theory of the independence of the church, or kirk, from the state, and suspicion of government involvement in religious affairs. Scottish ministers emphasized the subordination of secular rulers to the kirk, most memorably summed up by the minister Andrew Melville's reference to James VI, Mary's son, as "God's silly vassal" (quoted in Mackie 1978, 181). (*Silly* at the time meant "weak.") The kirk was headed by a general assembly rather than an individual.

James (1566–1625; r. 1567–1603) overcame a traumatic childhood to become one of the most successful Scottish kings. His mother left Scotland when he was only a year and a half old. His tutor was George Buchanan (1506–82), author of *De Jure Regni apud Scotos* (1579), one of the greatest anti-imperialist tracts of the 16th century, but a harsh man who harped on the sinfulness of James's entire family. Unsurprisingly, James hated him. When he was in his minority, James was kidnapped by noble factions, as was common in Scotland, and he was the subject of assassination attempts, both by violence and by sorcery—which made him an avid hunter of witches. Large-scale Scottish witch-hunting began after the passage of the Witchcraft Act in 1563, and over its course to the late 17th century, between 1,000 and 1,500 witches were executed—a large number for a small country. About 85 percent were women.

James's reign saw a complex struggle between the king; the great noble houses, some of which were still Catholic; and the ministers of the kirk. The king was the main winner, advancing centralization and the rule of law in Scotland. In response to church ministers' antiroyalist political theory, James elaborated a theory of divine-right monarchy that became very influential in both Scotland and England. As the cousin and heir of Queen Elizabeth of England, James maintained a policy of friendship with England that not only helped keep the peace between the two countries but smoothed his own way to the succession after the queen's death.

Elizabethan England

The reign of Elizabeth I from 1558 to 1603 saw the formation of a distinctively English Protestantism and conflicting religious parties. Sometime after 1570, England became a predominantly Protestant country. The generation that grew up under Elizabeth was the first to have no experience of a Catholic England. Her reign was also a key period in the definition of "Englishness" and the source of many of England's historical myths.

Three portraits of Elizabeth show her in youth, middle age, and old age. (Library of Congress)

Only Protestants believed Henry VIII's marriage to Anne Boleyn was legitimate and therefore that Elizabeth was the rightful heir to the throne. The queen's own religious feelings seem to have been more similar to her father's national Catholicism—following Catholic doctrine but rejecting the supremacy of the Pope or any earthly non-English authority—than anything else, but her allies in Mary's time were mainly Protestants concerned about Mary's Catholic restoration. Once Elizabeth ascended the throne in 1558, she set to work to mend the division between Roman Catholicism and Protestantism in the country. She created a new religious practice that brought together elements of both traditions and issued a new statement of church beliefs, the Thirty-nine Articles of Religion, and a new prayer book, the Book of Common Prayer, guiding worship in the Church of England. Her middle way became the distinctive perspective of the Anglican Church. Elizabeth accepted the separation from Rome but was a conservative on church discipline and order. The church was led by bishops, but its doctrine tended toward Protestantism.

However, not everyone was happy with the compromise. The crucifix Elizabeth kept in her chapel irritated many Protestants, and she had a difficult time dealing with her married bishops. The church's problems were aggravated by Elizabeth's contemptuous attitude. She confiscated church lands for financial purposes and often left bishoprics vacant for years so that their revenue went to the government. Many Protestants, including bishops appointed by Elizabeth at the beginning of her reign, wanted a much more radically Protestant church, without elaborate vestments or the formal liturgy set forth in the Book of Common Prayer. Others argued that vestments and ceremonies could be tolerated for the sake of preaching the true word. Few Protestants argued that these practices were actually good until late in the reign.

As resentment of lingering Catholic practices grew, an English Presbyterian movement emerged that saw the institution of bishops as tainted with Catholicism. Early connections between the English and Scottish Presbyterian parties would bear fruit in the next century. Some defenders of the church responded by rediscovering the value of some Catholic traditions. Their intellectual leader was the Reverend Richard Hooker (1554–1600), author of *Of the Lawes of Ecclesiastical Politie* (1594–97). Hooker and his followers emphasized the role of church rituals and the church as a religious gathering of the whole community rather than of the elect, that small proportion of the Christian community that Calvinists believed God had singled out for salvation. By the very end of Elizabeth's reign, Presbyterianism had been suppressed.

There remained a steadily shrinking but considerable Catholic population. Numerous Catholic priests from Mary's reign continued to practice as chaplains to Catholic noble and gentry families. Catholic landowners could greatly advance Catholicism among their tenants and dependants, and in many territories—particularly in the north, where the central government had less authority—there was hardly a Protestant to be seen. Elizabethan Catholicism became a religion of rural gentry, setting a pattern that would last until the 19th century. The slowly diminishing Catholic gentry community eventually became isolated from the mainstream of the English landed aristocracy, marrying among themselves and sending their children to be educated in Catholic institutions on the Continent. Catholics were in a particularly dangerous position as Pope Pius IV (1499–1565; pope, 1559–65), in his 1570 bull *Regnans in Excelsis,* had declared Elizabeth to be an illegitimate monarch to whom her Catholic subjects owed no allegiance. Loyalty to the pope could now mean treason to the queen. Some English Catholics, although not a majority, plotted and intrigued against Elizabeth and her successor, King James I.

Anti-Catholicism advanced in the Elizabethan era, as the memories of the persecution of Protestants under Elizabeth's sister Mary created an image of Catholicism as cruel and intolerant. John Foxe (1517–87), a Protestant minister, published a gigantic church history called *Acts and Monuments* (1563), better known as the *Book of Martyrs,* explaining how the true church through the centuries had always been persecuted

WILLIAM SHAKESPEARE, ENGLISH PATRIOT

The literary life of Elizabeth I's reign was distinguished by England's greatest poet and dramatist, William Shakespeare (1564–1616), many of whose plays are devoted to English and British historical subjects. He gave memorable voice to English patriotism in *Richard II* (ca. 1595). Like many English people throughout history, he referred to England as an "isle," or island, ignoring the fact that England shared the island of Britain with Scotland and Wales:

> *This royal throne of kings, this scepter'd isle,*
> *This earth of majesty, this seat of Mars,*
> *This other Eden, demi-paradise,*
> *This fortress built by Nature for herself*
> *Against infection and the hand of war,*
> *This happy breed of men, this little world,*
> *This precious stone set in the silver sea,*
> *Which serves it in the office of a wall,*
> *Or as a moat defensive to a house,*
> *Against the envy of less happier lands,*
> *This blessed plot, this earth, this realm, this England,*
> *This nurse, this teeming womb of royal kings,*
> *Fear'd by their breed and famous by their birth,*
> *Renowned for their deeds as far from home,*
> *For Christian service and true chivalry,*
> *As is the sepulchre in stubborn Jewry,*
> *Of the world's ransom, blessed Mary's Son,*
> *This land of such dear souls, this dear dear land, . . .*

Source: William Shakespeare, *Richard II*, act 2, scene 1.

by the false papal church. It became very popular and was frequently reprinted in the following centuries, often with gruesome illustrations of the torture and execution of heretics. It would help shape the self-image of English Protestants for centuries.

The struggle between Protestantism and Catholicism on the international level led the pope to encourage the king of Spain, Philip II (1527–98; r. 1556–98), to invade England. Philip had been married to Mary Tudor and had a tenuous claim on the throne. For Philip himself, however, the fundamental problem was not English Protestantism per se but English support for the Dutch rebels against Spain and the attacks against Spanish shipping by English pirates, such as the legendary Sir Francis Drake (1540–95). Conflict between England and Spain led to the attempted 1588 invasion by the famous Spanish Armada, a fleet of Spanish warships whose defeat caused national rejoicing in England.

Elizabeth did not care for parliaments and summoned them as seldom as possible. Parliaments early in the reign were arenas for pressuring the queen to marry and provide an heir to the throne, which she did not wish to do, or to further reform the church.

Elizabeth's reign saw a fundamental realignment of English external relations. The loss of Calais in 1558 had ended the 500 years of English history, beginning with the Norman Conquest in 1066, when English monarchs had ruled lands in France, but there was little interest in recovering it. Instead, English expansionism was refocused from Europe to both global and British contexts. After an abortive effort under Henry VII, England had not participated in the first thrust of European expansion, but conflict with Spain, which had used its New World resources to become Europe's dominant power, led the country to global involvement. The English acquired a taste for many New World and Asian commodities, of which the most famous was the American plant tobacco. Tobacco was introduced to English high society by one of Elizabeth's favorites, Sir Walter Raleigh (1552–1618), and eventually became widely popular, promoted as a health drug. Narratives of experiences of foreign lands sold briskly, and there was wide interest in problems of navigation and economic development.

Closer to home, in Ireland, the Elizabethan period saw the English government's first organized effort to control the whole island, along with the first definition of the struggle as a religious one. The Tudor policy of strengthening English control over Ireland, which had declined badly in the later Middle Ages, was complicated by religious issues. After defeating rebels and using the Irish parliament to impose the Reformation on Ireland, Henry VIII had been the first English king to take the title King of Ireland, in 1541. Henry's policy seems to have been to encourage Irish nobles to assimilate English ways (paralleling the far more successful Welsh policy), but after his death this was replaced with a more aggressive policy of colonization and the remaking of Irish society, strongly resisted by many Irish. Eventually the English put down the last organized Irish resistance in the last year of Elizabeth's reign.

The Elizabethan era was a remarkable age for English culture, particularly literature and theater, although in music and the visual arts England remained largely an importer. Until the Reformation, the English theatrical tradition had been oriented around cycles of sacred plays at religious festivals. Condemned by Protestantism as conducive to idolatry, religious theater had been wiped out, making room for a popular secular theater whose illustrious names included Christopher Marlowe (1564–93), author of *Dr. Faustus* and *Tamerlane*; Ben Jonson (1572–1637), author of *Volpone* and *The Alchemist*; and William Shakespeare (1564–1616), whose greatest plays include *Hamlet, King Lear,* and *As You Like It.* Shakespeare's genius drew particular nourishment from English history, the subject of his "history plays," including *Richard II,* the two parts of *Henry IV, Henry V,* the three parts of *Henry VI, Richard III,* and *Henry VIII.* An episode in 11th-century Scottish history provided the subject of Shakespeare's *Macbeth,* performed to welcome the Scottish king James VI to his new kingdom of England as James I (r. 1603–25).

Lay education and lay male attendance at universities increased in the 16th century. This process continued 15th-century trends and was greatly enhanced by the personal example of the first two Tudor monarchs, both of whom extensively educated their children, even the girls. Attendance for a few years at a university, though not usually culminating in the taking of a degree, came to be expected of young noblemen. Literacy at all levels of society was also advanced by the Protestant emphasis on Bible reading. By the end of Elizabeth's reign, the illiterate gentleman was becoming very rare, and even the illiterate gentlewoman was uncommon.

The Elizabethan era also saw the beginnings of English witch-hunting. The total number of witches executed in the witch hunt that began after the passage of a law against witchcraft in 1563 and lasted until the late 17th century was between 500 and 1,000, although many more died while awaiting trial in filthy jails or as the victims of mob violence. About 90 percent of the witches executed were women, a higher percentage than in most European countries.

The Union of Crowns and the Formation of the British State

The death of Elizabeth in 1603 was followed by the succession of the Scottish king James VI, who ruled as James I until his death in 1625. The same year saw the English suppress the last Irish rebels, for the first time subjecting the whole island to English rule. During James's reign, the first British state—with England, Wales, Ireland, and Scotland all ruled effectively by the king in London—was created.

James, founder of the Stuart dynasty in England, was widely welcomed. A family man with children, his rule promised to be free of the marriage and succession troubles that had plagued the Tudors since Henry VIII. James's reign over England is referred to as the Jacobean period, after the Latin equivalent of James, Jacobus.

The concept of a personal union—two countries with the same ruler but otherwise separate—had many medieval precedents and contemporary European parallels. Yet James wanted more than this, and he employed and promoted the title King of Great Britain. James's project for a closer union of his two kingdoms failed early in the reign due to English reluctance to be associated too closely with Scotland. This was not simply a matter of anti-Scottish prejudice, great as that was, but also the issue of whether the common law of England would continue to hold in a new kingdom. The only form of British union the mainstream of English public opinion would accept followed the model of Wales—an incorporation of Scotland into England with the subjection of the Scots to English laws, which according to the English were the best in the world. The Scots—who, unlike the Welsh, had never been conquered—were unenthusiastic about this idea.

Despite the failure of the union project, James was successful in other moves toward unity, such as the collusive Calvin's law case of 1608, which established that James's subjects in Scotland born after his accession were allowed to reside and trade in England. James was also successful in maintaining some unity between the English and Scottish churches, which despite their differences recognized each other as legitimate Protestant bodies on substantive doctrinal issues. On a practical level, the subordination of Scotland and England to one monarch led to far more effective law enforcement on the border, and the lawless border society dating back to the Middle Ages began to be tamed. James set up a swift postal service to cut the time for a round-trip between London and Edinburgh to a week and encouraged the use of English in Scotland. Intermarriage between Scottish and English noble families began to create an Anglo-Scottish nobility.

In England James continued the late Elizabethan religious peace and began to rebuild the Church of England from the economic devastation it had suffered in the Reformation and under Elizabeth. James's bishops, with some exceptions, were hardworking men respected by the different parties in the church. He tried to provide a preaching min-

KING JAMES ON TOBACCO

James I's reign saw the foundation of the colony of Jamestown in Virginia, which became a center of tobacco production. The king himself, however, was one of the foremost opponents of the new plant. His *A Counter-Blaste to Tobacco* (1604) denounced it in scorching terms as unhealthy, sinful, and disgusting.

> *And for the vanities committed in this filthie custome, is it not both great vanitie and uncleanenesse, that at the table, a place of respect, of cleanelinesse, of modestie, men should not be ashamed, to sit tossing of Tobacco pipes, and puffing of the smoke of Tobacco one to another, making the filthy smoke and stinke thereof, to exhale athwart the dishes, and infect the aire, when very often, men that abhorre it are at their repast? Surely Smoke becomes a kitchin far better then a Dining chamber, and yet it makes a kitchin also oftentimes in the inward parts of men, soiling and infecting them, with an unctuous and oily kinde of Soote, as hath bene found in some great Tobacco takers, that after their death were opened. And not onely meate time, but no other time nor action is exempted from the publike use of this uncivill tricke.*

Source: Neil Rhodes, Jennifer Richards, and Joseph Marshall, eds. *King James VI and I: Selected Writings.* Aldershot, England, and Burlington, Vt.: Aldershot, 2003, 291.

ister in every parish, but with an emphasis on Christian life rather than theological disputes. A small group of extreme Protestant, or Puritan, ministers were expelled from the church, but most accepted James's leadership. The king's later parliaments were almost all free of trouble about religion, as Elizabeth's never were. His greatest contribution to British religion was the sponsorship of the King James version of the Bible, translated by a committee of bishops and scholars on the basis of previous translations. James also seems to have lost his interest in witch-hunting after inheriting the English throne, and in some cases he intervened to defend accused witches.

James's major political problems were financial, with both long-term and short-term causes. The English taxation system was archaic, unable to raise the money that the state needed. Parliamentarians who wanted a more aggressively Protestant foreign policy (as they imagined

Elizabeth's to have been) were unwilling to vote for the vast sums necessary for a major war. Taxation in Tudor and Stuart England, with the exception of customs, was primarily taxation on land. The landowners who dominated both the House of Lords and the Commons frequently blocked tax increases. Tax collection was entrusted to local landowners, who were reluctant to rate each other's properties at their full value. Elizabeth had controlled the problem by exploiting the church and being parsimonious, but this was not an option for a new king seeking allies among the English aristocracy. The political need for generosity was compounded by James's fiscal irresponsibility. After the relative poverty of Scotland, the king never acquired a sense of responsibility in spending England's greater wealth.

James's extravagance was partly enabled by England's noninvolvement in European wars for most of his reign. The war with Spain ended in 1604 due to both Spanish and English exhaustion. James managed to keep his kingdoms out of the great European Thirty Years' War that began in 1618, even though it involved his German son-in-law Frederick of the Palatinate (1596–1632). James was a very unwarlike king, with a vision of himself as a great peacemaker in Europe. This policy had some successes early in the reign but failed during the Thirty Years' War. Some suspected James of an overly friendly policy toward Spain, particularly when he was negotiating for the marriage of his son and heir, Charles, to a Spanish princess. These negotiations failed due to Spanish insistence that any children of the match be raised as Catholics.

Like other British and European thinkers, James believed kings were divinely appointed and ruled by divine right. However, he was the most intellectual of British kings and wrote books on many subjects, including kingship, so he is more identified with the idea of divine right than other monarchs. His divine-right theories were not of absolute monarchy unfettered by the law. Many of his strong divine-right statements were put forth in a Scottish context, where their target was not the Scottish parliament, which James actually strengthened while keeping it under much tighter royal control than the English one, but radical Scottish Presbyterians who believed in the church's primacy over the state. For James, the divine right of kings was mainly a theological concept, compatible with political limits on the king's power. He did not view himself as above the law, nor did he attempt to levy taxes without a parliament or make law himself. There were some legal problems in his reign with the jurisdiction of various courts, but they were mostly contained.

The debauchery of James's court provoked some resentment among Englishmen, particularly those not invited to the party. There were prominent scandals, as when a woman at court, Frances Howard (1596–1632), was accused of poisoning Sir Thomas Overbury (1581–1613). James, whose predilection for handsome young men was widely known, was also suspected of being a sodomite. But there was little or no open opposition in his reign, which was one of the few in the early modern period with no serious popular disturbance. The defeat of a 1605 plot by some disaffected Roman Catholics to blow up the king and Parliament, known as the Gunpowder Plot, would have bad consequences for English Catholics, who faced more intense persecution in its wake, but the anniversary of its discovery on November 5 became a major Protestant and, eventually, national holiday.

In Ireland James continued on a massive scale the colonization that had started in the 16th century. While the medieval and early Tudor strategy had been to superimpose an English or anglicized ruling and landowning class on the Irish peasantry, James's policy was to settle the country with large numbers of British—mainly Scottish Calvinist—peasants. His policy in Ireland was similar to the one used in the Scottish highlands, to whose traditional society he was quite hostile. There were far too few colonists to simply replace the Irish peasants, but the new colonies functioned as garrisons for British rule in Ireland. This colonial policy built on the traditional connection between northern Ireland and western Scotland, and it inextricably involved the three kingdoms with one another in ways that reverberate to the present day.

The Reign of King Charles

James I always remained a Scotsman, on friendly terms with many Scottish nobles and intimately involved with his northern kingdom even when in London. His son Charles I (1600–49; r. 1625–49) was very different. Despite his Scottish birth, Charles was thoroughly English, and his religion was a very ceremonialist and conservative version of the Church of England.

Charles's reign culminated in the greatest disaster ever to befall the British monarchy, including civil war, his execution, and a temporary end to the monarchy. There were many reasons for this, from the complex relations of England and Scotland to the continuing religious divisions in England, but a major reason was the personality of Charles himself. The complete opposite of his father, Charles was a man of correct and sober personal life; even his enemies acknowledged that his court was a model of decorum after the disrepute of James's reign. He had superb aesthetic tastes and built one of the finest art collections of any English ruler. But he was weak personally, and he believed that any theoretical claim he could make about the power of the monarchy was practically enforceable. Charles thought that anyone opposing him must be motivated by malice or another unworthy emotion. That made it difficult for him to negotiate, something he was always reluctant to do. Even his aesthetic tastes became a personal liability. Under Elizabeth and even James, court life had been much more in touch with English life in general. Under Charles, court culture was influenced by the baroque culture of Continental Catholicism. Married to a French Catholic princess, Henrietta Maria (1609–69), Charles never shared the strong anti-Catholicism of many of his subjects. The misogynist and xenophobic prejudices of most of his opponents often led them to exaggerate the queen's influence, but it was nonetheless substantial.

Unlike Elizabeth and James, who had tried to be impartial mediators of the church's different factions, Charles identified himself with the High Church Party, which emphasized ceremony and the beauty of holiness. He had very extreme views on the divine right of bishops for a 17th-century Protestant, holding that bishops were absolutely necessary for a true church. This position was far too radical for most English bishops, who viewed those Continental Protestant churches organized without bishops as true churches, even if their organization was less than ideal.

The set of changes Charles attempted to enforce were associated with the archbishop of Canterbury, William Laud (1573–1645). They are often referred to as Laudianism, although they are at least equally due to Charles himself. Laudians emphasized the integrity and good repair of the church's physical structure and its freedom from lay control. Many churches were in bad shape after the Reformation and the impoverishment of the church under Elizabeth; one church was actually used as a hog sty. Laud and Charles wanted to improve the situation, but their emphasis on church furnishings led to charges of Romanizing and idolatry. Laudian emphasis on prayer and ritual activity in the ministry rather than the traditional Protestant emphasis on sermons seemed to point in the same direction. There were increased efforts to enforce the strict following of the Book of Common Prayer, as opposed to the de facto toleration of diverse practices under Elizabeth and James. The changes led to great resentment among the population. Some Puritans even migrated to America to find more tolerant climes.

Charles's early reign saw a more vigorous foreign policy in contrast to James's passivity. However, it was a diplomatic and military disaster, involving England in war with both of the great powers of the time, France and Spain, which were also at war with each other. Following military defeat, Charles adopted an isolationist policy similar to his father's but without James's conception of himself as an international mediator. This policy coincided with the so-called personal rule during the 1630s, an attempt to rule without calling Parliament after a series of failed parliaments in the 1620s. The lack of parliaments contributed to a growing alienation between the leaders of English society in the localities and the central government.

In the contentious Europe of the Thirty Years' War, Charles wanted to raise money for a navy but did not want to call a parliament to raise taxes for it. Instead, he revived and extended an old tax called *ship money*, ordinarily levied on port cities but now extended throughout the country. This eventually caused great resentment, both because of the question of the unconstitutionality of a tax levied without Parliament's consent and the increased administrative burden on the local notables who had to collect the tax in the absence of a centralized tax-collection bureaucracy.

Charles thought of himself as king of England, referring to Scotland as "your country" when addressing Scottish nobles. His rule in Scotland began badly. In 1625, shortly after his accession to the throne, he revoked all land grants since the accession of Queen Mary in 1542. Since Scottish nobles had acquired much church land in the Reformation, this ruling posed a threat to nearly every noble family. Subsequently, some compromises were reached, allowing owners the continued use of some lands. Charles also attempted to force through changes in the Scottish Church, not necessarily in the direction of making it more English but in the direction of making it more ritualistic than centered on preaching. Charles did this solely on his own authority, without bothering to get the consent of any Scottish body, either kirk or Parliament. His high-handedness aroused Scottish fears of creeping Catholicism and subjection to England. The 1638 Prayer Book Riot began when Edinburgh parishioners attacked a minister reading from the Book of Common Prayer, accusing him of bringing back the Catholic mass. According to legend, the riot began when a woman named Jenny Geddes threw a wooden stool at the minister's head. The riot was followed by a rebellion of Scottish Calvinists, with the support and leadership of Scottish aristocrats. The sleeping dragon of Scottish Presbyterianism awoke, as the Scottish bishops were strongly identified with Charles's policies. In 1638 the rebels gathered to formulate and agree on the Scottish National Covenant, a defiant declaration of Scots' intention to maintain their traditional Presbyterian religion and resist all attempts at Anglican invasion and modification. They became known as Covenanters. The Covenanters took over Scotland with relative ease, as the king had few supporters.

The War of the Three Kingdoms

The ensuing conflicts between Scotland and England in 1639 and 1640 became known as the Bishops' Wars. Charles's response to the Scottish rebellion was to mobilize Irish and especially English resources against it. England was a wealthier and more populous country, but the English military was severely underfunded, disorganized, and untested in war, whereas the Scots had generals with experience in the Thirty Years' War. Furthermore, many English people believed that the king's quarrel with the Scots was unjust, which further hindered the royal effort. The Bishops' Wars were the first attempt in centuries by an English king to fight a war without parliamentary approval, which limited Charles financially. His failure forced him to call a parliament, in which political and religious reformers dominated. This parliament lasted, with considerable gaps, for 20 years, becoming known as the "Long Parliament." A broad coalition emerged between those troubled by Charles's political innovations and those troubled by Laudianism, a coalition that reached out to the Scots. The rapprochement between the Scots and some of the English, however, led to the formation of an English anti-Scottish party who viewed the Scottish actions as interference in English affairs.

In 1641 there was a great Catholic revolt in Ireland precipitated by the anti-Catholicism expressed by both the Scots and the English party dominant in the London parliament. Ireland had been seething for a long time due to the harsh government of Charles's deputy in Ireland, Thomas Wentworth, earl of Strafford (1593–1641), who in his attempts to increase Irish revenue had managed to alienate every social group in Ireland, leaving the Crown with no effective allies. The situation worsened as Irish rebels massacred some Protestant settlers. Vastly exaggerated accounts of the atrocities reached England, further inflaming English Protestant anti-Catholicism. The Irish problem involved the Scots as well as the English due to the heavy representation of Scots among the Irish settlers and the political connections of Ulster and the Scottish highlands.

The Civil War in England began over the issue of whether the king or Parliament should control the army being raised to fight the Irish rebels. The two sides in England were known as the Parliamentarians and the Royalists, or "Roundheads" (after the cropped haircuts favored by many Parliamentarians) and "Cavaliers." The Solemn League and Covenant of 1643 brought Parliament and the Scots together in a military alliance, but whereas the English saw the alliance as essentially political, many Scots saw it as a religious agreement for the establishment of Presbyterianism in both kingdoms. Many English found Scottish Presbyterians excessively dominated by ministers and favored "Independency," vesting power in individual congregations. The Westminster Assembly of Divines, a gathering of theologians, hammered out common religious positions. One result was the Westminster Catechism, which is still used in Presbyterian and Reformed Churches in the British tradition.

As the Scots saw that the English were fundamentally uninterested in adopting Scottish-style Presbyterianism, and the English resented Scottish interference, the alliance declined. The English disliked the independent power of a Scottish Presbytery, and even English Presbyterians wanted to keep any Presbyterian church under Parliamentary control. The Scots themselves were divided with the rise of a Scottish Royalist party. The poorly supplied Scottish army, now having to fight on two fronts, was less of an asset to the English.

Superior organization and generalship, particularly from the cavalry commander Oliver Cromwell (1599–1658), and control of the navy and the kingdom's economic center at London, led to the Parliamentarians' victory in the Civil War. (Ironically, after all the talk about the horrors of ship money, Parliament taxed the country harder than it had ever been taxed before.)

The king was strongest in Wales and the south and west of England, the less economically developed areas where Catholicism had also been strong. The Parliamentarians were strongest in London and East Anglia, controlling the more economically developed parts of England. In 1646, after military defeat, King Charles surrendered to the Scots rather than the English parliament; the Scots turned him over to the English. However, divisions among the Scots and within the Presbyterian-dominated Parliament, horrified by the social leveling that was one consequence of the war, in addition in to an independent and Cromwellian-dominated army that wanted its massive back pay, all led to a second and far more vicious civil war allying the Scots, the king, and the English royalists. This culminated in the king's execution in 1649, provoking horror in ordinary people and gentry alike. People told stories of the miracles worked by the king's blood and wondered if the kingdom was now cursed. The ghostwritten book of the king's meditations and prayers, *Eikon Basilike* (The image of the king), became a best seller, going through numerous editions despite Parliament's best efforts to suppress it.

Revolutionary England

The violence of the 1640s was accompanied by great cultural innovation in England. The collapse of censorship after the revolutionaries took over London early in the war as well as popular interest in the political and military struggle led to the creation of the first English newspaper press with multiple and competing newspapers. England was opened up to many new religious and political movements. One religious sect, the Diggers, believed that land should be shared out equally. Another, more secular and influential sect, the Levellers, believed that all men should have a vote, or at least all men not dependent on someone else for wages. The Levellers were for some time powerful in the army, but radical movements were ultimately suppressed or marginalized. The most famous and influential of radical movements emerged after the Parliamentary victory, although its roots were in the 1640s. This was the Society of Friends, also known as Quakers, originally a derogatory name based on their alleged habit of "quaking" before the Lord. Its founder, George Fox (1624–91), was a religious quester who adopted pacifism and taught reliance on the spirit of God within each individual, what Fox called the Inner Light. Friends opposed all aspects of organized church including church buildings—which they called "steeple-houses"—a ministry as a separate order, tithes, and any structured authority. They also challenged authority in state and society. Friends would not take oaths, which they believed the bible forbade. They shocked people by refusing to take off their hats in the presence of a superior, as they considered "hat honor" inappropriate for a mere human. Many were beaten for refusing to take off their hats. Quakers were seen as radical and troublemakers, and persecuted for decades.

The Government of Oliver Cromwell

The victory of the English Parliament over their king was followed by the victory of England over Scotland and Ireland. The victorious "Rump Parliament"—so called because only a minority of the original Parliament was left after the successive divisions and purges of the civil war—imposed relatively mild English rule on Scotland and quite harsh rule on Ireland. Cromwell defeated both the Irish rebellion and a Scottish attempt to restore Charles I's son Charles as a Presbyterian ruler. Wales, legally incorporated into England, had also been a strongly royalist area, and it was subjected to intense evangelization. For the first time the British Isles were a political and administrative unity ruled from London. Much of Oliver Cromwell's reputation had been made by his defeats of the Irish and the Scots. Using his control of the army to overthrow Parliament in 1653, Cromwell took the title Lord Protector of England, Scotland, and Ireland.

Like other revolutionary regimes, Cromwellian rule was faced with the basic problem of finding a basis for legitimacy comparable to that of the old monarchy. Cromwell's efforts to establish a parliament that lived up to his own standards of godliness and public spirit were failures. He subjected England to its only phase of outright military rule in 1655, when he divided the country into 12 regions, each under a major general. This experiment was extremely unpopular and ended in 1657 when one of Cromwell's parliaments refused to fund it. It left

This contemporary Dutch cartoon shows Oliver Cromwell as a Hercules dissolving the Long Parliament. (Library of Congress)

England with a pronounced distaste for rule by an army. The traditional landowning elite continued to reassert itself in the parliaments of Cromwell's protectorate, even offering him the royal crown, which he refused due to army opposition.

The establishment of peace in the 1650s was accompanied by increased repression. The once-vibrant newspaper press dwindled to a few officially approved organs. Parliament attempted to suppress many aspects of Anglican parish worship, particularly the Book of Common Prayer, replacing it with a new liturgy, the Directory of Public Worship. Puritan iconoclasm and distrust of sensuality in worship also led to the smashing of images; destruction of musical instruments; and removal of candles, tapers, and basins from communion tables. The observance of Christmas, Easter, and saints' days was banned, although in practice there was little effective enforcement. Much of the church's cultural and social infrastructure was preserved. Despite the banning of church ownership of the Book of Common Prayer, more than one-third of all church inventories during the time show possession of it. Even in London there was an active underground Anglican religious life, and many Anglican ministers who had been ejected from parish churches obtained jobs as chaplains in the houses of conservative aristocrats and gentry.

Two events in Cromwell's protectorate that would influence British history for centuries were the conquest of Jamaica from the Spaniards in 1655 and the readmission of Jews to England. The conquest of Jamaica was a product of Cromwell's "Western Design," an assault on the Spanish Empire in the Caribbean. His goal was to conquer Hispaniola, but when that failed, Jamaica was viewed as a consolation prize. It subsequently became the linchpin of the British Empire in the Caribbean. Cromwell's anti-Spanish policy extended to an alliance with the Catholic French, who proved more than willing to swallow their reluctance to ally with the English king killer.

Edward I had expelled England's Jews in 1290, and those few Jews that had lived in England since then had either hidden their religious identity or had been short-term visitors under special arrangements. Motives for English people who favored the readmission included hopes that Jewish commercial skills and connections would benefit English trade and the millenarian belief that the end of the world could not come about until the Jews were scattered throughout everywhere in the world. Increasing scholarly interest in Hebrew had also led to contacts between English scholars and foreign rabbis. Anti-Semitic opposition, in part fueled by London merchants' fear of Jewish competition, meant that Cromwell's parliament did not pass a law formally readmitting the Jews to England. However, since Edward I's expulsion of the Jews was not actually a parliamentary law but a royal act, it could be simply ignored rather than repealed. Under Cromwell's de facto toleration, a small Jewish community developed in London, and subsequent governments continued to tolerate the growing Jewish presence.

Cromwell died on September 3, 1658 (the anniversary of two of his greatest victories against the Scots), and like a king he was succeeded by his son, Richard Cromwell (1626–1712). But Richard lacked both the legitimacy of the old dynasty and his father's force of personality and military prestige. He stayed in power for only nine months, and his fall was followed by different and unsuccessful attempts to form a military regime. The Long Parliament, elected before the revolution, remained the most legitimate body of authority, and its surviving members were now recalled. However, the real decision maker was another general, George Monk (1608–70), who had fought for the Crown during the Civil War but later assisted Cromwell in his campaigns against Ulster and Scotland. After Cromwell died, Monk brought his army from Scotland and spoke out in favor of a restoration of the Stuart monarchy, thus settling the matter.

Charles II and the Restoration Monarchy

The Restoration of 1660 was the restoration not only of the king but also of the institutions that had been abolished by the victorious Parliamentarians and that remained central to British life, such as the House of Lords and the episcopally organized Church of England.

The Restoration was popular among ordinary people, and there was much rejoicing. Maypoles, banned by the Puritans, became a symbol of the Restoration and the rejection of Puritan rule. The Restoration Church of England created new holidays, including January 30 as a day of mourning and repentance commemorating the execution of Charles I and May 29 as a day of rejoicing marking the Restoration of his son, Charles II (1630–85; r. 1660–85).

The original idea of the religious restoration was to combine the bishops, their supporters, and the moderate Presbyterians into a church that would allow some local variation in styles of worship. Having failed due to the Presbyterians' stubbornness and the growing confidence of hard-line Anglicans, it was replaced by a harshly repressive Anglican order. The so-called Clarendon Code was named after Charles's first lord chancellor and the head of his government, Edward Hyde, earl of

Clarendon (1609–74). The code was enacted by Charles's first parliament, called the Cavalier Parliament, which was dominated by old royalists. Local officials, ministers, professors, and schoolmasters were required to denounce the Solemn League and Covenant, refuse to take up arms against the king, and take the Anglican sacrament. The Corporation Act of 1661 required all those elected to serve as officers of a city or corporation to take the sacrament—that is, consume the bread and wine of the Eucharist—at an Anglican Church, to denounce the Solemn League and Covenant, and to take oaths of allegiance and supremacy. As of August 24, 1662, all ministers were required to use the Book of Common Prayer and swear consent in all things to it or be deprived of their livings.

Nearly 2,000 ministers were forced out of the church, which created a nonconformist clergy. To prevent the deposed clergy from starting their own congregations, the Conventicle Act of 1664 banned conventicles (religious gatherings) of five or more persons (excluding families) who were not in conformity with the Church of England. These acts were supplemented with the Test Act of 1673, which required all officeholders to take the Anglican sacrament, the Oath of Supremacy, and the Declaration against Transubstantiation, in force until 1829. However, enforcement of all these acts, which continued to depend on local authorities, was sporadic. A new religious order emerged in which, instead of different factions competing for control of the Church of England, the Anglican Church coexisted with marginally legal Dissenting churches. Although not yet centrally organized, the three largest groups were Presbyterians, Independents (who became known as Congregationalists), and Baptists. Quakers, while harshly persecuted, were also prominent in Restoration England.

The House of Lords was also restored, with its traditional complement of hereditary peers and bishops. The exclusion of the bishops from the House of Lords had taken place early in the revolution and had received the assent of Charles I, but the exclusion was quickly repealed after the Restoration.

Charles II's experience in exile on the Continent had shaped his personality in many ways. He became one of the least insular of early modern British kings. He did not share the anti-Catholic prejudices of many of his subjects and in fact converted to Catholicism on his deathbed. Charles was particularly attracted to the rich and sophisticated culture of the France of Louis XIV (1638–1715; r. 1643–1715), then Europe's dominant political, military, and cultural power. A constant stream of French visitors came to Charles's court, and his favorite mistress was

Louise de Kérouaille (1649–1734), a Frenchwoman to whom he eventually gave the title duchess of Portsmouth. More significantly, Louise subsidized Charles, and for much of the reign Britain was basically a French satellite, particularly in the French wars against the Dutch Republic. Charles's wars against the Dutch were mostly unsuccessful. In 1667 there was a famous incident when Dutch warships entered the Medway and burned English ships. However, in the course of the wars the English acquired New York, their most enduring consequence.

The Restoration introduced some Continental culture to Britain. The theater, banned by the Puritans, was restored, and for the first time English theater allowed actresses to appear onstage. Another aspect of foreign culture was the coffeehouse; although first introduced in the 1650s, coffeehouses now became associated with a certain degree of social egalitarianism, political conversation, and the availability of news and periodicals. In 1675 conversation in the establishments was deemed so threatening that the government attempted unsuccessfully to close all coffeehouses in England, but this effort was a failure.

The Restoration was also a golden age for British science. The world's oldest existing scientific organization, the Royal Society, received a royal charter in 1662. Its members in the late 17th century included the chemist Robert Boyle (1627–91) and the physicist and mathematician Isaac Newton (1642–1727) as well as a host of lesser lights. Newton's

RESTORATION WIT

One of the most prominent courtiers of Charles II was John Wilmot, earl of Rochester (1647–80). His epigram on the king's character exists in several forms, among them:

> God bless our good and gracious king,
> Whose promise none relies on;
> Who never said a foolish thing,
> Nor ever did a wise one.

Charles is reputed to have responded by pointing out that although his words were his own, his actions were those of his ministers.

Source: James William Johnson, A Profane Wit: The Life of John Wilmot, Earl of Rochester. Rochester, N.Y.: University of Rochester Press, 2004, 219.

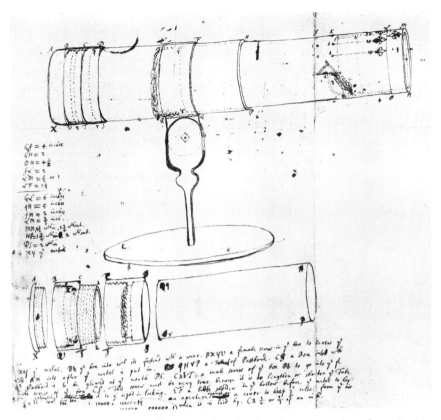

Isaac Newton was less interested in practical applications than other early modern scientists were, but he did devise one of the first reflecting telescopes. (Library of Congress)

Mathematical Principles of Natural Philosophy (1687), setting forth his theories of universal gravitation and the laws of motion, is the foundation of physics until the 20th century.

In the British Isles the Restoration marked the end of the parliamentary and Cromwellian policy of incorporative union and English military rule over Scotland and Ireland in favor of a return to multiple kingdoms, but with much closer supervision of Scotland and Ireland than before the revolution. The Scottish situation was particularly difficult, as the restoration of bishops was quite unpopular throughout much of the country.

Whatever glamour attached to the Restoration was dimmed by disasters, most notably the great plague and fire of London. The year 1665 saw the last major outbreak of the plague in the British Isles, with perhaps 110,000 deaths, a quarter of the London population. The next

119

year saw the Great Fire of London, spread by the city's wooden housing stock and the slowness of the city government to respond. More than 13,000 houses were destroyed, as well as some of London's most important buildings. The fire created the opportunity for rebuilding, the most important example being Christopher Wren's new St. Paul's Cathedral.

The greatest political crisis of Charles's reign is usually referred to as the Exclusion Crisis of 1678–81. Charles and his wife, the Portuguese princess Catherine of Braganza (1638–1705), had no children (although Charles had several children by his mistresses). That made his brother James, a Catholic, the heir. Many English Protestants, already paranoid about Catholics (many blamed the Great Fire of 1666 on Catholic plotters), were even more worried after the Popish Plot scare in 1678. This was an alleged Catholic plot to murder the king and reimpose Catholicism by force. In this situation, the idea of a Catholic exercising royal powers alarmed many Protestants in the three kingdoms. Some said that the legitimate heir should inherit, regardless of religion. Others had various schemes, ranging from letting James inherit with legal limitations on his power to excluding him and all Catholics from the succession.

Two groups that would long influence British politics, the Whig and Tory parties, were formed at this time. Although both were English parties, they drew their names from elsewhere in the British Isles. The Whigs were originally called Whiggamores—Scottish covenanting rebels—while the word *Tory* originally referred to Irish Catholic bandits. Although there were many political shadings, and people moved from Whig to Tory and vice versa, the Whigs generally stood for exclusion and the Tories for the legitimate succession of a powerful monarch. Charles II, James, and the Tories eventually won, as the broad middle of English opinion believed that Whig rebelliousness, threatening a revival of civil war, was more dangerous than James's Catholicism. On his brother's death in 1685, therefore, James succeeded to the English and Scottish thrones with no difficulty as James II (1633–1701; r. 1685–88).

James II and the Revolution of 1688

James's personality was the opposite of Charles's. James was straightforward, unsubtle, and completely insensitive to other people. He inherited a very strong position from the Tory victory in the Exclusion Crisis, yet lost it all in a few years. Rebellions at the beginning of his reign in both England and Scotland were easily crushed.

James's main political goal was to get toleration and legal equality for his fellow Catholics. He encouraged the open printing of Catholic books, both of liturgy and theology, and the open performance of Catholic services. People knew that conversion to Catholicism was a way to win James's favor, and his accession was followed by a small wave of conversions. However, the king realized that no matter what success he had with conversion, Catholics would remain a small minority of British people, and thus he tried to build a tolerationist coalition between Dissenters (those Protestants who did not accept the doctrine or observe the rites of the Church of England, including those of the Baptist, Independent, Presbyterian, and Quaker faiths) and Catholics. There were two major problems with this idea. One was the distrust and hatred many Dissenters felt for Catholics, and the other was the politically entrenched position of the Church of England, which commanded the allegiance of the majority of both the people and the political nation, and whose leaders opposed any toleration. Getting rid of the laws against other churches would require a major political effort.

James encouraged Dissenting leaders to attend his court, and he won some of them over to belief in his sincerity, including the founder of Pennsylvania, the Quaker William Penn (1644–1718). However, many remained suspicious of his motives. The impasse between the Anglican parliament, determined to maintain restrictive religious laws, and the king, who retained control of the central administration and the military, was difficult to resolve. The solution was foreign intervention.

The Dutch stadtholder and staunch Protestant William of Orange (1650–1702) was James's son-in-law and nephew. He was the husband of James's older daughter, Mary (1662–94), the heir presumptive to the throne as James had no legitimate sons. Since William was the dominant partner in their marriage, everyone knew that when Mary reigned, William would rule. William's life was dominated by his hostility to Louis XIV, who had attempted to smash the Dutch Republic. William spent much of his career building coalitions of European states alarmed by Louis's ambitions, including Catholic states. During James's reign, more and more English and Scottish exiles arrived at William's court, and as James was already in his fifties, there was hope that his death and Mary's succession would quickly end the pro-Catholic campaign.

This hope was ended by the birth of a son to James and his wife, the Italian princess Mary of Modena (1658–1718), in 1688. As a male, the new prince, named James, immediately jumped to the head of the line of heirs, and since he would be brought up as a Catholic, he opened the door to a line of Catholic successors. Many of the Catholics around

This cartoon shows William and Mary as Protestant crusaders, holding the pope's nose to the grindstone. (Library of Congress)

James saw the birth of the young prince as a divine blessing. Some Protestants spread the false rumor that the child was an impostor, that the real child was a girl or born dead, or that the whole pregnancy was fake and the boy had been smuggled in in a warming pan—the myth of the "warming-pan baby."

In 1688 William invaded with the support of many Whig and Tory elements who had asked him to come. Even with English support, his invasion was a desperate gamble; the key question was whether the English fleet and military would support him. The "Protestant wind," as it was described by Protestants claiming divine support for their cause, kept the English fleet in harbor and therefore unable to turn back this Dutch ships. William's agents managed to win key army leaders to his side. The most important was John Churchill (1650–1722), later to be the first duke of Marlborough.

The king's regime collapsed quickly, and James escaped to France with William's connivance. Although the Glorious Revolution was bloodless in England, it was quite a different story in the rest of the isles. Scottish supporters of James, or Jacobites, were forcibly and brutally suppressed, and a war in Ireland in 1690, in which both William and James directly participated, ended the military power of Catholic Ireland and ushered in a century of Protestant domination.

The Revolution Settlement

After the Glorious Revolution, the English elite wanted to focus their energies on domestic English problems, such as religious toleration. English supporters of the revolution ranged from radical Whigs who looked back to the "English republic"—the brief period under the Rump Parliament between the fall of the monarchy and Cromwell's coup (although most people accepted that England would stay a monarchy)—to Anglicans who wanted to preserve as much as possible of the Anglican monopoly. William, a patriotic Dutchman, was basically interested in bringing England into his coalition against Louis XIV.

Fear of another civil war lay behind the push for an agreement between the different parties supporting William's takeover. William had actually allowed James to escape to France to avoid another trial like that of Charles I. The rapidity with which the revolution took place meant that there was no need, and no desire, to appeal to popular support.

The first problem was who was going to decide who was going to be king. Most people agreed that Parliament should make the decision, but no one knew how to call Parliament without a king to summon it. The eventual solution was for William to call a convention, elected on a parliamentary franchise (and including the House of Lords). The Whigs did quite well in the election, which was bad news for those who wanted to keep James on in some kind of capacity, ranging from treating William as a conqueror to installing him as a regent for James. James could also be declared legally dead, abdicated, or having forfeited the crown. The crown could be given to William or devolved to Mary as hereditary successor, an option favored by many Tories suspicious of both James and William. William, however, wanted royal authority, not the role of a king consort. The convention declared that James had abdicated by fleeing the country and offered the crown to William and Mary as joint monarchs, a situation without precedent or sequel in English history.

Some Whigs were reluctant to offer the crown without conditions, believing that monarchy was a contract with rights and responsibilities on both sides. William was reluctant to accept the crown with conditions. The compromise was a document called the Bill of Rights, presented in such a way during the coronation that it could be viewed as either a condition or not. The bill banned the practices of suspending laws or raising money without the consent of Parliament, and it guaranteed the king and queen's Protestant subjects the right to have arms suitable for their defense. It also included guarantees of the rights of subjects to petition Parliament and other individual rights. The Bill of Rights was largely enacted into law by Parliament in 1690. There was also a major change in the coronation oath, which now included a promise to govern according to the statutes of Parliament—the first time this had been mentioned in the oath. The revolution settlement also enshrined religious toleration (for Protestants) in law in the Toleration Act of 1689, while leaving the Anglican monopoly of public offices untouched. Catholics were tolerated on a de facto rather than de jure basis.

The crowns of England and Scotland remained separate, so the whole process had to be repeated in Scotland. The Scottish settlement was more radical than the English one. The Whigs who dominated the Scottish parliament deemed that James had forfeited rather than abdicated the crown and offered the monarchy to William and Mary on certain conditions. The situation was complicated by a Scottish revolt dominated by highlanders, but it was defeated by forces loyal to William. Revolutionary Scotland was run by an alliance between the prorevolution forces in England, some of the Scottish political leadership, and the Presbyterians. The Scottish bishops had been much more strongly and uniformly pro-James than the English bishops, which was a factor in their elimination during the settlement. Presbyterians took over the Scottish kirk in a sometimes violent process that presented the revolutionary government with a fait accompli. At the same time, the Catholic challenge had finally been beaten back, the dream of a uniform Protestant church covering all of Britain was abandoned in favor of toleration, and very different churches were established in the two kingdoms.

Many of the religious and political issues that stemmed from the Reformation had been settled, and Protestantism in its Anglican English and Presbyterian Scottish forms had won decided victories. Although the monarchy was still powerful, the battle to impose limits on it had been won. However, the arrival of King William meant that the British kingdoms had been brought into his anti-French coalition. The conflicts with France would shape the next century of British history, which would see the formation of the greatest global power the world had ever known.

6

INDUSTRY AND CONQUEST (1689–1851)

After the 17th century, when most of the major shocks to Britain had been internal, 18th-century Britain displayed political stability while facing major challenges from outside the country. In the process of overcoming or surviving these challenges, Britain built the world's most advanced economy and largest empire. The benefits of these triumphs, however, were concentrated among the upper classes. The quality of life for ordinary Britons improved only slowly or even declined.

The Roots of World Empire

Britain in the 18th century was more deeply involved with the world beyond its shores than ever before. British ships plied the world's oceans, displacing the Dutch from their leadership in world trade. African slaves, Indian cotton textiles, and Chinese tea all served to fill the coffers of British merchants. Not only British trade but British dominion was rising. The Royal Navy was establishing a virtually insurmountable lead over all rivals and a global network of bases. The colonies in North America changed from isolated outposts to complex societies expanding into the American interior. The British colonies of the Caribbean, Jamaica, and Barbados, with their vast, slave-worked sugar plantations, were the source of immense wealth, even as slavery itself was increasingly controversial by the second half of the century. The Hudson's Bay Company, founded in 1670, traded with Native Americans for furs, although in the first part of the new century it was outpaced by French rivals. The East India Company, founded in 1600, had established a firm foothold in Bengal in northeastern India that became a base for further expansion by the mid-18th century.

Knowledge went with power. Along with other strong European nations, Britain amassed knowledge of global navigation, cartography, and hydrography. British captains followed in the wake of the Elizabethan captain Francis Drake, but with an emphasis on knowledge rather than mere plunder. The most notable of these explorers was James Cook (1728–79), who charted the coast of Newfoundland and the Pacific Northwest coast of America, circumnavigated New Zealand, and was the first European to encounter the islands of Hawaii. Like other British explorers, Cook was accompanied by cartographers and natural historians who made the layout and resources of the newly discovered lands and peoples known to Britain and Europe.

War, Union, and the House of Hanover

After taking power in the Glorious Revolution of 1688, Britain's new king, William III (r. 1689–1702), planned to use England's resources against Europe's most powerful ruler, Louis XIV of France (r. 1643–1715). The War of the League of Augsburg, or Nine Years' War, was fought from 1688 to 1697 between France and William's coalition, which included Spain, the Holy Roman Empire, and the Dutch Republic. The war itself was inconclusive, but it marked Britain's arrival as a great power. British society became increasingly militarized, as both the army and the navy grew in the 18th century.

The wars between England and France did not end with William's death in 1702. A widower when he died, he was succeeded by Mary's sister Anne (1665–1714; r. 1702–14), the last Stuart monarch. Following the 1701 death of James II, the exiled Catholic sovereign, Louis XIV had violated previous agreements by recognizing James's son, also Catholic and also named James (1688–1766), as the legitimate king of England and Scotland. (James III also became known as the Old Pretender.) The French refusal to recognize the "Protestant Succession"—the English and Scottish refusal to allow a Catholic on the throne—continued to poison relations between the two powers.

The next great conflict between Britain and France, the War of the Spanish Succession, was prompted by the death of Carlos (Charles) II of Spain without a direct heir in 1700. The grandson of the king of France, Philip, had a claim on the throne that the British feared would result in an effective union of France and Spain. By bringing low France's power, the war would also secure the Protestant Succession. It lasted from 1701 to 1714 (although Britain, the Dutch Republic, and France ended their participation by the Treaty of Utrecht in 1713). The British war effort was marked by amazing victories at Blenheim (1704) and Ramillies (1706) under one of the greatest of British generals, John Churchill (1650–1722), who was made duke of Marlborough in recognition of his achievement. British gains from the Treaty of Utrecht included French recognition of the Protestant Succession; the expulsion of the pretender James III; Newfoundland; the island of Gibraltar between Spain and Africa (a British possession even today); and the *asiento*, the exclusive right to trade slaves to the Spanish American empire.

One important consequence of the war was domestic: the Act of Union of 1707, which made England and Scotland one country under the new name of United Kingdom of Great Britain. The Act of Union was essentially forced through by the English, who were concerned that after the death of Queen Anne, the Scots would give the crown to James III. If the Scots made James king, he could then threaten to use Scotland's resources against England, possibly with French support. There was not much popular support for the union in Scotland, despite Scottish government propaganda about the economic benefits Scotland would receive. The act abolished the Scottish parliament, replacing it with elected representatives to the English House of Commons and

THE LAST WITCH HUNT: PAISLEY 1697

The last mass execution of witches in Britain, and indeed in western Europe, took place at the Scottish town of Paisley in 1697. Christian Shaw, the young daughter of a local landowner, was taken to having violent fits and vomiting, which she blamed on local witches. The Presbytery of Paisley, the council of Church of Scotland clergy with jurisdiction over the area, asked the Scottish Privy Council for a commission to try the case. The first commission, to a group of magistrates, landowners, and lawyers, authorized them to investigate. Shaw and an accused witch turned accuser, Elizabeth Anderson, accused several dozen people. A second commission with authority to try the case tried 24 accused witches, sentencing three men and four women to death. They were hanged, and their bodies burned on June 10. Other accused witches were still being held in jail two years later. Two pamphlets were published on the affair in England and one in Scotland. Christian Shaw fully recovered, and went on to found the commercial spinning industry in Paisley.

House of Lords, theoretically a new British parliament but in practice the English parliament with the addition of Scottish members. The Scots were left with their own Presbyterian church and legal system. In the 18th century, Scottish politicians, notably the house of Argyll, managed Scotland for the London government.

The right to inherit the crown of the new kingdom was settled on Queen Anne's closest Protestant relatives, the German rulers of the Electorate of Hanover, a north German principality that would be held by British monarchs until 1837.

Anne died in 1714 and was succeeded by the German prince George, the elector of Hanover, first of the Hanoverian dynasty. (*Elector* referred to the right of Hanover to participate in the election of Holy Roman Emperors.) George I (1660–1727; r. 1714–27) was an unprepossessing man with no knowledge of English or familiarity with English institutions, but he was a respected statesman in much of central Europe and the Baltic.

The British Parliament

Although monarchs continued to wield great influence throughout the 18th century, power was increasingly shifting into the hands of Parliament and its leaders. Continuing its traditional division into elected House of Commons and a mostly hereditary House of Lords, the Parliament now met every year and controlled government finances. By this time the Commons was growing in importance relative to the Lords, as "money bills" relating to taxes could only originate in the Commons. The House of Lords consisted of many of the most powerful men in the country, holders of broad acres and palatial country houses, but as an institution it took second place to the Commons. However, members of the upper house had great influence over the Commons through use of family connections and patronage, which was a means of influencing elections.

There was no uniform franchise for election to the Commons. Instead, it was divided into county members, two elected for each county on the votes of those adult men owning land assessed at at least 40 shillings a year—the "forty shilling freeholders." The vast majority of members of Parliament (MPs) were elected from boroughs on a wide variety of franchises; in some boroughs less than a dozen men elected their representative, while in others all or nearly all adult men could vote. Some of the small boroughs were "pocket boroughs," where a single local landowner could effectively name the representative—he had the borough in his pocket. Other small boroughs could be controlled or heavily swayed by the government of the day.

Contested elections were frequent and decided by the House of Commons itself, leading to many disputes in the first days of a new parliament. The importance of the political parties of the 17th and early 18th centuries—the Whigs and Tories—was diminishing, mostly as a consequence of Whig victory in the Hanoverian succession. The Tories were increasingly, and in many cases unfairly, identified with Jacobitism (those supporting Stuart claims to the throne), and despite the ability to elect dozens of MPs, they were politically irrelevant. Politics became a contest between Whig factions, and successful politicians were those who could manipulate elections to benefit their own causes or maintain coalitions of different Whig factions. The most successful of these politicians in the 18th century was Sir Robert Walpole (1676–1745), the most powerful man in Britain as the head of the king's government from 1721 to 1742. Walpole is often identified as the first "prime minister," although the title of prime minister did not officially exist at that point. However, the overall tendency in the 18th century was toward a single individual at the head of a parliamentary government.

Whig Ascendancy

The period roughly between 1714 and 1760, the year George I's great-grandson George III ascended to the throne, is often referred to as the Whig ascendancy. The Whigs were less popular in the country than their rivals the Tories, who could rely on the support of the influential Church of England clergy, but they seized power shortly after George I's succession. The Whigs considered themselves the party of the Hanoverian succession, and they supported an aggressive anti-French foreign policy, both positions highly congenial to George I, while the Tories were compromised by their association with Jacobitism and the Peace of Utrecht that ended the War of the Spanish Succession. The acquiescence of Queen Anne's Tory government in Philip V's retaining the throne of Spain enraged many English people, who viewed it as throwing away the duke of Marlborough's victories. Whig leaders, headed by Sir Robert Walpole, continued to present themselves as the defenders of the Hanoverian claim against the Stuarts. They also had a personal ascendancy over George's son, who succeeded him on his death in 1727 as George II (1683–1760; r. 1727–60), and a good relationship with George II's wife, Queen Caroline of Anspach (1683–1737).

Despite their royal connections, Whig leaders were not court figures the way that 16th- and 17th-century governmental leaders had been. Parliament met every year and controlled taxation, so any leader was ultimately dependent on parliamentary support. Since the government—the politicians entrusted by the king with the management of public affairs—could nearly always control the House of Lords through the bishops and the elected Scottish peers, the key problem was controlling the House of Commons. Even the most successful Whig minister, Walpole, was forced to resign in 1742 when the Commons turned against him, though the king still supported him and reportedly wept when accepting his resignation.

Electorally, the Whigs discouraged voter participation. The Septennial Act of 1716, allowing parliaments to sit for seven years before facing a new election, meant that elections were infrequent. It replaced the system under Queen Anne, in which new elections were required every three years. The requirement of frequent elections had kept voters interested and political organizations mobilized. The Septennial Act meant that for long stretches of years, politics was in the hands of professional politicians, which decreased public interest in affairs of state. The Whig ascendancy also saw efforts to interpret the franchise in favor of fewer people being allowed to vote. Much of the Whig leadership was corrupt and known to be so, particularly during the long period when Walpole was first lord of the treasury, the office that eventually became known as prime minister. Accusations of corruption accentuated the inevitable struggle of Whig factions and gave a platform for those Whigs who opposed others in power. Opposition Whig factions often clustered around the heir to the throne, who in the Hanoverian period almost never got along with the king.

Toryism steadily diminished throughout this period, although it never entirely disappeared. Its main focus remained the defense of the Church of England. The fact that the episcopal church of Scotland had been replaced by Presbyterianism after the Glorious Revolution of 1688 greatly concerned English Tories. However, Presbyterianism was not as popular a movement in England as it was in Scotland, and as it became clear that the Whigs, despite some of their differences with the leaders of the Church of England, were not going to destroy it, Toryism began to lose its point. The control the Whigs exercised over the Hanoverian kings made it unlikely that Tories would ever come back into power. The Tory party as an organized grouping was gone by mid-century, and even the word *Tory* was going out of use.

Opposition Parties

The weakening of the Tories did not mean that the dominant Whigs faced no competition. Parliamentary opposition was led by proponents of the so-called country ideology, which took both Tory and opposition Whig forms. Country ideology was essentially about distrusting government. Country members introduced measures such as place bills, which forbade government officeholders from also holding seats in the Commons, one of the chief government strategies for controlling that body. Country members, mostly rural, opposed taxes and a vigorous foreign policy, arguing that Britain should stay out of Continental affairs, thus reducing the tax burden. They often charged Whig leaders with excessive concern for Hanover. During wars they supported a "blue water" strategy, preferring naval arms and warfare in the colonies over expensive armies in Europe. Country patriots suspected commercial and financial wealth and believed that political power should be in the hands of those with a stake in the country—namely, landowners.

However, the most widespread form of opposition was that of the lower classes, often expressed during this period in riots. Eighteenth-century British common people were largely free from the threat of starvation but continued to lead hard lives of heavy work and poor diet. They rioted frequently, often over mundane issues such as taxes or the price of bread, but also over religious issues. There were also politically inspired anti-Catholic and anti-Semitic riots, including one against a bill for the simplified naturalization of foreign Jews, the so-called Jew Bill, in 1753. English culture generally was quite violent. Capital punishment was used extensively as literally hundreds of offenses applying to children as young as the early teens could be punished by death. Leaders of riots were sometimes punished with death, but authorities also sometimes made concessions to the rioters' demands, as when the Jew Bill was dropped.

The most radical and probably the least effective form of opposition to the Whig ascendancy was Jacobitism. Jacobites denied the legitimacy of the Hanoverian dynasty and held that the Stuart heirs, living abroad, were the rightful rulers of Britain. Scottish Jacobites had a particular animus against the Act of Union and emphasized the Scottish origin of the Stuart dynasty. Although they viewed Scotland as a base of operations, the Stuarts themselves were fixed on the goal of London and the British throne.

Since Jacobitism was essentially about supporting a particular person, Jacobites could and did take different political and religious positions. Scottish Jacobites emphasized repealing the union and restoring

ONANIA

The great medical crusade against masturbation, which lasted into the 20th century, began in early 18th-century England. Christians had long considered masturbation a sin but had not treated it as very important. During the Enlightenment, "solitary pleasure" moved to the forefront of medical and pedagogic concern. The creation of medical antimasturbation discourse began with the anonymous pamphlet *Onania,* which probably first appeared in 1715, although the earliest surviving edition is the fourth, from 1718. The title is derived from the biblical character Onan. Although Onan was condemned for "spilling his seed upon the ground" as a contraceptive measure rather than masturbation (Genesis 38:8–10), his story was increasingly interpreted as divine condemnation of masturbation.

The word *onanism* first appeared in 1719. The author of *Onania* blamed masturbation for ulcers, epilepsy, consumption, impotence, sterility, debilitation, and early death. As treatment, he recommended repentance, cold baths, and a drug available from the bookseller for a fee—a standard feature of quack pamphlets. *Onania,* which continued the focus on male activities, was a best seller, going through 15 editions by 1730 and many more thereafter, in addition to a German translation in 1736. The editions swelled with letters purportedly sent by suffering masturbators begging the author's assistance. Such was the horror it produced that the philosopher Bernard de Mandeville argued that it was better that young men visit brothels than masturbate. This exaggerated fear of masturbation spread to the European continent and America and lasted into the 20th century.

Scottish independence, English Jacobites hoped to clean up the corrupt political system, and Irish Jacobites hoped to restore Catholic Ireland. Both die-hard Tory defenders of the Church of England and deists who hoped for greater religious toleration could support the Stuarts. Many common people were attracted to the Jacobite movement because of its promises of lower taxation and religious tolerance. The largest pockets of support for the Stuarts were in Ireland and Scotland, especially in the Highlands. Catholic Ireland was kept down during most of the 18th century by the government's rigid repression as well as by English and Scottish Protestant settlers, and it had little to give to the Jacobite cause. Jacobite difficulties were the Stuarts' unbending Catholicism and the fact that a second restoration would require foreign, and probably

French, assistance. Jacobites were constantly intriguing with whatever powers were in conflict with Britain, making it easy for Whigs to
portray them, often accurately, as foreign agents. Whig governments,
particularly Walpole's, were paranoid about the Jacobites and kept an
extensive network of spies and informers.

The heights of Jacobite activity in Britain were the invasions of
1715 and 1745 (also known as "The Fifteen" and "The Forty-Five").
Both of these invasions, the first led by James III and the second
by his son, Prince Charles Stuart (1720–88), initially landed in the
Scottish highlands, where the government had little military presence
(particularly during The Forty-Five, when much of the army was on
the Continent fighting the War of the Austrian Succession) and where
there was the most popular support due to the cultural alienation of
many highlanders from the lowland Whigs who dominated Scottish
politics. After some initial successes, both risings were defeated due
to bad luck, the failure of the English to rally around (one defeated
Jacobite claimed that the lesson he learned from failure was never to
believe a drunken Tory), and the superior leadership of the government forces. The Forty-Five did leave a romantic legend of its leader,
Bonnie Prince Charlie.

The end result of the invasions was much closer government control of the Scottish highlands and a successful strategy of recruiting
highlanders into the British army, one of the great integrative forces in
the British Isles. Traditional highland society was broken up by government repression and also by the actions of highland chiefs, many
of whom dispossessed their clansmen to free land for more lucrative
enterprises—essentially exchanging their roles as traditional chiefs for
a new one as improving landlords. These so-called highland clearances
would persist well into the 19th century, depopulating large areas of the
highlands and encouraging the emigration of highlanders to other parts
of the British Empire or America.

Religion in 18th-Century England and Wales

The Church of England still attracted many dedicated clerics, but
unquestionably some of the fire had gone out. There was very little
extempore preaching, which had become associated with Dissenters—
Protestants outside the Church of England. Anglican preaching was
often from written discourses, or preachers recycled classic sermons
from famous clerics. The so-called plain style, popular among preachers of both the Church of England and the Dissenters during that time,

made little use of gesture or of variation in pitch and intonation and often appealed to reason rather than emotion. Church of England controversialists ably defended Christian orthodoxy from attacks within and without the church, but there was a less religious focus to much Anglican preaching and scholarship. Interest in the church fathers, a major preoccupation of the Church of England since the Reformation, was diminishing. The cooling of intellectual zeal in the church was reflected in the decline of English universities.

Structurally, the church was failing to deal with the increase of English population and urbanization. There was little interest in building new churches or expanding old ones. Bishops were often appointed for political or patronage ends, neglecting their dioceses as they spent time in London supporting the government in the House of Lords. There was less observance of Sunday as a holy day, as more and more social and political events took place on Sunday afternoon and evening. Many claimed religious indifference was spreading among both the upper and the lower classes.

The major Dissenting bodies, such as the Presbyterians and Congregationalists, also saw a slackening of both membership and religious practice. Whigs did try to lighten the burden on Dissenters, who were the most loyal Whig voters, but usually stopped short of anything that would ruffle the Church of England's feathers. Toleration, although sometimes attacked, was never seriously threatened during the century, and even the ban on Dissenters' political participation was not insurmountable. The lack of serious persecution contributed to the overall shrinkage of religious fervor, as did the introspective nature of most Dissenting communities, which were no longer looking to make converts. Some Dissenters, particularly the English Presbyterians, even converted to rationalist theology, namely Unitarianism, which denied the Trinity and the divinity of Christ.

The most important new religious movement of the 18th century was Methodism. Its founder, John Wesley (1703–91), was the 15th child of a Church of England minister. Devout from his youth, Wesley found the Church of England, with its worldly clergy and emphasis on reasonable religion, unsatisfying. He rebelled against the movement toward reasonableness in religion to the extent of believing that only a deception of the devil could explain why people had stopped believing in and preaching against witchcraft. At Oxford University Wesley led a small group known as the Holy Club, or Methodists. The early Methodist leaders included his brother Charles Wesley (1707–88), considered by many to be the greatest hymn-writer in the

English language, and another famous preacher, George Whitefield (1714–70).

In 1735 Wesley went on a preaching trip to Georgia, then a British colony in North America, but his preaching against the slave trade and the community's sins aroused fierce opposition. Shortly after he returned to Britain, he began the field preaching that would bring him fame. In the economically dynamic Britain of the 18th century, many people were outside the church's reach. Rapidly growing communities lacked parish churches, and many Church of England clergy were reluctant to minister to the poor and uneducated. Wesley preached in open fields and halls to coal miners and other poor workers and their families. He faced sometimes violent opposition from church and state authorities who opposed his preaching outside the church, as well as ordinary people who disliked his call for renouncing sin. Traveling preachers, as opposed to parish clergy, were viewed with great suspicion in England. Although Wesley himself never formally broke from the church, he was a great organizer and built his own institutions outside of it. After his death, that organization became the Methodist Church.

Wesley's preaching focused neither on reasonableness nor on church doctrine, but on the need for conversion. His sermons appealed to the emotions rather than the intellect with a simple message of repentance and faith in Christ. "From hence it manifestly appears, what is the nature of the new birth. It is that great change which God works in the soul, when he brings it into life, when he raises it from the death of sin to the life of righteousness" (Wesley 1840, 1:403). Wesley's emphasis on being "born again" still influences contemporary evangelical Christianity in Britain and throughout the world.

Calvinistic Methodism developed in Wales, which was poorly served by the Church of England. Wales's bishoprics were poor and were usually held by absentees seeking transfers to richer sees. Many of its clergy could not preach in Welsh, the language of the common people. There were exceptions, such as Griffith Jones (1683–1761), a Carmarthenshire rector who sponsored and led a remarkable group of male and female teachers who fanned out into the Welsh countryside to teach basic literacy in Welsh to the poor and uneducated, with the goal of encouraging reading the Bible and the church catechism. The Calvinistic Methodists, led by Howel Harris (1714–73), built on Jones's work to deepen the Christianity of ordinary Welsh. They promoted revivals, an emotional style of worship and small group meetings for converts to strengthen each other's faith. The Calvinistic Methodists remained in the Church of England until 1811.

Kirk and Enlightenment in 18th-Century Scotland

Eighteenth-century Scottish religious history was different from that of England in that the principal issues were fought out within the Church of Scotland itself. Patronage—that is, the right of an individual or institution, often a local landlord, to present or appoint a parish minister—was common and accepted in the Church of England but controversial in the Church of Scotland. Many Scottish Presbyterians were suspicious of the power patronage gave laypeople over the clergy. Another issue was the division between strict Calvinists and those who placed more emphasis on morality—the last often viewing themselves as the enlightened element in the church, while the strict Calvinists had a greater following among ordinary people. Tensions between the two groups led some of the strict Calvinists to establish a separate church in 1733 in what came to be known as the First Secession from the Church of Scotland—the first in a series of splits and reunifications that would recur throughout the world of Scottish Presbyterianism into the 20th century.

The so-called moderates in the Church of Scotland were also the leaders of the Scottish Enlightenment. The celebrated Enlightenment historian William Robertson (1721–93)—author of *The History of Scotland during the Reigns of Queen Mary and King James VI* (1759) and *The History of the Reign of Charles V* (1769), which included a famous survey of the Middle Ages that was one of the first attempts at writing the social history of Europe—was also principal of the University of Edinburgh and moderator of the General Assembly of the Church of Scotland, effectively its head.

Scottish enlightened thinkers believed that the future of their country lay in the development of a more modern civilization that was less bound by the strictures of tradition and religion. Part of the reason the moderates supported patronage was the hope that it would introduce an educated and civil clergy into Scottish communities. Sometimes this got them into trouble, as in 1756 when, in an attempt to promote an indigenous Scottish theater, leading moderates and the philosopher and historian David Hume (1711–76) supported a tragedy, *Douglas*, written by John Home (1722–1808), a clergyman of the Church of Scotland, and performed at Edinburgh's Canongate Theater. The play was violently condemned, both for being authored by a clergyman and also because of the values it promoted, as when the heroine commits suicide after her husband kills her son by her first husband. She should have displayed Christian patience rather than pagan despair, argued the play's opponents. The controversy provoked church condemnation of

DAVID HUME

David Hume (1711–76) is best known today as a philosopher, but he also excelled as a historian and social analyst. Born into a family of Scottish gentry and lawyers, he attended the University of Edinburgh and originally intended to go into law himself. Instead, he drifted from job to job in Britain and France while reading intensively and gradually losing his religious faith. His first book, the anonymously published, two-part *Treatise of Human Nature* (1739–40), attracted little interest despite being now viewed as a philosophical masterpiece. The disappointed Hume concluded that the book was too difficult to be widely read, and his subsequent philosophical books, including *Essays, Moral and Political* (two volumes, 1741–42) and *Philosophical Essays Concerning Human Understanding* (1748), were written in a more accessible style.

As a philosopher, Hume was a skeptic, not just of religion (although that was what made the greatest impression on his contemporaries) but of many things people took for granted, such as how one thing causes another. Hume's philosophy was rooted in human nature rather than transcendent reality. He based morality not on divine commands but on the pleasure or displeasure humans take in particular character traits. Religion itself, as he theorized in *Natural History of Religion* (1757), emerged in human societies due to fear of the future and the unknown. Hume's rejection of religion involved him in several controversies and was probably the reason he never received a position in a Scottish university.

The work Hume was best known for in his own lifetime was not his philosophy but his six-volume work *The History of England,* published from 1754 to 1762. It quickly became the standard history and enabled Hume to become the first writer in English to support himself by selling books on the market rather than being supported by a patron. Hume's history was politically controversial because many found it too conservative. His approach to history and politics differed from that of the British philosopher and activist John Locke (1631–1704) and others who based it on a social contract. In keeping with his generally naturalistic approach, Hume placed greater weight on custom and tradition than on abstract rights. However, conservatives in England and Scotland could not fully embrace his history due to its mockery of Christianity.

Hume's rejection of religion made his death particularly interesting. Many people believed that no one could continue to be irreligious

(continues)

DAVID HUME *(continued)*

when faced with imminent death. Hume's serenity and acceptance of his own end were remarkable to believers and nonbelievers alike, although there is some evidence that in private he was not as composed as he appeared to visitors. His friend Adam Smith (1723–90), the economist, wrote a posthumous evaluation of Hume as the ideal of a wise and virtuous man, shocking many who viewed religious skeptics as necessarily immoral.

the play, the theater in general, and the play's sponsors, although the moderates were able to contain the damage through their control of the General Assembly, the Church's highest council. In general, the evangelicals were able to make great polemical use out of the moderates' association with such religiously suspect persons as Hume.

Scottish concern with modernization contributed to interest in the historical development of society, a subject that emerged frequently in Scottish Enlightenment writing, from the histories of Hume and Robertson to Adam Ferguson's *An Essay on the History of Civil Society* (1767) and Adam Smith's *The Wealth of Nations* (1776). The close proximity of the highlands—where herding and, for much of the century, warfare were still prevalent—and the commercial metropolis of Edinburgh made the contrast between different types of society particularly apparent.

The Enlightenment in England

The 18th century is often identified as the century of the European Enlightenment—the rise of reason. Many of the most characteristic elements of the Enlightenment originated in England, including Newtonian physics, John Locke's approach to politics and epistemology, and limited monarchy. However, for a long time historians doubted whether there was an "English Enlightenment." Some of the most important thinkers of 18th-century England, such as John Wesley or the London essayist and journalist Samuel Johnson (1709–84), were opponents rather than representatives of the Enlightenment. However, while it did not always take center stage in the intellectual history of 18th-century England, the Enlightenment was definitely a strong presence.

English intellectuals operated with certain advantages that others lacked. In 1695 the Licensing Act, which had established censorship in England, expired, and Parliament never renewed it. English writers could still be persecuted for what they published, but they no longer had to receive permission for publication. Although the Church of England remained a force to be reckoned with in the 18th century, it lacked the institutional power and cultural hegemony wielded by the French Catholic Church or the Scottish Presbyterian Church. Not only were deist and anti-Christian positions aired with relative openness, the church also coexisted with other religious bodies, including a marginalized Roman Catholicism as well as several Dissenting Protestant churches, including Congregationalists, Presbyterians, Baptists, and Quakers. Perhaps because the Church of England was ineffective at repressing dissent, one characteristic of the English Enlightenment was that it produced few outspoken opponents of Christianity. Indeed, some of the most prominent Enlightened intellectuals of late 18th-century England, such as the chemist and materialist philosopher Joseph Priestley (1733–1804) and the Welsh political philosopher Richard Price (1723–91), were Dissenting ministers. (The difference between the English and French Enlightenment can be seen in the shock of many Parisian intellectuals, who admired Priestley as a scientist, in finding that he was a sincere Christian.) Price and Priestley targeted not the doctrine so much as the privileged position of the Church of England, which held a de jure monopoly on political power. This led them to support political reform and, eventually, sympathize with the French Revolution.

The 18th-century English writer most strongly identified with the Enlightenment was the historian Edward Gibbon (1737–94), author of *The Decline and Fall of the Roman Empire* (six volumes, 1776–88). An admirer of the French anticlerical radical Voltaire and the Scottish historians David Hume and William Robertson, Gibbon took a skeptical approach to the early history of Christianity. The famous 15th and 16th chapters of volume 1 of *The Decline and Fall of the Roman Empire,* on the early church and its rise to power in the empire, took a dim view of Christianity and its early champions, despite Gibbon's reliance on the work of earlier, devout church historians. Volume 1 aroused great opposition from some Church of England clergy; however, there was no possibility of church opposition preventing subsequent volumes of the history from being published.

England did not have the network of state-sponsored academies characteristic of France and other continental European countries, and unlike Scotland, its universities were not intellectual leaders. In science the gap was filled by Britain's major scientific organization, the Royal Society, and by a variety of informal clubs and groups. Although the Royal Society claimed a footing of equality with France's Royal Academy of Sciences as a leader of the scientific world, it was a very different organization, with voluntary, unpaid membership and little state support. A similar organization, aimed at technological improvement rather than scientific discovery, was the Society for the Encouragement of Arts, Manufacturers and Commerce, familiarly known as the Society of Arts and founded in 1754.

Many of the informal groups that spread Enlightenment ideas and values in England were based outside London, in the provinces and particularly in the north, where Dissenting was strong. There was a pronounced emphasis on the contributions of science and philosophy to economic development, as these areas were also cradles of the Industrial Revolution. The Lunar Society of Birmingham, one such provincial gathering of intellectuals and businessmen, included a leading Enlightenment philosopher and scientist, Priestley, as well as the great engineer James Watt (1736–1819), inventor of the steam engine with separate condenser, his business partner Matthew Boulton (1728–1809), and the great porcelain manufacturer Josiah Wedgwood (1730–95).

The Rise of the English Novel

The 18th and early 19th centuries were an age of entertainment as well as enlightenment. The period saw the rise of a new form of literature, long prose stories about common people, often appealing to a working-class or middle-class audience. The first best-selling novel in English was Daniel Defoe's *Robinson Crusoe* (1719), based loosely on the story of a man marooned on an island. *Robinson Crusoe* was an examination of an important 18th-century theme, sociability, by telling the story of someone deprived of it. Defoe (1660–1731) was a popular writer and journalist writing for a market, not to attract the attention of an aristocratic patron.

Subsequent best-selling novelists in the 18th century included Samuel Richardson (1689–1761), author of *Pamela* (1740) and *Clarissa* (1748), "epistolary novels," told in a series of letters, about virtuous heroines in stressful situations who kept their virtue. Richardson's work, often called sentimental due to its skillful tugging of the heartstrings, had a particularly strong appeal to women, a growing audience for literature in the 18th century. Henry Fielding (1707–54) mocked Richardson and wrote vigorously comic novels with male protagonists, such as *Tom Jones* (1749). The Scottish author Tobias Smollett (1721–71) wrote picaresque narratives of adventuresome heroes such as *The Adventures of Roderick Random* (1748).

The modern historical novel is largely the creation of the Scottish writer Sir Walter Scott (1771–1832). Scott specialized in stirring action set against great historical events, such as his first novel, *Waverley* (1814), which tells the story of a young Englishman of Jacobite sympathies who fights in the rebellion but is finally reconciled to the Hanoverian regime. Much of the sentimentalization of both the Jacobites and the Scottish highlands can be traced to Scott's works. He also wrote novels of the Middle Ages, such as *Ivanhoe* (1819), which greatly influenced the common picture of the period as an age of knightliness and chivalry.

A very different author from Scott, but one whom he admired, was Jane Austen (1775–1817), whose works were set in contemporary England and recounted not deeds of male courage but the sedate lives of English gentry from a female perspective. Often denigrated in her own time as a writer of light literature for amusement, Austen's critical star has steadily risen in the 20th century as her *Pride and Prejudice* (1813) has become a cultural touchstone, frequently adapted and presented in different media, as have her other works.

The Wars with France and the Rise of the British Empire

The 18th century is sometimes referred to as the Second Hundred Years' War due to the many conflicts between Britain and France. However, there were also long periods of peace, and Britain and France were in some ways culturally closer than they had been since the Middle Ages. Many British people knew French, the international language of European culture, and the French were even beginning to take an interest in English. Visits across the Channel were common, and the religious difference between Protestant Britain and Catholic France meant less than it had in the 17th century. None of this prevented a long and bloody series of wars. Conflicts between Britain and France included the War of the Austrian Succession (1740–48), the Seven Years' War (1756–63), and the War of the American Revolution (1775–83). The first was basically a draw, the second a great British victory, the third a British defeat. The wars of the 18th century were world wars, with battles in Europe, the Americas, and India as well as across the world's oceans. British victories led to the exclusion of its European rivals from India and most of North America. Even though the thirteen colonies and Florida were lost in the American Revolution, Britain retained the vast lands of Canada, which it had won from France in the Seven Years' War, as well as its rich Caribbean slave colonies. By the end of the century, an entire continent—Australia—had been added to the diverse collection of territories that made up the greatest empire the world had ever known.

British assets in the wars with France included its geographical position, which meant that any French invasion would have to be seaborne; its navy's control of the seas; and its dynamic economy, which made it the paymaster of the anti-French coalitions. One reason for the British defeat in the War of the American Revolution was that despite the British government's best efforts, it could not find a European country willing to attack France on the Continent. Lack of Continental engagement freed the French, for the only time in the 18th century, to concentrate their forces on Britain's colonial possessions by supporting the American rebels.

Britain in the Revolutionary Age

The triumphant Britain that emerged from the Seven Years' War was fundamentally challenged by the forces unleashed by the American and French revolutions. Not only was British military power stretched to the limit, but new ideologies and bases for opposition were disseminated in Great Britain itself as well as its satellite kingdom of Ireland.

Despite the growing impact of industry, Britain's ruling class continued to derive its power from the land. Its political center was the unreformed Parliament, both of whose houses, Lords and Commons, were dominated by landowners. Domestically, the British elite was challenged by radical movements for parliamentary reform; more frequent elections; and, in the most extreme formulations, manhood suffrage. Radicals, often Protestant Dissenters, charged the British parliament with subservience to royal despotism and, more credibly, with corruption. Despite the popularity of many reformers, such as the notorious demagogue John Wilkes (1725–97), and the embarrassing defeats Britain suffered at the hands of the American rebels and their French and Spanish allies in the American Revolution, Britain's rulers usually managed to contain dissent. The worst political disturbance in Britain itself during the war in America was the 1780 Gordon anti-Catholic riots in London. The riots, led by the erratic Scottish demagogue Lord

George Gordon (1751–93), lasted four days and resulted in extensive property destruction, although little loss of life. Newgate Prison was razed and the prime minister's house attacked. Troops were called in to disperse the rioters. Gordon himself later converted to Judaism.

Damaged by American defeat, the loss of its richest North American colonies, and civil unrest, Britain was often seen as irreversibly declining, although the expansion of British power in India compensated for losses elsewhere. The nation's recovery began during the long prime ministership of William Pitt the

This idealized portrait of George III shows him bathed in celestial light. (Library of Congress)

Younger (1759–1806), from 1783 to his death, with one interruption from 1801 to 1804. Pitt emphasized economic and administrative reform while leaving irregular and undemocratic parliamentary franchises and the Church of England's privileged position untouched. He relied on his own great ability and the support of the king, George III (1738–1820; r. 1760–1820). Pitt's great rival, Charles James Fox (1749–1806), was forced to ally with the dissolute and irresponsible heir to the throne, George, prince of Wales, the future George IV (1762–1830; r. 1820–30). Fox briefly came within sight of power in the Regency Crisis of 1788, when George III's brief fit of madness nearly made the prince of Wales regent. Fox's shrinking body of followers kept the designation *Whig*, while Pitt's followers were first referred to by the revived term *Tory* and later as *Conservatives*.

The French Revolution of 1789 added to the polarization of British politics. Many British people greeted it with the hope that France would now adopt a parliamentary government on the British model, and those sympathetic to the Revolution made Thomas Paine's *The Rights of Man* (1791–92) a best seller, with more than 200,000 copies sold, far exceeding sales of the antirevolutionary *Reflections on the Revolution in France* (1790) by Edmund Burke. However, horror at

French excesses accelerated the conservative reaction that had begun with Pitt's coming to power. Sympathy for exiled French Catholics and Catholic priests in Britain even muted British anti-Catholicism. On the political side, Pitt's government crushed the radicals by suspending habeas corpus and vigorously prosecuting them in Pitt's "reign of terror" in 1793–94. The repression was particularly harsh and successful in Scotland, with its different legal structure that gave less protection to individual rights. Not all of the opposition to radicals was directed from above, however. British sympathizers with the French Revolution also inspired popular opposition, partly because they were revolutionary and partly because they were associated with France, the traditional enemy. Mobs loyal to church and king, encouraged by local gentry and Church of England clergy, attacked Dissenting chapels and individual French sympathizers.

On the religious side, the evangelical movement in the Church of England drew in many upper-class men and women. Evangelicals furnished much of the leadership for the popular movement for the abolition of slavery, but they abominated the French Revolution and were conservative on other issues.

The Industrial Revolution

The British economy in the late 18th century was transformed by the so-called Industrial Revolution, although the term itself was not used at the time. England had several advantages in being the first country to industrialize. It was well supplied with coal and iron, and it was a rich society by premodern standards, with a surplus of capital available for investment and a developed system of capital markets, making it relatively easy to get capital to entrepreneurs through joint-stock companies and other financial arrangements. British domination of the seas was actually strengthened by the wars with France. British colonies were exploited both for cheap raw materials and as captive markets. England also had mechanics and engineers who combined practical experience with some training in Newtonian physics. The enclosure movement, in which Parliament handed over common community land to private landowners, coupled with rapid growth in the English population, meant that a large surplus workforce, unable to sustain itself on the land, was available for industry.

Industrialism first emerged in the production and trade of textiles, particularly cotton—known as light industry. Economic expansion in textiles was initially based on a series of technical and organizational innovations in spinning and weaving, including the spinning mule, the spinning jenny, the power loom, and the steam engine with separate condenser. Cotton was not as absolutely central to the British Industrial Revolution as it is often presented, but there is no question that it was very important. The origin of the factory system is closely associated with the cotton industry, and factory organization did not spread to other industries until after 1830. The quantity of raw cotton imported into the British Isles went from 11 million pounds in 1785 to 588 million pounds in 1850, and the output of cloth went from 40 million to 2,025 million square yards. This was an export-oriented trade, and it was efficient to the degree that, notwithstanding attempts by the French ruler Napoleon Bonaparte (1769–1821) to block British goods from the European continent, even the French army was clothing soldiers in English cotton cloth. British colonies in North America, India, and Africa were also British markets. After it won independence from Spain and Portugal in the early 19th century, Latin America became virtually an economic colony of Britain. Even the United States continued to be a major market for British manufactured goods after the American Revolution. Other British industries that were expanding included iron and coal, which would receive a powerful stimulus from the demands of war.

The Industrial Revolution led to powerful social changes, especially in the growth of urbanization and new forms of labor. English urban areas, particularly London and the cities of the industrial north, grew at an astounding rate, and by the mid-19th century Britain was the first large nation to have a majority of its population living in cities. Thousands of people abandoned the daily and seasonal rhythms of agricultural work in favor of a life regulated by machinery and the clock and subject to the iron rule of factory owners. Owners forced workers to work long hours in harsh and dangerous conditions, paid the lowest wages they could get away with, and enlisted the state to prevent workers from organizing to better their conditions. Children were employed doing exhausting physical work from a very young age. The new cities were overcrowded, with shoddy, quickly built housing for the working population and poor hygiene and waste disposal.

The Last Great Anglo-French War

The outbreak of war with revolutionary France in 1793, precipitated by the French conquest of the Austrian Netherlands, caught the British militarily unprepared. The revolutionary and Napoleonic wars between France and its European neighbors would last until 1815, when Napoleon—who had become consul in 1799 and emperor in 1804—was finally defeated at the battle of Waterloo. At the war's outbreak, the British army had fewer than 50,000 men, and the navy, while still the world's most powerful, had deteriorated since Britain's last major conflict, the war of the American Revolution. Both the creation and the maintenance of a large military force and the endless subsidies required by Britain's Continental allies strained the British treasury, forcing Parliament to adopt an income tax in 1799. However, revolutionary France faced the same disadvantages by sea that royal France had faced in its 18th-century wars and never successfully challenged British naval supremacy. A planned French invasion across the channel in 1797, for which Napoleon Bonaparte was appointed military commander, was abandoned as impractical due to Britain's naval power. The following year, however, saw a much more dangerous threat to British naval supremacy from a different quarter—its own sailors.

In April and May 1797, mutinies by sailors at Spithead and the Nore were precipitated less by sympathy with the French Revolution than by low pay, often in arrears, and poor food and working conditions. The government under Pitt resolved the mutiny with concessions to the sailors and punishment of the ringleaders of the Nore fleet, which had actually blockaded London and proclaimed its sympathy with the French.

The naval mutinies of 1797 and the French-aided Irish Rebellion of 1798 precipitated another wave of repressive legislation, including the Unlawful Oaths Act of 1797, which was aimed at secret societies; the 1798 Newspaper Act, establishing tight controls over the press; and the 1799 Corresponding Societies Act, suppressing political committees of correspondence that circulated radical writings. The Combination Acts of 1799 and 1800 were aimed at workers' organizations and combined the government's desire to repress popular organizations with employers' desire to crush workers' taking advantage of the war and its increased demand for labor to organize for improved wages and working conditions.

The need to control Ireland effectively, whose restiveness against British rule made it both a site of rebellion and a target of French invasion, led to the Act of Union of 1801, which joined Great Britain and Ireland into the United Kingdom. The incorporation of Ireland, with its enormous Catholic population, into the British polity led to the rise of Catholic emancipation as an issue in British politics. Pitt and much of the political elite, including the Whig opposition, supported the granting of political rights to Catholics as a quid pro quo for Irish Catholics' acceptance of the union, but they were firmly and effectively opposed by the king and most of the Protestant population.

The navy, recovering from the mutinies, won an important victory under the greatest admiral of the time, Horatio Nelson (1758–1805), at the Battle of the Nile in 1798, which forced Napoleon to abandon his Egyptian expedition. Napoleon organized another attempt at an invasion of England in 1805, this time with Spanish aid. Nelson's greatest victory, the Battle of Trafalgar in 1805, cost the admiral his life but destroyed any possibility of a French invasion and established Britain's complete domination of the seas.

The struggle by land was initially far different. At first British forces played only a minor role in the war in Europe. In the Caribbean, many soldiers were lost to both disease and the enemy in an unsuccessful intervention in Haiti. The army's relatively minor role only changed with the Peninsular War from 1808 to 1814, when Britain, led by Arthur Wellesley (later duke of Wellington), formed an alliance with Spain and Portugal, who were fighting against French occupation of their countries. Wellesley established his reputation as Britain's leading general despite inadequate support from the British government, but the

This cartoon shows Napoleon complaining that the British have taken him away from his wife, while George IV wishes he could get rid of his. (Library of Congress)

British army was still small compared to those of the great Continental powers. Even Wellington's victory over Napoleon at Waterloo in 1815, which ended the wars, was achieved with an allied force of which only a third were British.

The confrontation between Britain and France was economic as well as military. The importance of the export trade for the British economy was also a weakness. Although Napoleon could do nothing to prevent Britain from exporting outside Europe, he did attempt to close the European market to British exports with a decree issued in 1806 that ordered all Continental ports closed to British ships; this embargo was called the Continental System. The British also had difficulty exporting to the United States, which under President Thomas Jefferson (1801–09) attempted to isolate itself from the European war. (Shipping-related disputes between Britain and the United States would eventually lead to the War of 1812.) Britain responded to the Continental System with a series of Orders in Council, which essentially put all French-ruled Europe under a blockade, demanding that all exports from neutral countries to Europe pass through Britain first. The Orders in Council aroused fierce opposition from the British business community, however, and were abandoned along with the Continental System in 1812.

Prime Minister William Pitt the Younger died in 1806, leaving no one dominant figure in British politics. A coalition that included Pitt's great rival, Charles James Fox, and was known as the "Ministry of All the Talents" proved short-lived. The most successful prime ministers in the later period of the wars were Tories; Spencer Perceval (1762–1812) and Robert Banks Jenkinson (1770–1828), earl of Liverpool. (Perceval was the only prime minister to be assassinated.) George III's descent into madness in 1810 brought his son into power as prince regent, but by that time the future George IV had lost most of his sympathy with the Whigs and his ascent had little impact on the war effort.

The wars cost Britain approximately £15 billion and 210,000 lives. Victory vastly expanded the empire. The British acquired many new territories, including the Dutch colonies in Ceylon and South Africa, the Spanish Caribbean colony of Trinidad, and the Mediterranean island of Malta. They also expanded their possessions in India. Britain's imperial predominance would not be seriously challenged until the late 19th century. The abolition of first the slave trade in 1807 and eventually slavery in the British dominions in 1833 provided Britain with an ideological justification for naval supremacy, as the Royal Navy took on the task of preventing slave trading, not always effectively. Caught up in consolidating their empire, the British in the post-Napoleonic period mostly refrained from active military and diplomatic involvement on the European continent while fighting many wars outside Europe.

Postwar Britain

Domestically, the postwar period was marked by violent repression of dissent, most notably the massacre of Peterloo in 1819, when 11 peaceful demonstrators for parliamentary reform with a broader franchise were massacred by the yeomanry, a local militia under the command of magistrates at a reform meeting outside St. Peter's fields in Manchester. One of the fastest-growing communities in Britain, Manchester lacked parliamentary representation, so interest in parliamentary reform was particularly keen there. Parliament, which continued to be dominated on both the Whig and the Tory sides by landowners, passed a series of protective tariffs, the Corn Laws, beginning in 1814, to maintain a high price for domestic grain. Resentment of the government's bondage to the aristocratic landed interest was high throughout the country on the part of both the poor and the middle class. George IV's accession to the throne on his father's death in 1820 also produced a vast popular campaign in support of his estranged wife Caroline, seen as a faithful and maligned woman who was a victim of the same evil forces that prevented parliamentary reform. In the end, however, the Caroline agitation came to little.

The development of the steam locomotive railroad caused major changes in the British environment and way of life. The country's first public railroad began service in 1825. The major milestone in the early history of the locomotive railway was the inauguration of the 30-mile run between the industrial centers of Manchester and Liverpool in 1830. The railway expanded dramatically over this period, with railway booms in 1835–37 and 1844–47 marked by speculative frenzies far in advance of actual profitability. The railway infrastructure itself grew from a few dozen miles in 1830 to more than 8,000 by 1850.

By the late 1820s, British government was becoming less reactionary. In 1828, a Tory government under the duke of Wellington repealed the Test and Corporation Acts, which had been in force since 1673; this opened many positions in national and local government to Protestant Dissenters. Despite vehement opposition from reactionary Tories, the so-called Ultras, Wellington also passed Catholic emancipation, granting political rights to Catholics in 1829. The law was passed mainly to appease the mass movement of Catholic Irish led by Daniel O'Connell (1775–1847), but it was applied throughout the British Isles and,

This cartoon shows reformers sweeping out the rats of corruption from "rotten," or corrupt, boroughs, although the actual reform bill was not passed until 1832. (Henry Heath, courtesy Library of Congress)

together with the repeal of the Test and Corporation Acts, dissolved the 18th-century Anglican "confessional state," in which members of the Church of England monopolized most offices.

Reformers wanted more, specifically the reworking of Britain's archaic parliamentary election system to more accurately represent the British people. This was a particularly sore issue in the industrial areas of the north, where vast urban agglomerations such as Manchester had tiny electorates and little representation. Scotland, too, had a very small electorate and disproportionately low representation in the House of Commons. The Tories, knowing that reform would alter the political landscape to their disadvantage, refused to budge, but the death of George IV in 1830 dissolved Parliament, and the Whigs won the election on a reform platform.

The passage of the Great Reform Bill of 1832 was difficult. The Whigs, led by Prime Minister Earl Grey (1764–1845) in an uneasy alliance with the radicals, got it through the House of Commons. Rejection of the bill by the Tory-dominated House of Lords touched off riots and attacks on the homes of antireform peers. In April 1832, after King William IV (1765–1837; r. 1830–37) had made his support for the Lords passing reform clear (despite his own doubts on the measure),

the lords gave way. The Reform Bill did not bring Britain democracy—
nor was it meant to—but it increased the electorate and provided a
more uniform set of qualifications based on property for the franchise.
Scotland's electorate shot up 14-fold, a stark contrast to that of England
and Wales, which went up only by about a third. Subsequently, the
Second Reform Bill in 1867 and the Third Reform Bill in 1884 further
broadened the parliamentary franchise, although it remained restricted
to males. Other Whig reforms in the 1830s included the abolition of
slavery in the British dominions in 1833, the very unpopular New Poor
Law establishing the workhouse system for poor relief in 1834, and
reform of local government in Scotland and England. The Factory Act
of 1833 limited the hours of child labor and set up a system of factory
inspectors. Meanwhile, the Church of England was losing institutional
and economic independence. Civil marriage was instituted in 1836,
although divorce still required a specific act of Parliament dissolving
the marriage, rendering it impossible for all but the very wealthy.

The Whigs in power continued to repress popular dissent. The
1830 Swing Riots of farm laborers in southern England, who sought to
stop the introduction of the new threshing machines that threatened
their livelihoods, were put down by force, as was the Grand National
Consolidated Trades Union Movement in 1834. The Tolpuddle Martyrs,
six workingmen sentenced to seven years in the penal colony in
Australia for having administered illegal oaths to fellow union members, were brought back to England only after a massive petitioning
campaign by workers forced the government to yield. Troops were sent
to Wales to put down the Rebecca Riots, a movement of small farmers
and workers principally aimed at the hated workhouses that lasted from
1839 to 1843. In England the focus of working-class political activity
shifted from trade unionism to politics with the goal of securing working-class representation in Parliament. The six demands of the "People's
Charter," published by a London group dominated by skilled artisans in
1838, included annual parliaments, universal male suffrage, equal electoral districts, the removal of property qualifications for parliamentary
membership, secret ballots, and payment of members of Parliament.
"Chartism" dominated working-class politics thenceforth.

The other grave political issue was free trade. A bad harvest in 1836
roused opposition to the Corn Laws, and the Anti-Corn Law League
was founded in 1839. The league's base was in northern industrial communities, particularly Manchester. Its leaders, Richard Cobden (1804–
65) and John Bright (1811–89), claimed to represent the intelligent and
hardworking middle class against the corrupt landed aristocracy. Many

free-trade supporters were industrialists who believed cheaper grain would enable them to lower their workers' wages, and there was little collaboration between the Anti-Corn Law League and the Chartists. The eventual victory of free trade was due to the conversion of the conservative prime minister, Sir Robert Peel (1788–1850). Peel was the first prime minister from an industrial background. His support for the repeal of the Corn Laws in 1846 was prompted by the beginnings of the Irish potato blight, to which British response was delayed and inadequate, contributing to the loss of a million lives. Peel's support for free trade cost him his office and divided the Conservatives into a Peelite faction and a larger but less distinguished Protectionist one.

Queen Victoria (1819–1901; r. 1837–1901), the longest-reigning monarch in British history, inherited the throne in 1837. Her accession dissolved the personal union between Britain and Hanover, which unlike Britain followed the Salic law that barred female inheritance. Few Britons regretted the loss. The young queen certainly presented a better face for the monarchy than either of her two immediate predecessors.

Despite glaring internal divisions, the British ruling class easily weathered the storm of 1848 when revolutions rocked the European continent. There was a tense moment in April when the Chartists

The state opening of the great exhibition of 1851 (Library of Congress)

152

brought the last of their "monster petitions" to London. Ten thousand special constables were sworn in to deal with them, but the Chartists dispersed without violence, and the movement declined rapidly thereafter. In 1851 the Great Exhibition—the first world's fair, initiated by Victoria's husband, Prince Albert (1819–61)—took place in London. Its hordes of peaceful visitors from all over the world bore witness to Britain's triumph as the workshop of the world and a model of social and political stability.

7

BRITAIN IN
THE AGE OF EMPIRE
(1851–1922)

I n the second half of the 19th century, Britain reached an unparalleled height of world power while also maintaining political stability. However, it had grave difficulties dealing with the challenges of the 20th century, prominent among them anti-imperial nationalism in the empire and Ireland, the rise of competing economies, and the impact of World War I.

The Empire at Its Zenith

The British Empire under Queen Victoria (r. 1837–1901) was at its zenith of power and prestige. The empire included the legacy of British victories in the wars against France in the 18th and early 19th century and the new conquests that had been made since then. It was also the product of Britain's world-leading industrial economy and unrivaled navy. The queen's assumption of the title Empress of India on January 1, 1877, was an assertion both of British splendor and of the centrality of India in the empire. Much British colonial activity, such as the acquisition of control over the Suez Canal in 1875, was driven by the need to secure India. Britons argued that it was only the possession of India that made their nation a first-rate power. The Indian rebellion of 1857, also known as the Indian Mutiny as it involved Indian troops in British service, briefly seemed to threaten the British position, but it was quickly and brutally suppressed.

Britain was also an avid participant in what was known as the "Scramble for Africa," the process from about 1880 to 1900 by which all of Africa, with the two exceptions of Ethiopia and Liberia, was divided among European colonial powers. Britain came out with more territory than any other power, including Nigeria, most of East Africa, and domination over Egypt.

The empire was neither acquired nor maintained peacefully, and Victorian Britain was constantly engaged in wars on the colonial frontiers. However, only one war was fought against a European power in this period: The Crimean War against Russia was waged from 1853 to 1856, with France and the Ottoman Empire as allies. Despite the blundering of British generals, which destroyed the reputation of some, and the appalling incompetence of much of the army, the war ended in victory. (However, it made the reputation of Florence Nightingale [1820–1910], who campaigned against the abysmally filthy and ill-run hospitals for wounded British soldiers. Nightingale went on to found the modern nursing profession.) After the Crimean War, British governments carefully avoided the possibility of engagement in European wars. Adopting a policy of "splendid isolation" (a phrase originally coined by the Canadian politician George Eulas Foster in 1896 but one that caught on quickly in Britain itself), Britain shunned formal Continental alliances that might have drawn it into war with European great powers. This enabled it to maintain a small army (although there was a large army based in India, paid for by the colony itself)

A British camp in the Crimean War (Library of Congress, Fenton Collection)

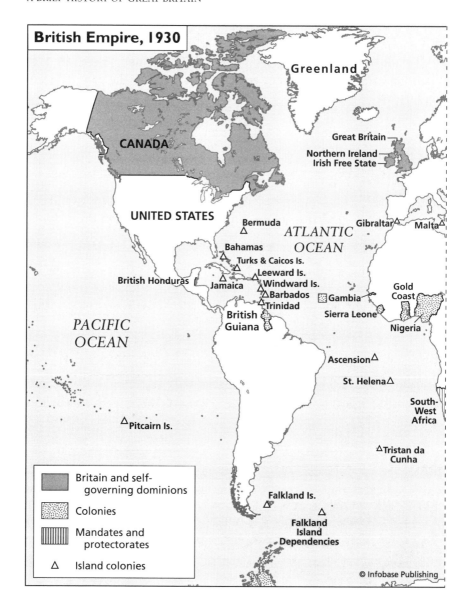

British Empire, 1930

Greenland

CANADA

Great Britain
Northern Ireland
Irish Free State

UNITED STATES

Bermuda
△

Bahamas
△

Turks & Caicos Is.
△

British Honduras

Jamaica
△

Leeward Is.
△

Windward Is.
△Barbados
△Trinidad

British
Guiana

ATLANTIC
OCEAN

Gibraltar△   Malta△

Gambia

Sierra Leone

Gold
Coast

Nigeria

PACIFIC
OCEAN

Ascension△

St. Helena△

South-
West
Africa

△Pitcairn Is.

△Tristan da
Cunha

Britain and self-
governing dominions

Colonies

Mandates and
protectorates

△   Island colonies

Falkland Is.
△

Falkland
Island
Dependencies
△

© Infobase Publishing

and devote most of its military budget to the world's dominant navy. Although there were also tensions and clashes between Britain and the United States, again the British avoided war, increasingly deferring to the United States in affairs of the Western Hemisphere.

Britain's main worldwide colonial rival was France, possessor of the world's second-largest colonial empire, but the two powers only

156

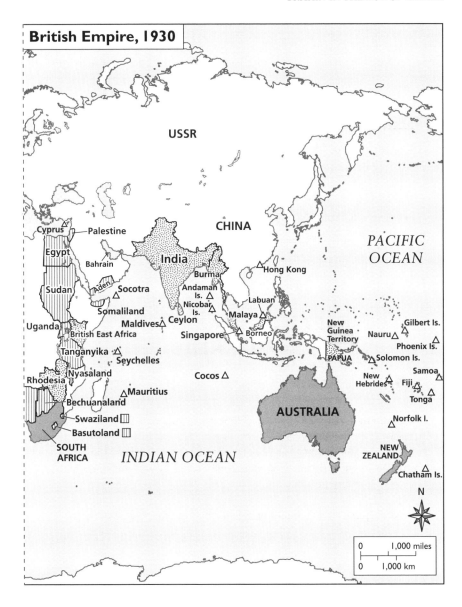

British Empire, 1930

USSR

Cyprus
Palestine
Egypt
Bahrain
Sudan
Aden
Socotra
Somaliland
Uganda
British East Africa
Maldives
Tanganyika
Seychelles
Nyasaland
Rhodesia
Bechuanaland
Mauritius
Swaziland
Basutoland
SOUTH
AFRICA

CHINA
India
Burma
Hong Kong
Andaman Is.
Nicobar Is.
Ceylon
Labuan
Malaya
Singapore
Borneo
Cocos

PACIFIC
OCEAN

New Guinea Territory
Nauru
Gilbert Is.
Phoenix Is.
PAPUA
Solomon Is.
New Hebrides
Fiji
Samoa
Tonga
AUSTRALIA
Norfolk I.
NEW ZEALAND
Chatham Is.

INDIAN OCEAN

N

0   1,000 miles
0   1,000 km

came close to war once, in the Fashoda Incident of 1898, when a small French military force coming northeastward from central Africa met British troops coming south from Egypt near the Sudanese town of Fashoda. Viewing their colonial empire as decidedly secondary to their European concerns, the French backed down rather than risk conflict with Britain.

By the end of the century, many Britons viewed the principal foreign threat as Germany, only recently formed into a united nation in 1871. Germany was a rising power both economically and militarily, and its leaders, particularly Victoria's grandson, the bombastic kaiser Wilhelm II (1859–1941; r. 1888–1918), occasionally made noises about challenging Britain for world leadership.

One of the empire's important roles in British culture was to provide a vehicle for British identity. Many Scots, Welsh, and Irish served in the colonial army or administration. The glory of the empire was presented as something that all Britons could be proud of, although this propaganda was more successful among the middle classes than among the workers. Imperialism also promoted racism, as the native inhabitants of various British colonies were presented as barbarous or comic figures, in need of British guidance. Rudyard Kipling (1865–1936), a poet and

KIPLING ON EMPIRE AND PRIDE

The 60th anniversary of Queen Victoria's accession to the throne—her Diamond Jubilee—was a great state occasion and an opportunity for Britons to celebrate the British Empire, then at its zenith. Rudyard Kipling, a firm supporter of the empire, took the occasion in his poem "Recessional" to remind his fellow British citizens of the transitoriness of earthly glory and power and the importance of humility before God.

> God of our fathers, known of old—Lord of our far-flung battle
>   line—
> Beneath whose awful Hand we hold
> Dominion over palm and pine—
> Lord God of Hosts, be with us yet,
> Lest we forget—lest we forget!

> The tumult and the shouting dies—
> The Captains and the Kings depart—
> Still stands Thine ancient sacrifice,
> An humble and a contrite heart.
> Lord God of Hosts, be with us yet,
> Lest we forget—lest we forget!

short-story writer, was particularly well-known for his writing on the empire, which glamorized—and sometimes mocked—British soldiers and administrators as well as those colonial subjects, like the fictional water bearer Gunga Din, who supported British rule.

Liberals and Conservatives

The politics of the 1850s were highly factionalized. However, the factions settled down into a two-party system when the aristocratic Whigs, radicals, and ex-conservative Peelites—supporters of the late prime minister Sir Robert Peel, who had broken with the Conservatives over the party's opposition to free trade—coalesced into the Liberal Party. As the electorate grew, politicians cultivated more of a mass appeal. No longer was it sufficient to be a master maneuverer in the backrooms of

---

Far-called, our navies melt away—
On dune and headland sinks the fire—
Lo, all our pomp of yesterday
Is one with Nineveh and Tyre!
Judge of the Nations, spare us yet,
Lest we forget—lest we forget!

If, drunk with sight of power, we loose
Wild tongues that have not Thee in awe—
Such boastings as the Gentiles use,
Or lesser breeds without the Law—
Lord God of Hosts, be with us yet,
Lest we forget—lest we forget!

For heathen heart that puts her trust
In reeking tube and iron shard—
All valiant dust that builds on dust,
And guarding calls not Thee to guard
For frantic boast and foolish word
Thy Mercy on Thy People, Lord!

Amen

Source: Rudyard Kipling, *The Writings in Prose and Verse of Rudyard Kipling.* New York: Charles Scribner's Sons, 1920. Vol. 23: 201–202.

Westminster: The politician who hoped to be leader of his party and prime minister had to cultivate a public image as well.

Often credited as the first politician to create an electorally powerful public image was Henry John Temple, third viscount Palmerston (1784–1865), who sat in the House of Commons for more than 50 years (while peers of the United Kingdom were barred from the Commons, Lord Palmerston's title was an Irish one) and served twice as prime minister, from 1855 to 1858 and from 1859 to his death in 1865. Palmerston, prime minister during the Crimean War, was identified with an aggressive foreign policy and a strong, uncomplicated English patriotism. The earl of Shaftesbury, an ally of Palmerston's, was amazed at his celebrity, writing of the election of 1857 "P[almerston]'s popularity is wonderful—strange to say, the whole turns on his name. There seems to be no measure, no principle, no cry, to influence men's minds and determine elections; it is simply 'were you, or were you not? are you, or are you not, for Palmerston?'" (quoted in Hodder 1971, 3:43). Palmerston was returned to office with a large majority.

Few British politicians have ever crafted such vivid public personalities as the leaders of the generation after Palmerston: Conservative Benjamin Disraeli (1804–81; prime minister, 1868, 1874–80) and his Liberal rival, William Ewart Gladstone (1809–98; prime minister, 1868–74, 1880–85, 1886, 1892–94). Disraeli, nicknamed "Dizzy," a novelist of Jewish descent and without landowning roots, was an odd choice for leadership of the Conservative Party. Gladstone, the "Grand Old Man" or the "People's William," whose political career spanned most of the century, served as prime minister on four separate occasions and traced a political pilgrimage from the right wing of the Conservatives to the left wing of the Liberals. The rivalry of Gladstone and Disraeli, who personally despised each other, gave British politics in this period an unequalled sense of drama.

One trend that can be traced in this period was the steady diminishment of the Whig landowning element in the Liberal Party. Landowners, even from traditional Whig families such as the Cavendish dukes of Devonshire, drifted to the Conservative Party, which better represented their economic interests by its support of protection for British agriculture rather than the free trade/cheap bread policies of the Liberals and shared their concern over the fate of the large landowners of Ireland, increasingly under assault from Irish nationalists who were in some cases supported by the Liberals. The Conservative Party was eventually renamed the Conservative and Unionist Party to reflect its support for the union of Ireland with Britain.

The Houses of Parliament are seen here with some of London's famous double-decker buses in the early 20th century. (Library of Congress, Carpenter Collection)

The Liberals did win one final triumph in the years before World War I (1914–18). This was the political marginalization of the House of Lords, a conservative stronghold where even Liberal majorities in the Commons could be frustrated. The Parliament Act of 1911 forbade the Lords from rejecting a "money bill" sent up from the Commons, gave the Speaker of the Commons the right to decide which bills were money bills, and stated that bills passed in three consecutive sessions by the Commons would become law regardless of the Lords. The act also shortened the time the Commons could sit without an election from seven years to five. Despite resistance by the Lords, they eventually passed the act, fearing that if they continued to hold it up, the new king, George V (1865–1936; r. 1910–36), would bow to Liberal pressure and create enough new peers to pack the Lords in its favor. Although the act did not completely marginalize the Lords, they were definitely off the main political stage. Shortly after World War I, a potential Conservative candidate for prime minister was rejected by the party leadership and the king because they considered it inadvisable for a prime minister to sit in the House of Lords.

The Decline of the Gentry

The Conservative gain from the landowning element moving from the Liberal to the Conservative Party was mitigated by the fact that landowners were a less dominant element in British life due to the decline of English agriculture and the rise of the industrial economy and financial services. The landed aristocracy and gentry, although still a formidable group at the end of the 19th century, had clearly waned in power socially, economically, and politically. All of Queen Victoria's prime ministers possessed or had acquired land during their political careers, but it was becoming less important in defining the ruling class. Instead they were increasingly defined by the possession of wealth, whatever form it took. Victoria's son and heir, Edward VII (1841–1910; r. 1901–10), was particularly notorious for his social preference for the nouveaux riches rather than the traditional landowning families. Among his best friends was Sir Thomas Lipton (1848–1931), the enormously wealthy self-made Scottish grocer who revolutionized the tea business by marketing cheap tea to the masses. Edward's friends also included rich Jews, which shocked many traditional aristocrats. The growth of cities, where landowners could not hope to have the same influence they did over the rural population, greatly diminished gentry and aristocratic power, as did the Reform Acts of 1867 and 1884 and the Redistribution of Seats Act of 1885, which broadened the parliamentary franchise to include many more poor and working-class people, who were largely insulated from landowning influence. The agricultural depression of the late 19th century was also particularly hard on landowners.

The gentry's political weakening can be seen in the process by which, moving from its position as a powerful group in both major parties, it became increasingly concentrated in the Conservative Party, where it shared power with businesspeople and the lower middle class. By the end of the 19th century, the gentry formed a shrinking minority in the House of Commons and the prime minister's cabinet. Even the traditional gentry stronghold of local government was increasingly shared with rich businessmen. By the late 19th century, what few new country houses were being built were erected not by traditional landowners but by millionaire capitalists, few of whom viewed their new estates as the basis of their wealth. They were likely to treat the principal business of their new country mansions as hunting rather than agriculture.

Politically, the gentry was redefined from being a ruling class to one interest group among others. Although the ladies and gentlemen of the landed class maintained their separate cultural identity, they were no longer unquestioned leaders of society.

Religious and Ethnic Diversity

British society, while still dominated by the Church of England and Church of Scotland, became much more religiously diverse. The Roman Catholic presence in Britain greatly increased with Irish immigration, driven partly by hunger and poverty in Ireland and partly by the labor needs of the British economy. By 1861 the Irish-born made up about 3 percent of the population of England and Wales and about 7 percent of the Scottish population. British workers resented Irish workers, who were often willing to take lower wages, but in England this resentment was not usually directed against their Catholic religion. In Scotland, however, the conflict between the mostly Protestant native people and the new Irish immigrants took sectarian form.

The Jewish community was also growing, particularly as eastern European Jewish immigrants, facing poverty and anti-Semitism in their native countries, settled in London. There was some tension between the new Jewish immigrants and the established Jewish leadership, mostly of Mediterranean (Sephardic) or German origin. Although anti-Semitism remained strong in many areas of British society, there was a growing acceptance of the Jewish community. Religious Jews were allowed to serve in the House of Commons in 1858, after a long and hard campaign led by Lionel de Rothschild (1808–79) of the London-based Rothschild Jewish banking family. Benjamin Disraeli, who came from a family of Christian converts but never hid his Jewish ancestry, actually became prime minister as leader of the Conservative Party. There is no parallel for his career elsewhere in the 19th century. In the early 20th century, Rufus Isaacs (1860–1935), a practicing Jew and the son of a London fruit merchant, became lord chief justice, ambassador to the United States, foreign secretary, viceroy of India, and first marquess of Reading.

Secularization

As Britain grew more diverse, it also grew more secular. There was increasing intellectual skepticism and disbelief among the educated. Secularizing forces included Charles Darwin's theory of evolution through natural selection. Darwin published *On the Origin of Species* in 1859 and *The Descent of Man* in 1871. The naturalistic theory of human origins he offered was controversial but eventually won the day among most scientists and intellectuals. A more significant force for intellectual secularization was the higher criticism of the Bible, a movement with German origins but one that had great influence among the British as well. By treating the Bible like any other ancient document, examining its sources and textual traditions, the higher critics diminished its authority as a religious text.

The most famous declared atheist of the late 19th century was Charles Bradlaugh (1833–91), who won a seat in Parliament in 1880 but refused to take the religious oath of allegiance. Bradlaugh's refusal to feign religious belief led to a series of controversies as Parliament, led by the Conservatives and the Church of England, kept refusing to seat him and the electors of the English city of Northampton kept returning him to Parliament. Eventually Bradlaugh and his supporters, including devout Christians such as William Gladstone, prevailed, and he was seated in 1886, The Bradlaugh case established the right of the nonreligious to serve in Parliament.

Secularization was also gaining in the educational field. Old institutions were remodeled to make them less religiously restrictive, and new and more secular institutions were created. Since the Middle Ages, England had had only two universities, Oxford and Cambridge. This was clearly not enough for its growing population. The first new universities—Durham University, founded in 1832, and the University of London, founded in 1836—retained religious affiliation. The older universities were reformed in the 1850s, as nonmembers of the Church of England were allowed to take degrees. The requirement that fellows of colleges be celibate, a holdover from the old days when they were considered clergy, was also dropped. The Education Act of 1870 created secular, universal, and compulsory education in England. A class system developed in education, with the lower classes attending the state schools and the upper and middle classes attending private, or public, schools. The educational system has often been credited with the peculiar importance of class background in England.

Among the working class, whose members were the most likely to be open disbelievers, unbelief built on anticlericalism as part of a general opposition to authority. The working-class population was also "unchurched" in many British cities, as church builders were hard-pressed to keep up with Britain's rapidly expanding urban population. British religious leaders were aware of the difficulty in reaching urban workers and the poor. The late 19th-century Anglo-Catholic or ritualistic movement in the Church of England, the official church of the English state, made some efforts to reach the unchurched poor with elaborate and visually appealing church services. Another effort to create a new form of Christianity appealing to the urban poor was the

Salvation Army, founded in London by William Booth (1829–1912). The Salvation Army was not a charitable organization but a Christian denomination. By combining emotionally revivalist preaching, music, a strict hierarchical organization built on explicitly military lines, and social services, the organization met with some success among the English—and later the American—poor.

Social Change and the English Novel

The second half of the 19th century was a golden age for the novel in England. The English novel of the period drew much of its strength from its relation to social change. Charles Dickens (1812–70), the most popular novelist of the age, examined problems of poverty and industrialization in *Oliver Twist* (1838) and *Hard Times* (1854). Dickens's 15 novels have never been out of print since their first publication. Anthony Trollope (1815–82) examined the confrontation between traditional rural values and the new values of commercial and urban society in the six novels he wrote set in the fictional county of Barsetshire, beginning with *The Warden* (1855) and ending with *The Last Chronicle of Barset* (1867). Trollope tackled Parliament, government, and the rise of a more democratic political culture with his six Palliser novels, beginning with *Can You Forgive Her* (1865) and ending with *The Duke's Children* (1880), and high finance with *The Way We Live Now* (1875). Trollope and Dickens frequently published their work in serial form before the appearance of a collected edition, adding to the suspense of their plotting; fans could not wait to get their hands on the next installment. The most prominent writer of the suspense novel was Dickens's friend Wilkie Collins (1824–89), author of *The Moonstone* (1868), whose plot dealt with the influence of empire on British domestic life.

Gender issues attracted the interest of a number of novelists, both male and female. Mary Ann Evans (1819–80) used a male pseudonym, George Eliot, in order to be taken more seriously. She wrote about the plight of women in marriage in *Middlemarch* (serialized in 1871–72 and published in one volume; 1874) and *Daniel Deronda* (1876), while George Gissing (1857–1903) wrote about their unmarried sisters in *The Odd Women* (1893). Sarah Grand (1854–1943) tackled both personal and public feminist issues in *The Beth Book* (1897). Like many writers of the later 19th century, Eliot, Gissing, and Grand reacted against the sentimentality and humor associated with Dickens to a more realistic and psychological style influenced by contemporary French literature.

Challenges to the Established Order

What seemed to be a relatively stable order of late 19th-century Britain, with two large political parties, Liberals and Conservatives, that competed for the support of moderates, was challenged on a number of fronts in the late 19th and early 20th centuries. The most important challenges were those by Irish nationalists, Welsh Dissenters, the working class, and the women's movement.

Irish Nationalism and British Politics

One of the biggest issues in British politics was Ireland. The rise of Irish nationalism, dating to the 18th century, had produced a parliamentary political movement focused on dismantling the apparatus of British government in Ireland and replacing it with Irish self-government, or home rule. Some more radical nationalists wanted an independent Irish republic, although many would have settled for home rule under the British Crown, as an equal of Britain. Others, such as Charles Stuart Parnell (1846–91), a Protestant and a landlord, were interested in pushing for home rule as a stage in the process for independence.

Many of the English ruling class hated the possibility of Irish home rule. Traditional anti-Catholicism; the fears of Irish landowners, many of whom were English aristocrats or connected with English aristocratic families, that their property would be lost in home-rule Ireland; and the belief that an independent Ireland would set a precedent for the dissolution of the British Empire all played a role in British resistance. Liberals were more sympathetic to home rule, and many of the aristocrats of the traditional Whig families left the Liberals for the Conservatives in order to defend English rule in Ireland. The greatest English supporter of home rule was Gladstone, but his strongest efforts resulted only in failure.

The Irish issue was complicated by divisions among the Irish themselves, principally on regional and sectarian lines. The majority of the Protestants of the north, many of them descended from Scottish settlers in the 17th century, abominated the cause of Irish independence, which they felt would put them under the authority of the hated Catholics—"Home Rule means Rome Rule" was a slogan they used effectively. Like the Catholic "Home Rulers," the Irish Protestants, or Orangemen, were represented in the Westminster parliaments, and they combined parliamentary activity with extra-parliamentary action and alliances with English unionists.

Welsh Disestablishment

Welsh nationalism in the late 19th century was centered on religious issues, particularly the privileged position of the established church. The Church of England in Wales was the church of a small minority, dominated by the landowning gentry. The vast majority of the population followed Methodism or one of the other Protestant Dissenting churches, and they deeply resented the obligation to pay tithes to the Church of England. The Church of England, on the other hand, was powerful in Parliament, particularly in the Conservative Party, and wished neither to lose its Welsh tithes nor to set a precedent for disestablishment in England, an idea that was occasionally circulated. A Welsh Disestablishment Bill was finally passed in 1914, but its operation was delayed until 1920. David Lloyd George (1863–1945), the most important Welsh politician since the Welsh-descended Henry Tudor had founded the Tudor dynasty in the 15th century, began his career as a supporter of Welsh disestablishment, and never lost his Welsh identity or connection with his Welsh roots.

The Working Class

The working class was an extremely diverse occupational group. Even at the height of the Industrial Revolution, most working-class people were not factory laborers. In the census of 1851, the two largest groups of laborers were in the traditional sectors of agriculture and domestic service. Even manufacturing workers were not always factory workers. In practice, factory culture was limited to the north of England. The principal center of population, London, remained much more oriented to small shops. Much of the leadership of the early working-class movement came not from factory workers but from skilled laborers and craftsmen in small manufacturing businesses, such as coachmakers. This so-called labor aristocracy formed about 10 percent of the working-class population.

Trade unions gradually grew more powerful and more legitimate as institutions in the late 19th century. Unions spread from the original skilled elite to semiskilled and unskilled labor and women workers. The central organization of the British labor movement, the Trades Union Congress (TUC), was founded in 1868. Unions engaged in both industrial actions such as strikes and political lobbying, particularly for liberalizations of the laws restricting strikes and other trade-union activities, and for extensions of the franchise to workers. A few workers were able to vote under the qualifications of the Reform Bill of 1832, but most continued to be barred from voting.

Male workers' access to the franchise was improved by the Reform Acts of 1867 and 1884.

The horrific living conditions of the early Industrial Revolution were somewhat alleviated in the second half of the 19th century. Although working-class life was still hard, workers received increases in wages and reductions in working hours. The Liberal Gladstone government in 1871 created bank holidays (public holidays in designated Mondays), offering workers a chance to head to the seashore and other places of amusement in throngs. Sanitary reform, although often unpopular due to its authoritarian implementation, helped make working-class districts more habitable with cleaner water and better sewage.

Increased prosperity and leisure contributed to the development of an autonomous working-class society and culture. Workers created friendly societies (credit unions) and building societies with mutual help for loans, home purchases, illnesses, and burials. A cheap working-class press emerged along with characteristic institutions such as the public house, or "pub"; the music hall (a kind of vaudeville); and Association Football, or soccer. Sport was generally booming in late Victorian Britain. There were divisions between the traditional footballing culture of amateurs and the new professional footballers, which eventually saw the formation of a league of professional teams. Rugby saw a split between the Rugby Union and the Rugby League, which actually developed different sets of rules. Gambling was also popular among male workers. These working-class cultural institutions were often opposed by religious and temperance movements, sometimes of working-class and other times of middle-class origin.

Socialism

Karl Marx (1818–83), the century's most influential socialist theorist, spent several decades in London but had much less effect in Britain than he did in his native Germany or other Continental countries. The Labour Party stood out among the major European socialist parties for its complete lack of interest in Marxist theory or revolution. All but the most radical Britons accepted the parliamentary system and worked to reform rather than overthrow it. British Marxism was always dominated by intellectuals, and compared with Continental working-class movements, there was very little coordination between intellectuals and workers in British socialism.

One of the most intellectually important of the British socialist movements was the Fabian Society, an organization dedicated to advancing socialism through Fabian strategies, emphasizing patience, reformism, and opportunism rather than revolution. The society took its name from the ancient Roman general Quintus Fabius, known for his cautious tactics in warfare. The Fabians attracted a stunning array of intellectual leaders, including the playwright George Bernard Shaw (1856–1950) and the novelist and founder of science fiction H. G. Wells (1866–1946). Its leaders, however, were a married couple: Sydney Webb (1859–1947) and Beatrice Webb (1858–1943), who issued a number of voluminous studies of English working-class society and history. The Fabian Society still exists today.

Working-Class Politics and the Labour Party

Nineteenth-century workers mostly supported the Liberals. Some Conservatives, notably Disraeli, dreamed of an alliance of the aristocracy and the workers against the middle classes, but their dreams were in vain. From 1874 to 1880, Disraeli's Conservative government passed several laws on factories, workers' dwellings, and pure food and drugs, but it was defeated in the next election as working-class voters supported the Liberals anyway. The real Conservative base in the lower classes was the white-collar lower-middle class of clerks, a growing segment of society.

The prophet of a labor party separate from the Liberals was Keir Hardie (1856–1915), an Ayrshire coal miner and member of Parliament (MP) who founded the Independent Labour Party (ILP) at Bradford in 1893. The ILP was a socialist party with the declared goal of collective ownership of the means of production, but not a revolutionary one. Its main areas of strength were industrial regions of northern England and Scotland. The ILP failed to find a mass base, and Hardie lost his seat in the general election of 1895.

The trade unions, both industrial and nonindustrial, were the key to a mass-based socialist party. The Labour Representation Committee (LRC), colloquially referred to as the Labour Party, was formed under trade-union auspices in 1900. Other participants in the Committee's creation were the Fabian Society; the Social Democratic Federation (SDF), a Marxist group; and the ILP. Despite the representation of socialists from the Fabians, the SDF, and ILP, the LRC was not a socialist body in its political platform and was more concerned with trade-union rights than reshaping the British economy and polity. British working-class politics would continue to be about getting a better deal for the workers in the capitalist system rather than overthrowing it. Until 1918, the Labour Party had no individual membership of its own; individuals joined through membership in a union or one of the affiliated

Poor Scottish children in Edinburgh (Library of Congress, Carpenter Collection)

groups. As Britain had no salaries for MPs, Labour members were paid by the unions. The close alliance between the Labour Party and the unions, who assumed the principal responsibility for its funding and overall direction, became a central characteristic of British politics.

The LRC drew strength from the response to the Taff Vale judgment of 1901, which made unions financially liable for damages charged against its officials during strikes. Union leaders and officials who thought that organized labor and the right to strike were under renewed assault supported independent political mobilization. The LRC's membership more than doubled by 1903. That year, although it was acquiring a more independent identity, the LRC formed an electoral pact with the Liberal Party wherein the two parties agreed not to oppose each other in constituencies where a competition for votes might return a Conservative. The LRC put up 51 candidates in the general election of 1906—the same year it formally adopted the name *Labour Party*—of whom 29 were elected, 24 in constituencies the Liberals did not contest. Labour reaped the rewards of its electoral alliance with the Liberals. In 1906 an act passed by a Liberal government, following LRC lobbying, granted trade unions immunity from being sued for damages related to a strike, a key union demand. After that achievement, the party suffered from the loss of the clear mission of union law reform and divisions between trade unionists and socialists as to what the purpose of a Labour Party was. It benefited from the adhesion of the Miners' Federation in 1909 and the institution of salaries for MPs in 1911, enabling those without an independent income to serve in the Commons, but continued to be a satellite of the Liberals until after World War I.

In the long run, the Liberals grew weaker. Much of the old Whig elite of Liberal aristocrats left for the Conservatives due to Gladstone's Irish policy, and now the Liberals faced a potential rival for the loyalties of the working class in the form of Labour. Most Liberal governments were dependent on Irish nationalist or Labour support, or both.

Women, Politics, and the Rise of Suffrage

The working-class challenge was paralleled by another assault on Britain's rulers, from their own wives and daughters. Middle- and upper-class women in the 19th century labored under many disadvantages. They could not be educated past the equivalent of high school, and they were educated to that level at a much lower rate than men. They could not participate in the recognized professions in law, medicine, or the church. They could not participate in the institutions of electoral politics, although women did participate in political movements outside the government, such as abolitionism. Under the English common law, a married woman could not possess property in her own name; unless special arrangements were made, her property was considered that of her husband. If a woman was stuck in a bad marriage, divorce was very difficult. It was almost impossible for a woman to divorce and receive custody of her children if the husband wanted to keep them. It was much easier, although still difficult by contemporary standards, for a man to divorce a woman than the other way around. The double standard was in full bloom: A wife's adultery was grounds for divorce and theoretically imprisonment, but a husband's was not unless accompanied by aggravating circumstances such as brutality or the establishment of the mistress in the marital home. (Open adultery could still greatly harm a man's reputation, and men publicly known to engage in extramarital sex could have their political careers ruined, the most notable case being the Irish nationalist and British parliamentarian Charles Stuart Parnell.) It was expected that the daughters in a middle-class family would sacrifice and go without an education in order to support the sons properly.

Middle-class women who did not marry also faced great problems in the early 19th century. Their main choices were to live off relatives as a "poor relation" or to be a governess, a woman charged with the education and disciplining of young children. The life of a governess was proverbially difficult and despised, with poor pay and garretlike living conditions; however, such a life was still better than being a maid. One aspect of the governess problem was the fact that members of the middle class had higher expectations than members of the working class. The situation began to improve with the expansion of the educational sector after the mid-19th century, which offered more women the opportunity to be teachers, a relatively more respected profession, but options were still very limited.

A women's movement, dominated by middle-class women and their concerns, emerged in mid-19th-century Britain for several reasons. Literacy and education among women was increasing. The organization of women taking part in political and humanitarian campaigns and for charitable work increased women's and men's awareness of problems caused by lack of education, access to the professions, and the vote. The key to suffragist and women's rights activities generally was the organizing of large numbers of mostly middle-class women.

By the last third of the 19th century, the new women's movement was winning some victories. The Married Women's Separate Property Acts of 1870 and 1882 gave married women with property or income some protection against greedy or irresponsible husbands, and women began receiving medical degrees. The first recorded biologically female Briton to receive a medical degree and practice as a surgeon was Dr. James Barry (d. 1865). Born Margaret Ann Bulkley, he spent his educational and medical career living as a man for more than 50 years; Barry's biological sex was only revealed in an autopsy after his death. The next, Elizabeth Blackwell (1821–1910), obtained her medical degree in

America, graduating in 1849 from the Geneval Medical School in New York. The first British woman to be qualified and to practice medicine in Britain itself was Elizabeth Garrett (1836–1917). A pioneer in opening the University of Edinburgh, Britain's leading medical school, to women was Sophia Jex-Blake (1840–1913). Partly through Jex-Blake's efforts, the London School of Medicine for Women was founded in 1874. Parliament gave medical examining bodies the right to certify women in 1876.

The two colleges of Cambridge University for women, Girton and Newnham, were founded in 1869 and 1871. Oxford followed suit a little later, with Lady Margaret Hall founded in 1878 and Somerville College in 1879. Entrance into higher education involved choices. At first, some advocated a separate curriculum for women in higher education with less study of classical languages, math, and science and more domestic skills, such as needlework. However, this curriculum would not enable women to enter universities. The movement for curricula closer to those of male students resulted in the founding of new institutions. The federal system of Oxford and Cambridge—known as the "ancient universities"—was well adapted to the addition of new colleges for women separate from the existing male colleges, but some advocated entry into existing male colleges. Even after the establishment of women's or coeducational institutions, females faced further institutional barriers and resistance from male students, who were generally misogynic and concerned that the entry of women into their institutions would lower their status. Institutions continued to drag their feet on issues such as whether women, once admitted, could take degrees or receive honors. Men still made up the vast majority of university population in the early 20th century, but this began to change during and after World War I.

Prostitution was an increasingly prominent public issue in the late 19th century. (The publicity attached to the Jack the Ripper murders of London prostitutes in 1888 both followed and caused this heightened public awareness.) The Contagious Diseases Acts of 1864 and 1866, prompted by the high rate of sexually transmitted diseases in port and garrison towns, gave the state the right to forcibly examine women the local police identified as prostitutes and hold diseased women in these communities in "lock hospitals," where they were kept under lock and key for up to three months. The lock hospitals became a prominent target of the English women's movement, who viewed them as an attempt to make sexual licentiousness safe for men by penalizing and confining women and forced examination as surgical rape. A women-led campaign, whose most notable individual leader was Josephine Butler (1828–1906), eventually secured repeal of the acts. The willingness of middle-class women to identify with prostitutes, at least rhetorically, was a strike against the absolute divide between respectable and unrespectable women. This did not mean that women campaigners necessarily supported a freer approach to sexuality—some did—but many were associated with temperance and moral purity movements and advocated a single standard of monogamy and chastity for men as well as women.

Arguments for women's suffrage were based on both the liberal model, in which women, like men, should have the right to participate in the making of the laws by which they are bound; and the separate-

OSCAR WILDE AND THE GAY UNDERWORLD OF LONDON

Like other cities, London contained an underground of homosexual men and lesbians. Although lesbians were ignored by the law, gay men were the targets of harsh punishments. The most famous gay martyr of Victorian England was the Irish playwright Oscar Wilde (1854–1900). He was skilled in a variety of genres, from drama to fairy tales to political writing. He was also one of London's most renowned wits.

Wilde had an affair with a young Scottish nobleman, Lord Alfred Douglas (1870–1945). The affair came to the notice of Douglas's father, the marquess of Queensberry (the inventor of the marquess of Queensberry Rules for boxing), who denounced Wilde as a "somdomite." Wilde sued the marquess for libel in 1895. He subsequently withdrew the charge, but the matter was now in the public sphere. Wilde himself was arrested, tried, and convicted of "gross indecency"; he was sentenced to two years of hard labor at London's infamous Reading Gaol (jail). His imprisonment was the subject of his poem "The Ballad of Reading Gaol." His wife, Constance, left for Switzerland, along with their two children.

Shortly after his release, Wilde, a broken man, left England for the Continent. Sick, broke, and unable to resume his writing career, he died and was buried in Paris. Douglas later repudiated his homosexuality and his relationship with Wilde and became a fanatical Catholic and anti-Semite.

spheres model, as some advocates claimed that women's superior virtue would elevate politics by making it more domestic. The issue was complicated by the fact that not all men had the vote. Some men who proclaimed sympathy with the suffragist cause wanted to wait until all men had the vote before extending it to women. The suffrage struggle was therefore a long, tough fight in which much effort had to be spent just getting men to take the idea seriously. When the idea of women's suffrage was brought before the English parliament of 1832, the one that passed the First Reform Bill, male politicians did not argue against it—they just laughed.

The first elections in which women were allowed to vote were local elections such as school boards and sanitary authorities. These electoral rights were put in the context of women's role of caring for homes and families. The franchise was also offered in colonial areas with a heavy male-to-female population ratio, such as New Zealand, as a way of attracting female settlers.

Antifeminist and antisuffragist arguments included those based on women's intellectual inferiority and poor emotional discipline, as well as religious arguments based on the divine origins of traditional gender roles. Some claimed that the vote would make women unfeminine and undomestic, and that a country that allowed women to vote would make men effeminate, unable to defeat the military forces of more manly nations. It was argued that even without the vote, women could participate indirectly in the polity by influencing the votes of their husbands or sons. Some women, usually supporters of the political right, opposed suffrage and even formed organizations such as the Women's Anti-suffrage League.

There were a variety of suffragist positions, ranging from moderate suffragists who believed in lobbying MPs and cabinet ministers to the more confrontational radical suffragists who, influenced by the Irish nationalist struggle, believed in disruptive tactics and the destruction of property. The largest radical suffrage organization was the Women's Social and Political Union (WSPU), founded in 1903 by Emmeline Pankhurst (1858–1928) and her daughters Christabel (1880–1958) and Sylvia (1882–1960). The founding of the WSPU was followed by a wave of militant suffrage activism. One woman slashed a painting in a museum; others mowed the words "Votes for Women" into a golf course, rendering it temporarily unfit for use. Another suffragette, Emily Wilding Davison, killed herself in 1913 by throwing herself in front of a racehorse owned by the king at the Derby, England's most prestigious horse race. When imprisoned, many suffragettes went on hunger strikes and were forcibly fed through tubes inserted into the throat. This agonizing practice provoked a new campaign against forcible feeding.

The Boer War and British Strategy in the Early Twentieth Century

The British governing class faced external as well as internal challenges in the early 20th century. The most draining colonial war Britain fought was against European-descended South African farmers, known as Afrikaners or by the derogatory nickname of "Boers," who sought independence from the British Empire. Britain, on the other hand, considered the Afrikaner states, rich in gold and diamonds, a priceless possession and had long wished to integrate all of South Africa into one British union. Britain could no more allow the upstart Afrikaners to win than it could anti-British subjects in any of its colonies.

The Boer War (also known as the South African War) from 1899 to 1902 not only brought home to Britain the limitations of its army; it also made clear to many how widely the country was disliked. The Afrikaners won the sympathy of virtually every other country, which admired the "plucky farmers" and their struggle against the world's mightiest empire. Horror stories of the concentration camps (the first use of the term) in which the British held Afrikaners, including women and children, circulated throughout the world. Particularly sympathetic was Germany and its erratic kaiser, William II (Wilhelm), who had a love-hate relationship with Britain, the country of his grandmother, Queen Victoria. Such was British power, however, that all the sympathy the Afrikaners received translated into very little actual support.

In the aftermath of its victory in the Boer War, Britain abandoned its policy of "splendid isolation" and started to look for allies. The first fruits of this new policy was the Anglo-Japanese alliance of 1902. It was principally directed against Russia, and it probably benefited the Japanese more than the British. But the traditional view of Russia as Britain's main potential enemy was giving way to fear of Germany, a fear that eventually led Britain to ally with its former rivals France and Russia. British strategic thinking was increasingly influenced by what is often described as history's first arms race: the competition with Germany to build more effective armored warships—the dreadnoughts. Britain also feared the German-financed Berlin-to-Baghdad railway, which, if completed, would have offered the Germans a way of getting an army to the Middle East and the borders of India.

In 1903 Edward VII, a well-known admirer of France and its culture, went to Paris, a visit often credited with smoothing the way for the Anglo-French ("Entente Cordiale") Entente between France and Britain concluded the following year. Edward's affability helped dissolve some of the French hostility to Britain engendered by the history of conflicts between the two states and ongoing colonial rivalries, but the real basis of the alliance was the desire for cooperation against Germany, whose kaiser posed perpetual diplomatic headaches for his government with his impulsiveness.

Alliance with Russia was a more difficult problem. Fears of Russian aggression against India persisted into the 20th century. British army officer Francis Younghusband (1863–1942) led a bloody but ineffectual expedition to Tibet in 1903 and 1904 based on rumors of Russian influence there. However, the defeat of Russia by Japan in the Russo-Japanese war of 1905 lessened British fear of Russian aggression against the empire. In 1907 Britain and Russia agreed on the Anglo-Russian Entente, which resolved various colonial questions by defining the two nation's relative zones of influence in Afghanistan, Iran, and Tibet. (The Afghans, Iranians, and Tibetans were not consulted.) Along with the existing agreements between France and Russia and Britain and France, this agreement constituted the Triple Entente, implicitly directed against Germany.

Britain and World War I

In 1914 the assassination of Archduke Franz Ferdinand of Austria-Hungary by a Serbian nationalist led to a war that lasted until 1918 and involved every major world power. Known at the time as the Great War, it is now known as World War I, and it had a deep effect on every European country. From the British point of view, the devastating conflict was the culmination of years of colonial and naval rivalry with the rising power of Germany.

The war's early days saw a great deal of enthusiasm. Most suffragettes, Irish Home Rulers, and trade-union leaders rallied behind the national banner. Masses of men volunteered, often with the hope that the war would be over quickly; in fact, it dragged on for four bloody years. The style of warfare practiced on the western front (as opposed to the eastern front, where the Germans were fighting the Russians) involved two parallel lines of trenches, one occupied by the Allied—British and French—forces and the other by the Germans. The use of machine guns, poison gas, and barbed wire ensured that casualties were appallingly high, and after the first few months of the war, the trenches moved very little. The British army had to change from a small force mainly designed and equipped to fight small colonial wars to a mass army like those of the Continental powers France and Germany.

In 1915 the British government attempted to break the stalemate on the western front and get supplies to its beleaguered ally, Russia, by an attack on Gallipoli in the Dardanelles, then in the possession of Germany's ally, the Ottoman Empire. Opening the straits between the Mediterranean and the Black Sea would allow the allies access to Russian ports. The first attempt, heavily backed by First Lord of the Admiralty Winston Churchill, was to force the straits by ships alone. The naval attack on March 15 failed as British and French ships ran into Turkish mines—a failure that led to Churchill's being forced out of the cabinet. The Liberal prime minister, Herbert Asquith (1852–1928), abandoned his attempt to run the war from a one-party Liberal government in favor of a coalition government with the Conservative party. The second Gallipoli attack, launched on April 25 after the Turks and their German advisers had had time to fortify the straits, involved troops. British and French forces were joined by the Australia and New Zealand Corps (ANZAC). The attack proved a bloody and expensive failure, and Allied forces completed their evacuation from Gallipoli on January 8, 1916. Many New Zealanders and even more Australians resented what they saw as poor British leadership, which had resulted in the wasted deaths of the ANZAC troops.

The British economy also had to gear itself for the mass production of munitions and other supplies of war. David Lloyd George was successful as minister of munitions, and he used that success to climb to the position of prime minister in 1916, displacing the ineffectual Liberal leader Asquith. He formed a coalition government of Liberal, Conservative, and Labour party members. It was under the Lloyd George coalition that Britain and its allies (including the United States, which had joined the war in 1917, but not including Russia, which had left the war after the Russian Revolution the same year) forced the surrender of Germany and its allies in 1918.

Casualties were massive: Between 750,000 and 800,000 Britons died in the war. Unlike World War II, these were overwhelmingly found among the military itself; there were relatively few civilian casualties. Scotland was particularly hard hit, as was the British aristocracy and gentry, which still made a disproportionate contribution to the officer corps. The western front accounted for most of the casualties.

Like other countries at war, Britain drew on the labor power of women during World War I. This photograph shows women in a shell factory. (Library of Congress, Bain Collection)

The war had profound cultural and social effects. It accelerated the decline of the gentry as a ruling force and the decline of the social order headed by aristocratic ladies and gentlemen. The traditional aristocratic bastion in the army, the cavalry, was revealed as militarily obsolescent on the western front. The predominantly upper-class military leadership was discredited in the war by the failure of most of the offensives and the endless, futile slaughter of trench warfare. The traditional military values of individual courage and heroism proved useless or even suicidal in the trenches. British military heroes tended to be drawn from peripheral fronts. T. E. Lawrence (1888–1935), also known as Lawrence of Arabia, who fought in the British-supported Arab revolt against Germany's ally the Ottoman Empire, was one such hero, despite the peripheral and minor contribution to Allied victory the revolt made. Other heroes were the "flying aces" of the air war. The top British ace was Edward Mannock (1887–1918), officially credited with 47 kills of enemy aircraft, although some have claimed a total as high as 73.

179

BRITAIN
HAS BEEN ALL
SHE COULD BE
TO JEWS
JEWS WILL BE
ALL THEY CAN
BE TO BRITAIN

ENLIST AT ONCE
IN ANY REGIMENT
APPLY AT THE NEAREST
RECRUITING OFFICE.

In addition to recruiting campaigns aimed at the general public, British recruiters also used targeted campaigns, such as this one aimed at young Jewish men. (Library of Congress)

The war set off a vigorous yet fleeting cultural reaction against things German, of which the longest-lasting legacy was the renunciation of all German titles by the British royal family and their relatives. In addition, the royal house was renamed from Saxe-Coburg-Gotha, after Queen Victoria's German husband Albert, to Windsor, after the royal palace of Windsor.

The exaltation of democracy as the war's ideological focus, although taken less seriously in Britain than in the United States, meant that what remained of the domination of the aristocracy and gentry no longer had any ideological justification. The United Kingdom was the last remaining "gentlemanly" power, but even in Britain the necessities of organizing the country for war had brought labor leaders, businessmen, and the middle classes generally to the fore. A famous description of the first postwar parliament, dominated by the Conservatives, is sometimes attributed to John Maynard Keynes (1883–1946), the great economist, and sometimes to the Conservative politician Stanley Baldwin (1867–1947): MPs were "hard-faced men who looked like they had done well out of the war" (quoted in Taylor 1965, 129).

Despite victory for Britain, World War I ended the optimism of 19th-century British civilization. It was no longer possible to believe that the growth of internationalism, the creation of international institutions, and the intertwining of national economies would make war obsolete. The great liberal European democracies, Britain and France, both lost the faith that they represented the future, which seemed to be American, Soviet, or even fascist (the first fascist leader, Benito Mussolini, took power in Italy in 1923). Wartime central direction of the economy further weakened 19th-century liberal faith in the free market. The prewar period came to be viewed through a roseate haze of nostalgia, causing many who looked back on it as a golden age to grossly exaggerate the social harmony of the period.

Postwar Britain

The years following World War I wrought a sea change in politics that made Britain a fully democratic country for the first time. Much the immediate legislation passed in the war's aftermath was a revival of initiatives put on hold in 1914. In 1918 women above the age of 30 finally won the right to vote and run for Parliament. Many British politicians put this action in the context of gratitude for women's participation in the war effort. The Fourth Reform Act of 1918 also broadened the suffrage to all men over age 21 capable of proving six months' residence. Women were eventually granted suffrage on the same basis as men in 1928. Female suffrage did not have much immediate effect on politics: Women tended to vote the same way as men of their class, sect, and region, and very few entered parliamentary politics for the first few decades it was open to them. The first woman to serve in the Commons was an immigrant from America, Nancy Astor (1879–1964). She was elected as a Conservative for Plymouth Sutton in a by-election in 1919. (A by-election is held when a seat falls vacant during a Parliamentary session.)

Welsh disestablishment went into effect in 1920. The Church of England in Wales became the Church in Wales. Its bishops lost their seats in the House of Lords and were severed from dependence on the archbishop of Canterbury, except insofar as they remained part of the worldwide Anglican communion of which Canterbury was the titular head.

Another problem whose solution had been put off until the end of the war was that of the relationship of Britain and Ireland. Unlike the suffrage and Welsh issues, it had actually become more difficult to solve during the war. In 1916 a Dublin rising, based on the hope of German assistance, had briefly proclaimed an Irish republic. British authorities had suppressed it with no difficulty, but execution of the leaders had made them martyrs for Ireland and alienated a majority of the Irish Catholic population. In 1922 British alienation of the Irish people and the terrorist activities of Sinn Féin, the Irish nationalist underground organization, forced the British to grant self-government to most of Ireland, while the Protestant-dominated north remained part of the United Kingdom with representation in Westminster. Although southern Ireland—Eire—had won de facto independence, it took more than a decade to transform it into de jure independence, and the Irish economy remained closely linked and essentially subordinated to the British one into the late 20th century.

Britain entered the League of Nations, a pet project of the American president Woodrow Wilson (1856–1924; president, 1913–21), with the purpose of putting an end to war through international cooperation. Since the United States did not join the league, and Soviet Russia and Germany were initially excluded, Britain was the league's dominant power along with France. The British Empire had gained huge new territories from its victory in the war in the Middle East and Africa. The new territories, mostly taken from the old German colonial empire or the fallen Ottoman Empire, were held as League of Nations mandates with the proclaimed goal of ultimate independence rather than colonies, but in practice there was little difference between the old colonies and the new mandates. A particularly problematic area was Palestine, where Britain formally supported the establishment of a Jewish homeland, as advocated by Zionism, the Jewish nationalist movement that had emerged in the late 19th century as a solution to the poor living conditions and shaky political situations in which Jews in the Diaspora often found themselves. The alliance between Britain and the Zionist movement was formally proclaimed in the Balfour Declaration of 1917, named after Foreign Secretary Arthur James Balfour (1848–1930). This conflicted with the promises that Britain had made to Arab nationalists during the war in order to gain their support against the Ottoman Turks. It also conflicted with the Sykes-Picot agreement between Britain and France in 1916, which allowed for a nominally independent Arab state or Arab federation in the Middle East but in practice divided the region into British and French mandates. (The agreement is named after the British and French negotiators, Sir Mark Sykes and Georges Picot.) The conflicting expectations of Britain, the Zionist movement, and Palestine's Arab population would bedevil the British until 1948.

The empire was under increasing strain in many places. The most important of all of Britain's colonies, India, had a rising nationalist movement with a charismatic leader, Mohandas K. Gandhi (1869–1948). A series of nationalist demonstrations and riots and British responses at the Indian community of Amritsar led to the Amritsar massacre of April 13, 1919, in which more than 300 unarmed Indians were shot down by British troops. Many British people were shocked and horrified when news of the massacre and the other cruelties inflicted on the people of Amritsar reached Britain, but many others approved of the military's action.

The postwar imperial situation brought about the fall of David Lloyd George and with him Britain's last Liberal-led government. Britain's ally Greece was attempting to establish control over Constantinople and a section of Asia Minor and facing a powerful and resurgent Turkish national movement. When Turkish forces confronted British and French troops at the town of Chanak on the southern coast of the Dardanelles in September 1922, Lloyd George believed that Britain should involve itself directly against Turkey, while a war-weary populace and the Conservative leadership favored working out an arrangement with the Turks and abandoning the postwar occupation. Labour had left the coalition after the war, and many Liberals continued to stand outside it, so Lloyd George was dependent on the votes of the Conservative Party to stay in power. His rashness led the Conservatives to leave the

LLOYD GEORGE'S POSTHUMOUS FATE

D avid Lloyd George was among the most hated of British politicians, particularly by Liberals who thought he had betrayed their cause by splitting the party and coalescing with the Conservatives. A famous anonymous bit of doggerel expresses this attitude by associating the "Welsh wizard" with the biblical liar Ananias.

> Lloyd George, no doubt,
> When his life ebbs out
> Will ride in a flaming chariot;
> Seated in state
> On a red-hot plate
> 'Twixt Satan and Judas Iscariot.
> Ananias that day
> To the Devil will say:
> "My claim for precedence fails.
> So move me up higher,
> Away from the fire,
> And make way for that liar—from Wales!"

Source: Trevor Wilson, *The Downfall of the Liberal Party, 1914–1935* (Ithaca, N.Y.: Cornell University Press, 1966), 380.

coalition, resulting in the fall of the government and the end of Lloyd George's career as a national leader.

The Chanak affair was also a milestone in the British Empire's disintegration. While the so-called white dominions—Canada, Newfoundland, Australia, New Zealand, and South Africa—had followed Britain into World War I without hesitation, they were much less willing to become involved in a prospective British war against Turkey. Prime Minister Mackenzie King of Canada refused to back Lloyd George, claiming that Canada had not been consulted. Australia and South Africa also refused to back Britain.

8

AN AGE OF CRISIS
(1922–1945)

From 1922 to 1945, Britain continued to face numerous challenges. Some, the most notable being the Great Depression and World War II, were surmounted successfully or at least endured, but by the end of the period Britain's steep decline from its former position of world leadership was apparent to all. However, the decline of British power was accompanied by many improvements in the lives of ordinary British people.

The Coming of Labour and the General Strike of 1926

The fall of the Lloyd George coalition in 1922 was followed by a short spell of Conservative rule. However, the election of December 1923 led to the formation of Britain's first government headed by the Labour Party. The Labour prime minister was the Scottish socialist Ramsay MacDonald (1866–1937). MacDonald was the illegitimate son of a Scottish farmworker and a housemaid, a background that was a startling departure from that of previous prime ministers. The mere fact of a Labour government was considerably more dramatic than anything the government actually accomplished. In many aspects, including financial, MacDonald and his cabinet were more concerned with demonstrating that Labour could run the country responsibly than with advancing a socialist agenda. The first Labour government was short-lived, lasting less than a year, but it did establish a precedent for Labour as a party of government. The Liberal Party lost its place as the main party of opposition to the Conservatives and never again formed a government.

Despite Labour's success in forming a government, electoral politics were not the sole weapon of the workers' movement. From midnight on May 3 to May 12, 1926, Britain endured a general strike in which the members of many of the unions belonging to the Trades

Union Congress (TUC) walked off their jobs. Although strikes were nothing new in the British labor movement, a general strike calling out workers in a broad array of industries was a new and untested weapon. The strike began as an expansion of one by the Miners Union, then locked in a bitter struggle against coal-mine owners who wanted to reduce wages and increase working hours. The TUC's leaders hoped that the threat of a general strike would cause the government to intervene to break the deadlock between miners and mine owners.

Negotiations between the TUC and the Conservative government led by Stanley Baldwin came to nothing. The TUC leadership called out some of its members or ordered them to strike—including the transport workers, workers in heavy industry, printers, and workers in gas and electricity—while it held in reserve members of other industries. Solidarity was nearly total, as all workers ordered to leave their jobs, about 2.5 million, did so. However, the government had also had time to prepare and was able to continue essential services with extensive use of middle- and upper-class volunteers who did such things as drive milk trains and trucks with food supplies. Volunteers also served as special constables to maintain order. Later, many volunteers would look back on the experience as an exciting adventure.

Although there was some violence, neither the TUC leadership nor the government (with the exception of the always pugnacious chancellor of the exchequer, Winston Churchill [1874–1965]) wanted a violent confrontation. Troops were not called upon to maintain order

This photograph of Winston Churchill in 1929 shows him rather cheerful, despite the failure of his political career at the time. (Library of Congress, National Photo Company Collection)

except in the London docks, traditional areas of violent labor disputes. In some areas, police and strikers played football matches, although there were also battles in the street. About 4,000 workers were arrested during the strike, and about another 3,000 were charged with various offenses afterward.

The strike ended when the government offered to sponsor an agreement between the miners and mine owners that required the owners to reorganize the mines and improve working conditions before wage reductions could be imposed on the miners. The TUC accepted and brought the strike to an end, much to the disappointment of many rank-and-file workers. The miners refused the settlement and held out for another six months. In the end they were forced to accept lower wages, longer hours, and no improvements in conditions.

The general strike was followed by a Conservative-led crackdown on unions that made striking harder and established the principle that there was no right to strike to exert pressure on the public at large.

The Great Depression

Britain faced the greatest economic challenge of the postwar years beginning in 1929, as the world was racked by the economic slowdown known as the Great Depression. Although Britain suffered from the depression, it was less affected than were some other countries, notably Germany and the United States. British unemployment remained concentrated in the working class rather than spreading into the middle class. At the worse time during the early 1930s, the country had only about 3 million unemployed, and the fact that the British economy was already suffering before the crash meant that they had less far to fall. Those British who remained employed also benefited from falling prices, and Britain recovered from the depression relatively quickly.

The Great Depression, like the Great War, led people to further question the viability of the bourgeois order based on parliamentary democracy and traditional liberal economics based on free trade. Britain even passed a tariff law, breaking with its free-trade tradition, and, in a move of great symbolic if not practical importance, went off the gold standard in 1931. The British economist John Maynard Keynes (1883–1946) put forth his new economic theories at this time. Keynes denounced the balanced-budget orthodoxy that treated government finance as household finance on a larger scale, claiming that in a recession or depression it was good for a government to go into deficit spending, in order to generate economic activity and pull the economy out of its doldrums.

187

This portrait of Conservative politician F. E. Smith (Lord Birkenhead) combines a modern suit with a traditional judicial wig, creating a striking image of the uneasy mix of British tradition and modernity. (Library of Congress, Bain Collection)

It is testimony to the depression's limited effect on British society and the stability of British political culture that no successful charismatic leaders with the influence of America's Franklin Roosevelt or Germany's Adolph Hitler emerged in Britain. The dominant political figure of the 1930s in Britain was the Conservative Stanley Baldwin (1867–1947). A shrewd parliamentary politician, Baldwin was able to present himself as rooted in English tradition. The leaders of the Labour movement were also cautious and not inclined to break with the parliamentary tradition.

Despite the persistence of parliamentarianism in Britain, not all were content. In politics, many, such as the Conservative-turned-Labour-turned independent aristocrat Sir Oswald Mosely (1896–1980), thought that parliamentary democracy, often stigmatized as a "talking-shop," was simply inadequate to solve the problems facing industrial society, and that more authoritarian or dynamic forms of rule were necessary. British intellectuals—such as the socialist Eric Blair, better known by his pen name of George Orwell (1903–50), or the writer, painter, and fascist sympathizer Wyndham Lewis (1882–1957)—became more willing to embrace radical solutions of the left or right (although not to the extent that Continental ones were). In their estimate the fascist and communist countries seemed to be coping with the depression better, and this was often adduced as evidence of the superiority of authoritarian government and a planned economy. Some conservatives, even though rejecting a fascist or non-democratic solution for their own country, admired Germany's fascist reich chancellor Adolf Hitler (1889–1945) and Italy's dictator Benito Mussolini (1883–1945) as dynamic men of action who were doing the best thing for their own countries. The maverick politician Winston Churchill could be counted among Mussolini's British admirers. He saw the Italian dictator as a man of action, a staunch anticommunist, and even a possible ally against Hitler's Germany. In 1937 he said of Mussolini, "It would be a dangerous folly for the British people to underrate the enduring position in world history which Mussolini will hold, or the amazing qualities of courage, comprehension, self-control and perseverance that he exemplifies" (quoted in James 1977, 531). Given the success of Hitler's diplomacy in the 1930s, during which Germany recovered much of what it had lost in World War I, dictatorships seemed to be politically as well as economically more successful. The pessimism that gripped many practitioners of traditional politics can be summed in the phrase used by Baldwin while prime minister in a speech before the House of Commons, that "a democracy is always two years behind the dictator" (quoted in Taylor 1965, 319).

There were several British fascist movements, of which by far the most successful was Mosely's British Union of Fascists (BUF), founded in 1932 as an amalgamation of several smaller fascist groups. Mosely, a former Conservative MP, Labour cabinet minister, and leader of the short-lived New Party, was frustrated by what he perceived as the inaction of parliamentary politics and attracted to the dynamism and authoritarianism of fascism. Following the model of Mussolini's Italian fascists, the BUF wore black shirts and came to identify themselves as Blackshirts. As time went on, Mosely's movement increasingly focused on anti-Semitism. The party had some success appealing to voters in the east end of London but abstained from running candidates in the parliamentary election of 1935 with the slogan "Fascism next time." The next Parliamentary election would be 10 years later, by which time fascism was resoundingly unpopular.

Like fascism, communism never became a mass movement in Britain; however, it was moderately more successful. Communism managed to attract enough support from isolated pockets of workers to elect an occasional MP, something the fascists never managed. Communism also became more popular among some British intellectuals and scientists, including the crystallographer J. D. Bernal (1901–71) and the poet W. H. Auden (1907–73). This was not necessarily based on concern for the workers, although sometimes it was. The idea of a planned society and economy, promoted by Soviet sympathizers, was also particularly appealing to those frustrated with the "irrationality" of British life and politics and hoping for a more technocratic society run by "experts" rather than politicians or press lords. Many of the leaders of the Communist Party of Great Britain (CPGB) put as much faith in the growth of science as they did in the revolutionary actions of the working class. Not all left-wing intellectuals were sympathetic to the Soviet Union. Bertrand Russell (1872–1970), the great mathematician and philosopher, was one of the first Western leftists to turn strongly against the Soviets, whose authoritarianism and violence he detested. There was also a British community of Trotskyists, followers of the defeated and exiled Russian communist leader Leon Trotsky (1879–1940), who believed that the Soviet Union was not a true communist state.

Like all communist parties of the time, the CPGB followed the party line—the directives laid down by the Soviets through the Communist International, or Comintern, the international organization of communist parties. Since the Soviets were primarily concerned with Russian interests, they were often oblivious of the effects of their decrees on communist parties in other nations. As one of the smaller parties in the Comintern, the CPGB had little effect on its decisions.

An important moment for the British left was the Spanish civil war (1936–39), in which the forces of the Second Spanish Republic, backed by communists, socialists, and anarchists, fought the conservative Falange led by Francisco Franco and backed by fascist Italy and Nazi Germany. Although the British government retained a neutrality that was pro-Franco in practice, British communists, Trotskyists, and leftists volunteered for the cause of the Spanish Republic (and British fascists volunteered for the other side.) Many British leftists came back disillusioned with the brutalities of the Republicans, and particularly the Stalinists. Franco's victory was seen as another triumph for fascism. The best-known British memoir expressing this disillusionment was George Orwell's *Homage to Catalonia* (1938).

Toward a Federal Empire: the Statute of Westminster (1931)

The so-called white dominions—British colonies of settlement that included Canada, Newfoundland (then administratively separate from Canada), Australia, New Zealand, and South Africa—had been growing increasingly eager for self-determination within the British Empire. World War I, in which colonial troops had died for what were perceived as narrowly British interests, had further alienated some people in the colonies. Australians were particularly resentful at what they viewed as poor British leadership contributing to the slaughter of Australians and New Zealanders in the Gallipoli campaign of 1915.

The growing independence of Britain's white dominions was formalized in the Statute of Westminster in 1931. The statute established the dominions' legislative freedom, as well as that of the Irish Free State, and it continues today to be the framework in which those states that acknowledge the British monarch as their head of state operate—although both Ireland (1949) and South Africa (1961) eventually became republics, and Ireland severed all ties to Britain at the same time. By restricting the new status to colonies of white settlement, the statute emphasized the racial nature of the British Empire. Britain and the dominions were joined in the "British Commonwealth."

The Abdication Crisis

The reorganized British Empire faced a crisis at the very top of its leadership in 1936. The death of King George V, who had restored respectability and a middle-class lifestyle to the monarchy after the reign of his raffish father Edward VII, was the first great royal occasion broadcast on the radio, followed by millions. His son and successor, Edward VIII (1894–1972; r. 1936), was initially very popular, but he eventually provoked one of the greatest crises in the history of the British monarchy.

The unmarried Edward had fallen in love with a twice-divorced American woman, Wallis Warfield Simpson (1895–1986). Edward's position was complicated by his role as supreme governor of the Church of England, which at the time did not allow divorced persons with living ex-spouses such as Simpson, to remarry. In addition, Edward was not only king of the United Kingdom but of the British Commonwealth. The Commonwealth prime ministers, representing societies more rural and socially conservative than England, were particularly resistant to the idea of Simpson becoming their queen. Various solutions were proposed, from Prime Minister Stanley Baldwin's suggestion that Edward keep Simpson as a mistress (rejected by Edward) to Edward's idea of marrying Simpson morganatically—that is, without her becoming queen.

The issue split British politics. Older members of the establishment—led by Baldwin; Edward's mother, Queen Mary (1867–1953); and Archbishop of Canterbury Cosmo Gordon Lang (1864–1945)—took an uncompromising position, putting all the pressure they could on Edward to abdicate. Other politicians, mostly political outsiders such as the anti-Baldwin conservative Churchill and the Canadian immigrant and newspaper magnate Max Aitken, Lord Beaverbrook (1879–1964), supported Edward. The eventual, but controversial, solution was for Edward to abdicate in favor of his brother George, duke of York, who became George VI (1895–1952; r. 1936–52). George was a solid, dull family man, a great contrast with his flamboyant brother. Edward departed Britain to marry Simpson, not to return for several decades. The couple received the title of Duke and Duchess of Windsor, although the royal family, with a touch of spite, denied the duchess the title of Royal Highness that she coveted.

Society and Culture in the 1920s and 1930s

The 1920s and 1930s were a time of cultural as well as political transformation. The period saw the enormous acceptance of many aspects of American popular culture in Europe. Britain was particularly receptive to the appeal of American culture due to its lack of a language barrier. Jazz music and the cinema were two particularly powerful American imports. Jazz became popular in the form of records, tours by American bands, and eventually British "dance bands" that played more or less faithful versions of American music. The "pictures" also became an enjoyable recreation that, unlike the football pitch or the music hall, catered to an audience of both sexes and all ages.

The fledgling British cinema had been nearly destroyed by the war, and Hollywood swept in to take its place However, the relationship between Britain and the United States in the production of movies was complicated and two-sided. British talent made vital contributions to the success of early cinema. The most popular star of all, often considered emblematic of the early silent cinema, was Charlie Chaplin (1889–1977), a Londoner whose distinctive garb and mannerisms were products of the English music hall. Unlike many British performers who relocated to Hollywood and became American citizens, Chaplin remained a British subject all his life and was eventually made a knight of the British Empire (KBE). Another English comedian best known for his work in American cinema was Stan Laurel (1890–1965), the partner of the American Oliver Hardy (1892–1957). British actors, directors, and writers were also valued by American producers who wanted success in the British market, as it was believed that they could better handle films with British settings or characters. The dramatic actor Ronald Colman (1891–1958) was one of many British actors who specialized in British roles in American films, giving idealized portrayals of British gentlemen with "stiff upper lips." The English director Alfred Hitchcock (1899–1990), whose early films often had British settings, became thoroughly identified with American cinema. Many

British writers also worked in Hollywood for shorter or longer periods of time, and by the 1930s there were enough British expatriates in southern California to form a British community. The close relationship between the British theatrical community and Hollywood was actually a hindrance in developing British cinema, as actors, directors, and writers headed for the greener fields of Hollywood rather than making films at home. France and Germany, separated from the American industry by language, were (and remain) far ahead of Britain in developing their own film industries.

The Formation of the BBC

The new technology of radio led to the formation of a state organization for broadcasting, the British Broadcasting Corporation (BBC). The BBC was chartered late in 1926 as the successor to the British Broadcasting Company. It was noted for its financing structure, in which owners of radios paid a license fee to support broadcasting. (This model would later be adapted to television when the BBC expanded into that field.) Advertising, viewed as crass and commercial, was shunned.

The BBC, dominated by its director general, the stern Scottish Calvinist John Reith (1889–1971), was a culturally elitist organization. It broadcast much classical music and required its newsreaders and other broadcasters to have a southern English, upper-class accent that came to be known as "BBC English." Regional dialects were to be used only by comedians. Politicians gradually came to employ radio for delivering speeches, adapting to it with greater or lesser degrees of success. The greatest of all British radio orations were Winston Churchill's addresses when he was prime minister during World War II, but Stanley Baldwin was another adept radio speaker who quickly learned that an intimate style was more effective than speaking to a political crowd in public.

The Automobile and Bus

Like other parts of the developed world, Britain in the early 20th century was shaped by the automobile. The motorcar went from being a toy for the rich to becoming a basic means of transportation for millions, although it was still restricted to the prosperous. There were approximately 200,000 motorcars registered in 1920; within a decade the number had increased around fivefold, doubling again during the Great Depression decade. Although workers could not afford their own automobiles, they were also directly affected by the rise of motorized transport. By the late 1920s, the motorized bus was beginning to replace the streetcar, leading to increased sprawl as the grid of streetcar lines ceased to shape British communities.

The British were not merely consumers of automobiles; they were also manufacturers at both the high end and the mass market. Two of the most famous luxury car brands of all time are originally British manufactures: the Rolls-Royce (founded in 1906) and the Bentley (founded in 1919). The two companies merged in 1931, as Bentley was underfunded and having a difficult time dealing with the shrinking market of the depression era. A leading mass-market British manufacturer was Morris Motors, whose founder, William Morris (1877–1963), had started with a bicycle shop, then went to motorcycles, and finally cars. Morris won the undying hatred of many nostalgic for preindustrial England by establishing a car factory in the Cowley district of

THE CONTRACEPTIVE REVOLUTION

Effective contraception was recognized as essential to women's emancipation. It was also one of the few issues binding together middle- and working-class feminists, although at first working-class people had economic difficulty acquiring condoms and diaphragms. Contraception was opposed on the grounds that it encouraged immorality and separated sex from its natural function of procreation. Promoters of contraception were persecuted as pornographers. Medical schools did not train doctors to dispense contraceptive advice, and contraceptive devices had to be bought surreptitiously.

However, World War I had introduced millions of men to the use of condoms, also known as sheaths or "French letters." The diaphragm was much less popular. Contraceptives were also promoted by the Scottish scientist Marie Stopes (1880–1958). Her book *Married Love* (1918), a frank treatment of heterosexual sex, was very popular and controversial. Her treatment of contraception, *Wise Parenthood,* was published the same year. In 1921 she founded the first British birth control clinic. Like many early writers on contraception, Stopes was a eugenicist who believed that the inferior should be discouraged from reproducing, as they would pass on inferior qualities to their offspring. The spread of contraception helped lead to shrinking families and a diminished birthrate.

Oxford, sharing the city with the university's medieval and Renaissance buildings. By 1926, Morris Motors was turning out more than 50,000 cars a year. A philanthropist, Morris was raised to the peerage as Lord Nuffield and founded the Oxford college of the same name as well as many medical institutions in Britain and the Empire.

Appeasement and Its Failure

World War II was a central event in both the politics and the culture of 20th-century Britain, but the British were drawn into war only reluctantly. The Conservative government under Neville Chamberlain (1869–1940), Baldwin's successor, made several attempts to prevent war between Britain and Nazi Germany. The Chamberlain government had been one of marked efficiency and centralization. Chamberlain was a top-down leader, more like an American president than a parliamentary leader like Baldwin, who worked by consensus. The Chamberlain government had made great strides on rearmament, but this was widely seen as a means of preventing another war rather than preparing to fight it. Chamberlain's strategy of appeasement was aimed at giving Hitler the territorial and other concessions that he wanted, with the hope that he, like Chamberlain and the leaders of Britain's main ally, France, ultimately wanted to avoid war. Some in Britain felt that the Treaty of Versailles (1919) following German defeat in World War I had been overly punitive, and that once Germany was restored to the dominant position in eastern Europe that it had held before the war, it would settle down into the community of nations. Some also argued that the real enemy was the Soviet Union, and that a strong Germany would be a bulwark against Bolshevism. These beliefs were more common on the Conservative side. Labour and the left generally, although strongly opposed to war, were not hostile to the Soviet Union and tended to believe in collective security and the League of Nations rather than appeasement. However, the league had lost authority in the face of German, Italian, and Japanese infringe-ments of its tenets in the 1930s, and by the end of the decade it was basically a relic.

The most controversial act of appeasement diplomacy was the Munich agreement of 1938, which arranged for the secession of the German-inhabited areas of Czechoslovakia to Germany, essentially leaving the rest of Czechoslovakia defenseless in the face of further German aggression. Appeasement remains historically controversial, but it was ultimately based on a misreading of Hitler's nature and intentions as well as an intense desire not to become involved in another war like World War I.

The British were very aware of the weak position in which they had come out of the last world war, despite winning it. Many British leaders thought that another major war, win or lose, would mean the destruction of Great Britain and the British Empire. Their fear of another war was accentuated by fear of new military technology, particularly of the bomber. Many exaggerated the damage that bombers would do to cities in the event of war. The British were actually pioneers in the use of bombing in war, having bombed the civilian populations of Iraqi villages to put down a rebellion in 1922. The government anticipated more bombing deaths in the first night of the war than would actually happen during the entire war and estimated that 100,000 tons of bombs would be dropped in the first 14 days, a total not reached in the entire war (Taylor 1965, 437). Many British people believed the deliberate German exaggerations of the power of the German air force—the Luftwaffe—and overestimated the German bomber resources that could or would be devoted to Britain.

Appeasement was generally supported by the British people. In the vast majority of cases, this was not because of sympathy for Hitler, a widely despised figure in Britain, but because of the desire to avoid war and a general lack of interest in foreign affairs. On his return from Munich, Chamberlain was met with wild cheering. Winston Churchill and the small band of politicians who also supported an increased military budget and a confrontational approach to Germany were politically marginalized.

The key moment in moving Britain to a more confrontational posture was the period after the Munich agreement, when Germany annexed what remained of Czechoslovakia in March 1939, thus violating the Munich understanding that Germany was not making further demands on Czechoslovakia. The pogrom against German Jews and their property on November 9–10, 1938—known as *Kristallnacht*—also aroused horror and disgust in Britain, hardening anti-German attitudes. The British people began to believe that war was necessary and inevitable rather than something to be avoided at all cost. After the German takeover of Czechoslovakia, it was clear that Hitler's next target would be Poland. Britain and Poland drew closer together and finally signed the Common Defense Pact on August 25, two days after a Nazi-Soviet pact aimed at the partition of Poland. What actually precipitated the outbreak of the war was the German invasion of Poland on September 1. Britain's declaration of war on Germany followed on September 3.

World War II
Disaster and the Coming of Churchill

The war's early stages were marked by widespread popular support. Even the British dominions, which had no vested interest in what happened in eastern Europe, declared war immediately following the British declaration. Pacifists became and remained a marked minority in the war. The one exception to this pattern were communists who followed the Moscow line, which directed that any potential war between Britain and Germany was to be treated as an imperialist war and thus to be opposed. However, many British communists were appalled by the cynicism of the nonaggression agreement between Germany and the Soviet Union and left the movement over the issue.

Early optimism ended with the quick fall of Poland and increasingly successful German attacks in western Europe. With Poland easily defeated in less than a month, the Germans in a strong position to invade France, the Soviet Union a partner of Germany in the division of Eastern Europe, and the United States neutral, the situation for Britain looked grim indeed. It looked even grimmer for the government of Neville Chamberlain, ill-prepared for war and embarrassed by the failure of appeasement. Winston Churchill, identified as the premier supporter of an aggressive policy that had been vindicated by events, was brought into the government in his old World War I position as first lord of the admiralty. With the failure of the campaign against the German occupation of Norway in May 1940, it became clear that the Chamberlain government was unwilling or unable to carry on the war seriously, and it was overturned in the House of Commons as dissident Conservatives joined with Labour. (Chamberlain was very ill at this time and died shortly thereafter.)

Britain was governed during the war by a coalition of all parties led by Churchill with a cabinet numerically dominated by Conservatives, including the new prime minister. Churchill's comeback was a stunning surprise, as he had been widely disliked in the Conservative Party for his association with the disastrous Gallipoli campaign during World War I. He was viewed as a brilliant but dangerous egomaniac, and Baldwin and Chamberlain had excluded him from Conservative governments during the 1930s. Labour also distrusted him due to his strong opposition to unions and nationalist movements in the British Empire. Churchill's strong support of rearmament and a confrontational policy with Germany had been perceived as another one of his eccentric crusades, like his support for Edward VIII during the abdication crisis. It took a threat to national existence to bring him back into power, and even then he was the second choice of the Conservative leadership, who would have preferred the ex-appeaser Edward Wood, viscount Halifax (1881–1959). However, in addition to the fact that Halifax suffered under what was now perceived as the handicap of a seat in the House of Lords rather than the Commons, Churchill was widely perceived as the one person with the vigor and leadership ability to carry on the war. Halifax quietly withdrew from consideration, and Churchill became prime minister on May 9, 1940. His government would be even more presidential than Chamberlain's, with unprecedented control over the military as well as the civilian branches of the war effort, and very different from the governmental arrangements of World War I.

After the formation of the Churchill government, the war was marked by electoral and parliamentary peace among all parties. General elections were suspended for the duration of the war, so there was no election for 10 years, from 1935 to 1945. In the coalition cabinet the Conservatives tended to focus on issues relating to war and diplomacy, while Labour concentrated on the home front. The Labour leader, Clement Atlee (1883–1967), was the deputy prime minister and chaired the Lord President's Committee, which ran the war's domestic side, while Churchill concentrated on the military and diplomatic side. The powerful union official Ernest Bevin (1881–1951) was particularly vital in the war cabinet as minister for labor and national service, with responsibility for the mobilization and allocation of labor. There was industrial peace for the duration of the war. The allocation of resources in both labor and matériel required unprecedented state involvement and the mobilization of much of society, including women and youth.

Almost immediately, the new Churchill government faced another disaster: the fall of France. One of the most heavily mythologized actions of the war was the evacuation of Dunkirk from May 26 to June 4, 1940. About two weeks after Churchill came to power, the bulk of the British troops in France had their backs to the English Channel, surrounded by the Germans. Most of them (along with many French and other Allied soldiers) were successfully evacuated by the Royal Navy, with the help of many civilian sailors in small boats. The "Dunkirk spirit" became a byword for persistence in the face of disaster. However, despite giving British morale a badly needed shot in the arm, Dunkirk was a catastrophe from a purely military point of view, as the British Expeditionary Force had to abandon nearly all of its equipment to the Germans. Shortly thereafter, Churchill, who was prepared to continue the war regardless of what happened at Dunkirk, rejected a peace offer

THE GERMAN OCCUPATION OF THE CHANNEL ISLANDS

The only portion of the British Isles to be occupied during World War II were the Channel Islands between Britain and France, which were occupied by Germany from June 30, 1940, to May 9, 1945. The British government deliberately abandoned the islands, believing that they were of no strategic value and that occupying them would waste German resources. The Germans did heavily fortify the islands for an attack that never came. After the D-day invasion of Normandy from England in 1944, the islanders and Germans alike were cut off from both German and Allied food sources, although the Red Cross brought some food. The occupation only ended after Germany's defeat, when German forces on the islands surrendered without firing a shot.

from Hitler without discussion and announced his war aim: total victory. Given the nearly uninterrupted stream of German victories that had made Hitler the master of the European continent, this seemed objectively insane.

Finest Hour?: The Battle of Britain

The next challenge was to Britain itself. The German plan for the invasion of Britain was code-named Operation Sea Lion, and its prospects for success remain a topic of controversy. In any event, invasion was never attempted, and the actual Battle of Britain was fought in the air.

The Battle of Britain, which lasted from July to October 1940, became another heavily mythologized wartime period. (The parts of World War II that resonate most loudly in the British memory were often from its early stages, before the British contribution was overshadowed by that of the United States and the Soviet Union.) In the first major military campaign to be fought entirely from the air, heavily outnumbered British fighter pilots defeated the attempt of the German Luftwaffe to establish dominance of the skies. In large part this was a matter of poor German leadership as the Germans could not settle on a consistent strategy concentrating on airfields, aircraft production, or radar stations. Superior British technology, including radar and the control of fighters from the ground, was also an important factor.

Although the Germans initially focused their attacks on British military targets, by late August they were attacking British cities (as the Royal Air Force [RAF] was attacking German cities). The attack on British cities, which intensified in December, is referred to as the Blitz. Although the Germans killed more than 20,000 British civilians and wounded more than 30,000, their bombing of cities did not bring them closer to the objective of destroying the RAF's capacity to fight, nor did it have the destructive effects on British morale that some German leaders, including Hitler, expected. By October, RAF air supremacy over British skies had been established, and the Germans had abandoned plans for an invasion. Despite being a defensive win, the Battle of Britain was the first victory of the war on the Allied side (although Britain at the time was actually without allies, other than the Commonwealth).

British victory did not end the air war, which continued for the remainder of the conflict, as both Germans and British dropped bombs on each other's cities, killing uncounted thousands of civilians in a way that made little contribution to ultimate victory. Dealing with air raids became an important part of the wartime experience, particularly for Londoners. The experience of the ordinary Londoner was shared by King George and his consort, Queen Elizabeth, who refused to leave the city.

Ordinary civilians were much less isolated from World War II than they had been from World War I, which had a relatively static front line and little in the way of attacks on the civilian population. With bombing, and also with the overwhelming presence of the state in allocating work and food, the ordinary British person felt the war as something in which he or she was personally involved. The extensive temporary relocation of children away from cities where they would have been the targets of bombers also contributed to class and regional mixing.

From European to World War

Once it had become clear that Operation Sea Lion could not work due to German failure to establish air and sea dominance, it was a question of how long the British could hold out until the Americans or possibly the Soviet Union would enter the war against Germany. Even aided by its dominions, Britain lacked the military might to challenge the German grip on Europe, although British and British Commonwealth forces remained active in the Mediterranean. What brought about Germany's defeat was the entrance of the two other world powers into the war. Once the Germans invaded the Soviet Union in 1941, the bulk of the German military effort was devoted to the massive war on the eastern front; the war with Britain became a secondary concern. By that time the United States had unmatched economic power and a large population that could be mobilized, and German defeat became virtually certain from after Hitler's catastrophic decision to declare war on the United States on December 11, 1941, four days after the Japanese attack on Pearl Harbor.

After the Battle of Britain, the principal area where British and Axis troops engaged was North Africa. The British fear was that the Germans and their Italian allies would be able to drive them out of Egypt, sever their communications with the Middle East and Asia through the Suez Canal, and eventually take over the oil fields of the Middle East. British and Commonwealth troops in North Africa faced one of Hitler's best generals, Erwin Rommel (1891–1944), nicknamed the Desert Fox. The campaign's decisive battle was El Alamein in the late summer of 1942, the first great Allied offensive victory of the war. The commanding Allied general at El Alamein, Bernard Law Montgomery (1882–1976), became the best-known British soldier of the war. After El Alamein, Montgomery led a masterly campaign that destroyed the German positions in North Africa. As a general he was an admirable leader of men and usually a clear and detailed planner, but he was sometimes criticized for being overly cautious and unable to work with superiors and peers.

The war put an enormous strain on the empire, particularly as Britain confronted Japan in Asia. As well as the American base at Pearl Harbor, Japan attacked the British in the Far East in 1941. Racism and Japanese remoteness had led the British to underestimate the Japanese threat, and Britain could spare little from its resources devoted to home defense to protect its empire from Japanese attack. The Japanese humiliated the British by taking their fortress at Singapore in the early days of the war, a loss that was felt particularly keenly in Britain, and they also conquered the British colonies of Hong Kong (1941), Burma (1942), and Malaya (1942). In their propaganda to Asian peoples, the Japanese emphasized the common struggle against European imperialism, although colonies occupied by Japan soon found that the new masters could be even harsher than the old.

Many Indians (and other colonial subjects) resented being dragged into another European war. The Quit India movement led by Mohandas Gandhi and the Congress Party leader Jawaharlal Nehru (1889–1964) called upon the British, unsuccessfully, to leave India to preserve its neutrality. More militant Indian nationalists led by Subhas Chandra

EL ALAMEIN (1942)

Perhaps the greatest victory of British and Commonwealth troops was the Second Battle of El Alamein from October 25 to November 3, 1942. El Alamein was a town in northern Egypt near which the British Eighth Army and associated Allied troops under the command of Bernard Law Montgomery defeated German and Italian troops, the famous Afrika Korps, under Erwin Rommel. Rommel's troops were undersupplied, as the Soviet front had first claim on German resources. Montgomery's troops were being reinforced and supplied with British and American matériel. The victory was overwhelming, with the Axis suffering more than 37,000 casualties as compared to about 13,500 Allied casualties. The battle ended Rommel's hopes of going on to conquer Egypt, take the Suez Canal and the Middle Eastern oil fields, and join up with German troops in southern Russia. It made Montgomery's reputation (he would later take the title of Viscount El Alamein when raised to the nobility) and placed the Allies on the offensive in North Africa, a position they were never to lose. Churchill later stated: "It may almost be said that before Alamein we never had a victory. After Alamein we never had a defeat" (Churchill 1949, 4:541). The fact that Alamein was a British and Commonwealth victory at a time when the burden of the war was increasingly on the Soviets and Americans made it particularly important in the British national memory of World War II.

Bose (1897–1945) attempted to disrupt the British hold on India by forming the Indian National Army in alliance with the Japanese; and a smaller force, the Indian Legion, under German command, formed from Indian prisoners of war taken by Germany. British mismanagement and indifference, along with wartime inflation, contributed to the massive Bengal famine of 1943, in which between 1.5 and 3 million Bengalis died. However, most of the Indian army stayed loyal to Britain and played a central role in the British land war effort against Japan, the so-called China-Burma-India theater, or CBI. Many Indians, in and out of the army, assumed that after the war the situation would improve.

Following a strategy that had won some successes in World War I, Germany attempted to strangle the British economy through the use of submarine warfare, the famous U-boats. The war against Germany was always the first priority for the British fleet, which meant it was unable to protect its dominions and colonies such as Australia, which turned to the United States for protection. The increased reliance of many parts of the empire, from the Pacific to the Caribbean, on American protection contributed to the dissolution of the British Empire as a functioning political unit.

British and Commonwealth forces participated in the invasions of Axis Europe in Italy, southern France, and Normandy, where Montgomery was the initial commander of Allied ground forces. British generals served under overall American command, although the American commander of the European theater, Dwight D. Eisenhower, was diplomatic in his accommodation to British sensibilities and became very popular in Britain. The nation played a much smaller role in the war against Japan, but British, Indian, and imperial troops in the CBI theater—under perhaps the finest British general of the war, William Slim (1891–1970)—tied down tens of thousands of Japanese troops and won a great victory at the Battle of Imphal from March until June 1944. Along with the United States and the Soviet Union, Britain remained one of the big three powers and participated in the wartime conferences. However, by then it was definitely the least of the big three.

The Wizard War

The British proved highly capable of applying their best minds to the problems presented by war. The invention of radar in 1935 proved absolutely vital in the Battle of Britain, giving British airmen advance warning of German air attacks. The pioneer of radar, the Scottish physicist Robert Watson-Watt (1892–1973), supervised the creation of radar stations along the British coasts. During the war itself, he served in the Air Ministry as director of communications. Fortunately, the Germans abandoned the tactic of bombing the radar stations after two nerve-wracking weeks. Radar was better adapted for bombers by John Randall's (1905–84) and Henry Boot's (1917–83) development of the cavity magnetron in 1940, which enabled night bombers to distinguish cities from the air. Another British technical triumph was in cryptography. Bletchley Park, the headquarters of the British cryptographic effort, has passed into legend in the history of computing. Ultra, the code name for the British breaking of the German military codes, was one of the best-kept secrets of the war. It was an enormously important contributor to the Allied victory. The British also conducted research into making atomic bombs.

British ingenuity by itself was not enough. Even before the American entry into the war after Pearl Harbor, the British sought to harness

American productive and technical capacity. The Tizard Mission of 1940, led by the scientist and civil servant Henry Tizard (1885–1959), essentially turned over all British developments and patents to be further developed and mass-produced by the Americans. Once given out, the knowledge could never again become a British monopoly. Atomic research passed nearly entirely into the hands of the Americans, who would produce the world's first nuclear bomb in July 1945. The jet engine, pioneered by the RAF engineer Frank Whittle (1907–96) in the 1930s, was also first made into an operational plane by the Americans, two years before the British.

The Home Front

The war was a transformative experience even for those British people who did not join the military or leave the island. Even more than World War I, World War II was a "total war" involving every person in the belligerent nations. Urban Britons continued to feel the might of German bombing. Toward the end of the war, German bombers were supplemented by the V2 rocket.

The war saw an unprecedented degree of economic centralization. The economy was completely organized for war, and the lifestyles of ordinary British people were severely cut back. Rationing was, in theory, universal; labor was also coordinated. The intake of men into the military left numerous jobs to be done. Some of the need for labor was supplied by temporary immigrants from Ireland, and the Colonial Office worked to encourage temporary migration from the British Caribbean colonies. Another source of reserve labor in Britain, as in other countries, was women, who were required to register as workers in 1941. The Women's Land Army, a revival of a World War I program, supplied women laborers for agriculture, informally known as Land Girls. A similar organization was the Women's Timber Corps, which did forestry work. The Air Transport Auxiliary, which ferried combat and transport aircraft, recruited pilots not qualified to fly in combat, including women, and it was the first British government organization to pay women and men the same wage.

Popular involvement was mobilized by scrap drives, although these were often more symbolic than a useful way of supplying needed metal. Ornamental iron gates were melted down, unless there was an historical or artistic argument for their preservation. The retired prime minister Stanley Baldwin, whom Churchill particularly loathed, strove in vain to preserve the iron gates of his country estate.

Wartime Britain saw an influx of people from all over the British Empire as well as allied countries. This photograph is of South African young women practicing to be dispatch riders. (Office of War Information)

One of the keys to popular mobilization was propaganda, and in Britain as in every other combatant country, the war led to the use of propaganda on an unprecedented scale, spread through radio, newsreels, posters, and numerous other media. In the interests of national unity, the BBC even abandoned its prohibition on the use of regional or lower-class accents by persons who were not comedians. Radio was a particularly important tool, as it made it possible to propagandize the other side as well as one's own. Rather than simply denouncing the Nazis, the British decided that since they had access to the Germans via radio, they would establish a reputation for trustworthy reporting so that what they said would be believed. German anti-British propaganda was much more crude, as in the work of William Joyce (1906–46), a former British fascist sympathizer (actually American by nationality) who became known as Lord Haw-Haw. Recognizing the BBC's power, the Nazis forbade anyone to listen to its German broadcasts. (Joyce was executed as a traitor after the war.)

Churchill was a master propagandist, particularly on the radio. His speeches during the war have become legendary, and he even won the respect of the German minister of propaganda Joseph Goebbels (1897–1945), who, when the war turned against Germany, recommended (in vain) that Hitler, when addressing the German people, adopt a realistic tone modeled on Churchill's during the darkest days for Britain.

After the United States entered the war, the American military became an omnipresent force in wartime Britain. This photograph shows American tanks on maneuvers in England. (U.S. Army Signal Corps)

Another transformative aspect of the war was the heavy presence of American and other foreign troops. After Dunkirk, Britain received many French and other Continental soldiers who had been evacuated along with the British. London became the base of numerous governments in exile and resistance military forces, most notably the Free French of Charles de Gaulle (1890–1970), who caused his British hosts unending headaches. Britain also served as the ideal base for American and Canadian troops preparing for the invasions of North Africa and Europe. British men often resented Americans whose money and exotic glamour was appealing to British women. Numerous British "war brides" married American soldiers and moved to the United States after the war.

Victory

Britain emerged from the war with much of its infrastructure destroyed and with massive casualties, including about 450,000 deaths from Britain itself and hundreds of thousands more from Empire and Commonwealth countries. It was also heavily indebted to the United States, to the point of having lost financial independence. The empire was increasingly unsustainable, British dominions were moving into the American orbit, and Britain itself faced a grim future of rationing for years. Poland, for whom the war had originally been started, had been liberated from Germany but now was under the grip of the Soviet Union. Nonetheless, as Churchill had said in the grim days after the fall of France, "Let us therefore brace ourselves to our duties, and so bear ourselves that if the British Empire and its Commonwealth last for a thousand years, men will still say, this was their finest hour" (quoted in Moss 2003, 185). And few would deny that it was.

9

THE AGE OF CONSENSUS (1945–1979)

The decades after the end of World War II were a time of cultural vitality and increasing pluralism. On the political side the era saw the formation of the welfare state, which attracted support from all parties but eventually also became the target of criticism. The period also saw the decolonization of nearly all of the British Empire and the weakening of key sectors of the British economy. Suppressed populations within Britain—Scottish and Welsh nationalists, Catholics in Northern Ireland, immigrants, people of color, sexual minorities, and women—increasingly began to make their voices heard.

Postwar Britain

Although the Allied victory had brought much rejoicing, Britain faced numerous problems after the war, both internally and externally. The war's expense was a major concern: Britain had used up all of its foreign reserves of currency and had to borrow immense sums of money from the United States. After the glow of victory wore off, life was drab, food rationing was still in force, and there seemed few economic opportunities. In the years following 1945, many Britons who could afford to do so emigrated to Australia, Canada, or the United States.

Many in Britain expected that the general election in 1945—the first in 10 years, called after victory in Europe—would be a triumph for the Conservatives and for their leader, the great wartime prime minister Winston Churchill (1874–1965). Instead it was a landslide victory for the Labour Party under Churchill's wartime deputy, Clement Atlee (1883–1967), who became the new prime minister. Labour won 394 seats to the Conservatives' 210, a nearly 2-to-1 majority that ensured Labour would govern with few political checks.

The reasons for the Labour victory were many. While Churchill remained personally popular, many continued to hold the Conservative Party responsible for the economic and diplomatic errors of the 1930s. In addition, Churchill's charge that Labour's economic policies would require more state control over business and could only be enforced by a "Gestapo" (Pugh 2002, 255), coming as it did after the hard-fought victory against the Nazis and the revelations of Nazi atrocities, alienated many British voters. Labour's dominance of the home-front administration during the war gave it credibility as a government for peacetime. The party's program of housing, full employment, and social insurance also appealed to many who hoped the war would be followed by a more socially just Britain.

The Atlee government (1945–51) was the most important peacetime British government of the 20th century, laying the foundation for the British welfare state whose pillars, if battered, remain to this day. The challenges the government faced were legion. One of the most basic was housing. Thousands of houses had been destroyed or rendered uninhabitable by the German bombing. In addition, much of Britain's housing stock was decrepit, poorly maintained, and in need of replacement. The government took the lead, building hundreds of thousands of "council houses" but attracting resentment for severe restrictions it placed on the private market.

The Atlee government carried out a vigorous program of nationalization of basic services. Nationalization faced surprisingly little opposition, in large part because it was seen as a continuation of the policies of close cooperation between government and industry during wartime. In its first two years, the Atlee government nationalized the Bank of England, the telegraph and radio, civil aviation, coal and electrical power, roads, and railroads. To the disappointment of many socialists in and out of the Labour Party, nationalization did not establish workers' control over their industries but instead created publicly appointed boards to replace private boards.

The Labour government did not see its mission merely as aiding Britain in its recovery from the war; it envisioned the creation of a new society, one that would provide for the welfare of all rather than letting each fend for him- or herself. Plans for a welfare state had been in the works for decades, but the most important, the 1943 Beveridge Report, dated to the war period. It was the work of the civil servant William Beveridge (1879–1963), who had been charged with planning for postwar social services in Britain. Beveridge was not a Labour man but a Liberal who firmly adjured socialism. His report laid down plans for eliminating poverty and unemployment through a universal welfare state. The wartime government, an alliance of all parties, approved it, although Labour's campaign for a stronger endorsement failed.

For many Labourites and other leftists, central planning was as important as social welfare. The war was widely held to have demonstrated the superiority of a centrally planned economy, whether Soviet-style communism or the combination of government coordination with a private sector characteristic of the British and U.S. wartime economies, over a purely capitalistic, free-market one. Although few wished to emulate the Soviet system, Soviet victory was also considered to be evidence of the superiority of a managed economy. Some believed that Britain could be the shining example of a "middle way" of democratic socialism, between Soviet tyranny and the selfish cruelty of American capitalism.

One of the most remarkable and long-lasting programs launched by the new Labour government was the National Health Service (NHS), created in 1945. Few institutions have had more influence on British life. The NHS was particularly identified with one man, Aneurin Bevan (1897–1960), a Welsh socialist and the minister for health. Bevan had a well-deserved reputation as a troublemaker that dated from the war, when he had been one of the few to oppose the collaboration of Labour with the Conservatives in the coalition government. The Welsh mining communities from which Bevan hailed were known for their uncompromising radicalism.

Bevan had his work cut out for him. He faced great resistance from the medical profession, which feared government control, and skepticism from the civil service. The National Health Service that emerged combined public provisions with the toleration of private practice. Although Britons have grumbled over NHS inefficiencies and delays for generations, its basic principle, that patients should not be forced to pay for medical services, remains widely popular.

Britain and the Cold War

The most important international conflict following World War II was the cold war between two coalitions, one led by the United States and the other by the Soviet Union. Britain was a leading member of the U.S.-led coalition of the "free world." It was Winston Churchill who, at an address given in Fulton, Missouri, in 1946, launched one of the dominant metaphors of the cold-war era when he spoke of an "iron curtain" that divided Eastern Europe, dominated by the Red Army and communist regimes, from Western Europe. One important aspect of

Winston Churchill in 1949, returning from a trip to America, where he was (and remains) very popular. (Library of Congress, New York World Telegraph and Sun Collection)

the cold war in Britain is that it meant the American military presence continued long after the end of World War II. The cold war also saw the continuation of the British military presence in Germany. Britain became an important part of the premier, American-led cold-war military alliance, the North Atlantic Treaty Organization (NATO).

The cold war was a struggle against both the internal and the external communist threat. Britain never went as far in domestic anticommunism as did the United States in the McCarthy era. Although British communism declined through the postwar period, the Soviet Union itself bore much of the responsibility, as it did for the decline of communism elsewhere. Soviet repression of Eastern European dissidents, most notably its crushing of the rebellion in Hungary in 1956, was followed by a large drop in membership in the Communist Party of Great Britain as communists grew increasingly disillusioned with Soviet power and the "party line" of unconditional support for the Soviet Union.

Sometimes the cold war became a hot war. The two most notable occasions were the Korean War (1950–53) and the Vietnam War (1959–75), during which an American-led coalition faced the communist-supported states of North Korea and North Vietnam. Britain participated in the Korean War as a member of the United Nations, the international body set up for collective security at the end of World

THE CAMBRIDGE SPIES

Ideological sympathy with communism helped cause the greatest spy scandal in British history, the case of the Soviet spies Guy Burgess (1911–63), Donald Maclean (1913–83), and Kim Philby (1912–88). The three, all Cambridge men and referred to collectively as the Cambridge Spies, passed on an enormous amount of information to the Soviet intelligence service, the KGB, in World War II and the early cold war. Burgess and Maclean defected to the Soviet Union in 1951, but Philby managed to keep his true loyalties secret for longer and only defected in 1963. The mysterious "fourth man," the eminent art historian Anthony Blunt (1907–83), was not publicly outed until 1979, by which point he had been appointed Master of the Queen's Pictures. The scandal was a huge embarrassment for the British intelligence community, and it impaired cooperation with U.S. intelligence agencies for decades. The Cambridge Spies have remained a source of fascination and numerous works of art and historical investigation for decades.

War II. Despite the U.S. government's urging, British leaders avoided participation in the Vietnam War, which unlike the Korean War was not waged by the United Nations. The Vietnam War was very unpopular in Britain and contributed to a growth in anti-Americanism.

One of the most controversial elements of the cold war was nuclear weapons. However, the idea that the British should obtain their own nuclear arsenal was not widely opposed on the left at first. Even Aneurin Bevan, the most left-wing figure in national politics, supported an independent British nuclear deterrent. Like many leaders of both parties, Bevan did not fully trust the Americans. (Clement Atlee's foreign minister, Ernest Bevin, a champion of nuclear research, at one point exclaimed that he wanted a bomb "with a bloody Union Jack on it" [quoted in Morgan 1992, 54].) At the end of the war, the United States had promptly reneged on its treaty obligations to share the results of its nuclear research with Britain. The Labour government had launched its own nuclear research program in 1946. The military nature of the research was secret, but when it eventually became known it was not very controversial.

Opposition to nuclear weapons along with fear of a nuclear Armageddon grew in the 1950s. The movement of opposition to the British nuclear arsenal broadened into the Campaign for Nuclear

Disarmament (CND), a mass movement for the abolition of all nuclear weapons founded in 1958. Unlike many previous movements of the left, the CND was dominated by the middle class rather than workers. It attracted some of Britain's leading intellectuals, including the philosopher Bertrand Russell (1872–1970), whose vocal opposition to war went back to World War I. Women played a larger role in CND leadership than in most previous movements of the left. Aneurin Bevan's followers, the "Bevanites," also joined the campaign.

The most radical suggestion of the CND was that Britain should unilaterally renounce and destroy its nuclear arsenal, in the hope of setting an example for other powers. This suggestion was enormously controversial in the Labour Party. The Labour leadership and the trade unions, suspicious of the middle-class CND, rejected the call for unilateral disarmament.

The Beginnings of Decolonization

World War II placed immense strain on all the European colonial empires. The Japanese promoted anti-imperialism in the territories they conquered, such as Malaya and Singapore, although they behaved like imperialists themselves. The Japanese conquest means that in the far-eastern part of the empire, the British were faced not merely with the problem of maintaining colonial rule but actually reinstating it after the Japanese left the territory. Britain was also involved in the colonies of other states. In the Middle East, where they had occupied the French colonies in Syria and Lebanon, they simply handed power over to the indigenous liberation movements. However, in the East the British supported the restoration of French imperial power in Indochina and Dutch power in Indonesia.

The future of the British Empire was one of the great questions hanging over postwar Britain. Impoverished by war, Britain, like other European imperial powers, was increasingly unable to pay the social and economic costs of running an empire as well as repressing nationalist movements in their dominions. Even though many, including the Labour government, believed that holding onto the colonies was necessary to preserve any pretense of great power status, it was also held to be impossible in the face of colonial resistance. Empires depended on the collaboration of a native elite that had become alienated from the imperial order. Although the Indian army had played a central role in British strategy for decades, fighting on battlefields across the world, it and other colonial armies, penetrated by nationalist ideologies, had become unreliable.

The global situation had also turned against empire. The two superpowers of the postwar world, the United States and the Soviet Union, both identified themselves as anti-imperialist. The United Nations became a force against maintaining colonial empires. The racial framework for imperialism, along with racist thought in general, had been declining for decades and had finally and irrevocably been discredited by Nazi atrocities. Racism survived and thrived as a prejudice in Britain, but it had lost its usefulness as a justification for colonial rule.

The abandonment of empire was supported at least ideologically by both British liberal and socialist political tendencies. War-weary Britons found the idea of more substantial sacrifices in blood and treasure to make an increasingly hollow claim to national greatness unappealing. Those wars that were fought to temporarily retain portions of the empire or shape the successor states, such as the successful war against communist insurgents in Malaya, received little publicity and did not rely on popular support.

The British were perhaps the most willing of all European imperialists to give up their overseas possessions. Britain's exit from India in 1947—although it had disastrous consequences for the colonized, leading to extensive massacres with more than a million casualties as India was divided into the two states of India and Pakistan—was carried out with little difficulty or lingering embarrassment for the British once the decision to abandon the colony had been made.

It was usually more difficult to withdraw from colonies that had seen extensive white settlement, especially when the number of settlers was too small to form a majority. Settlers both resisted decolonization on the ground and built lobbies that influenced the British government's actions. British colonies of settlement where the indigenous population was outnumbered by a mostly British majority had been working toward gradual and peaceful independence since the 19th century, culminating in the 1931 Statute of Westminster, which had essentially given them self-government with the British monarch as head of state. These colonies included Canada, Australia, and New Zealand. South Africa, where British settlers coexisted with both a larger group of Dutch-descended white settlers, the Afrikaners, and an indigenous majority shared this dominion status. The worst postcolonial situations in the British sphere were in southern Africa and Israel/Palestine, both of which had settler populations out of the political or cultural control of a metropolitan power. Afrikaners and Zionist Jews had no road to a home elsewhere, while at the same time they were large, powerful, and organized enough to maintain a colonial form of rule without being a

In 1946 the Irgun, a Zionist underground terrorist group, blew up part of the King David Hotel in Jerusalem, the headquarters of the British Mandatory authorities. (Library of Congress, Matson Collection)

colony. Britain, faced by violent resistance from Jews and Arabs, left Palestine in 1948. In 1961 South Africa became a republic and severed its last ties with Britain. Elsewhere in southern Africa, the British-

215

descended settlers of Southern Rhodesia, modern Zimbabwe, declared independence themselves in 1965, maintaining white rule outside the colonial framework for many years.

The most conspicuous institutional continuation of the British Empire was the Commonwealth of Nations, or British Commonwealth. This originated as a term for Britain and it dominions, countries recognizing the British monarch as their head of state. In 1949 the word *British* was dropped from the Commonwealth's name, and a procedure was established for states that became republics or monarchies with indigenous monarchs to remain Commonwealth members as long as they recognized the British monarch as its head.

Britain and the European Community

The loosening or dissolving ties between Britain and its colonies were not replaced by closer ones with continental Europe. Outside of participation in NATO, the British were remote from the first movements for European unity, which were dominated by Belgian, French, and German diplomats and politicians. The gradual process of unification began with the six-nation European Coal and Steel Community founded in 1951, which set the pattern for the European Economic Community, or Common Market, founded in 1957, also without British participation. Britain's aloofness was partly due to hopes that ties with its former colonies and dominions would provide markets for British goods and help keep the economy afloat. It was also influenced by British mistrust of Continental peoples, particularly after World War II, when many viewed the Continent as an abode of fascists and collaborators.

In 1960 Britain and other powers outside the Common Market—Denmark, Norway, Austria, Switzerland, and Portugal—formed the European Free Trade Association (EFTA), pledged to the mutual reduction of tariffs and the fostering of commerce between members. As the largest economic power within the EFTA, Britain benefited from being able to export to its markets, but the EFTA markets did not rival the larger markets of the European Common Market.

The distrust between Britain and continental Europe was mutual. When the British changed their minds and sought entry into the Common Market in 1961, the president of France, Charles de Gaulle (1890–1970), vetoed the idea. He feared that Britain was too close to the United States and that British admission would undermine the community's independence. Britain finally joined the Common Market in 1973, leaving the EFTA at the same time, but few Britons were enthusiastic about it.

Britain Celebrates Its Britishness

Britain's problematic relations with its empire and with Europe contributed to a revival of British identity as separate and apart. As the 1950s began, the nation enjoyed two national celebrations: the 1951 Festival of Britain and the 1953 coronation of a new queen, Elizabeth (b. 1926), following the death of her father, King George VI, the previous year. (The new queen's numbering would provoke some controversy. England, but not Scotland, had had a previous Queen Elizabeth. Elizabeth was and is officially Elizabeth II, but some Scots resented her use of that number in their country, even defacing mailboxes with the hated "II.")

The Festival of Britain, which marked the 100th anniversary of the London Great Exhibition, had a distinctively nationalist message. The uniqueness of British culture, not its connections to Europe or to the world, was what was being celebrated. The festival was also nostalgic, focusing on the greatness of the British past rather than its transformations in the future. A project of Labour deputy prime minister Herbert Morrison (1888–1965), the festival was also designed to mark the country's recovery from the long postwar period of austerity. Most of it was based in south London, but there was also a branch in Glasgow dedicated to industry and numerous traveling exhibitions. The Festival of Britain attracted tens of thousands of visitors.

Many Britons remember the coronation on June 2, 1953, as the first time they watched television. Retailers pushed customers to buy televisions, and television owners invited their neighbors in to witness the great event. The young queen and her husband (and distant cousin), Prince Phillip, duke of Edinburgh (b. 1921), were presented as symbols of British continuity and icons of British patriotism. (The young couple's marriage in 1947 had also been a great public occasion.)

The Conservative Comeback

The Conservative Party, led by Winston Churchill, won the general election of 1951, and Churchill became prime minister for the second time. But the real power behind the aged Churchill was Foreign Secretary Anthony Eden (1897–1977).

Churchill's hope of restoring Britain to a place among the world's leading powers was doomed to disappointment. The Conservative

THE ORIGIN OF WICCA

Wicca has been described as the only religion invented in England. A form of neopaganism, Wicca drew from roots in 19th- and 20th-century English culture. One of its origins can be found in the histories of medieval and early modern witchcraft written by the Scottish scholar Margaret Murray (1863–1963). Murray wrote several books, beginning with *The Witch-Cult in Western Europe* (1921), in which she described how the witches persecuted in the 16th–18th centuries practiced a secret nature religion that was the rival to Christianity. Although Murray's original books fit in with the anthropological mainstream of the time, her interpretations grew more eccentric until she claimed that medieval English monarchs were secret supporters of the pre-Christian religion. The "Murray thesis" has been rejected by historians of witchcraft but retains great cultural influence.

Murray's interpretation was taken up by an English civil servant named Gerald Gardner (1884–1964) in the 1950s. In *Witchcraft Today,* Gardner claimed that the nature-worship tradition of witchcraft described by Murray had not been destroyed during the persecutions but survived as an underground cult. Gardner referred to this religion as *witchcraft,* not *wicca,* although he referred to initiates as *wica.* He claimed to have been initiated into a coven of surviving witches in Dorset. There is no actual evidence of this, and historians who have studied the subject agree that Gardner was lying. Freemasonry influenced Gardner's picture of witchcraft as a religion with degrees of initiation and an organization of local groups bound together. Gardner's witchcraft, like Murray's, was oriented around the worship of a great goddess, who was the personification of nature, and her male consort, the horned god. Gardner became a media celebrity in England, and a number of groups formed essentially using his work as a manual. Wicca eventually diverged into numerous branches and traditions in Britain and elsewhere.

government took power during another balance-of-payments crisis, and the country simply could not afford the kind of imperial status that Churchill wanted. On the domestic front, many leaders, such as Chancellor of the Exchequer R. A. Butler ("Rab") (1902–82), believed that Labour's policies on the welfare state should be maintained, in some cases out of ideological sympathy and in others out of fear that any attack on the achievements of the Atlee government would be followed by a Labour comeback in the next general election. The government was cautious in privatization, reprivatizing iron and steel but leaving the railroads in public hands. The British economy did improve, although the reasons for its improvement had little to do with the government. Churchill's resignation after a series of strokes in 1955 was followed by Eden's accession to the prime ministership and another general election, won by the Conservatives.

Eden's prime ministership was destroyed by the most high-profile milestone in the decline of the British Empire after the independence of India and Pakistan: the Suez Crisis of 1956. The root of the crisis lay in British control of the Suez Canal, a vital waterway for international trade. Along with France, Britain controlled the majority of shares in the Suez Canal Company. Egypt, which had been dominated by the British while nominally independent, had thrown off British indirect control and was now led by the military officer and Arab nationalist Gamal Abdel Nasser (1918–70). Nasser nationalized the Suez Canal Company on July 26, 1956.

Eden seems to have thought of Nasser as another Mussolini or Hitler, believing that if the Egyptian ruler was not stopped from seizing the canal, he would continue expansionist policies. The ludicrousness of this comparison—Nasser did not control a small fraction of Nazi Germany's military power—discredited Eden and the British case, already questioned as a reassertion of an increasingly disreputable imperialism.

In October and November 1956 Egypt was invaded by an alliance of Egypt's enemy Israel, Britain, and France. Despite the attack's military success, it provoked worldwide condemnation as a reassertion of colonialism. The Americans, who had not been informed of the British and French plan and had no fondness for Britain's imperial tradition, shared this condemnation. U.S. president Dwight Eisenhower (1953–61), who had worked closely with British generals as Allied commander in World War II, strongly opposed the Suez adventure. The combination of American pressure and a run on the pound forced British withdrawal, and the whole Suez affair came to be a gigantic embarrassment for the Eden government; Eden was eventually forced to resign the following year. The fact that the British withdrew without informing their French allies added to the distrust between the two powers.

The Suez affair is often seen as the definitive end of Britain's career as a global power (and France's as well). With a few exceptions, Britain's future military ventures abroad would be as a leading member of a U.S.-led alliance rather than as an independent power.

The Age of the Harolds

British politics between the Suez Crisis and 1970 were dominated by two Harolds: Harold Macmillan (1894–1986) of the Conservative Party and Harold Wilson (1916–95) of Labour. In their public presentation the Harolds fit the stereotypes of their parties. Harold Macmillan was an aristocratic and brave ex-army officer, while Harold Wilson, the academically brilliant son of a Yorkshire chemist and a schoolteacher, presented himself as a man of the people who wore a workingman's raincoat, supported, Huddersfield Town, his local football team, and loved simple British fare.

Macmillan was prime minister from 1957 to 1963. He came to power after the Suez Crisis, outmaneuvering Eden, discredited by the crisis and in poor health, and Rab Butler (1902–82), his rival for the succession. As prime minister, Macmillan was the beneficiary of British economic recovery in the 1950s. In 1959 he led the Conservatives to victory in the general election under the slogan "Life's Better under the Conservatives," and he was frequently associated with the phrase "You've never had it so good." Macmillan's governments practiced what he called "One Nation" Conservatism, maintaining the welfare state Labour had built and aspiring to maintain a high level of employment. In foreign affairs he tried mending the rift with the United States over the Suez Crisis; his good personal relationship with President Eisenhower, with whom he had worked in North Africa during the war, was useful in the process, but he was considerably less successful with Eisenhower's successor, John F. Kennedy (1917–1963). He also presided over the early stages of Africa's decolonization. Macmillan's "Winds of Change" speech in 1960 is often considered an important moment in British public acceptance that the African empire was going the way of the Indian.

Macmillan's government was hurt, if not destroyed, by the Profumo scandal. John Profumo (1915–2006) was a Conservative politician and junior minister who was having an affair with a high-class prostitute named Christine Keeler (b. 1942). One of Keeler's other clients was a naval attaché at the Soviet embassy, Yevgeny Ivanov (1926–94). When this question was touched on in the House of Commons, the married Profumo denied any improper relations with Keeler. Lying to Parliament was an unforgivable offence, and it was for this, not for the affair or for any leaking of national secrets (there was never any evidence that any secrets had been leaked) that Profumo was forced to resign from the Commons and the government. Harold Macmillan was blamed for his apparent obliviousness to the whole affair. He also faced health problems, which, due to inaccurate diagnoses, he believed worse than they actually were. He resigned on October 18, 1963, and was replaced by a caretaker government under the Scottish aristocrat Sir Alec Douglas-Home (1903–95). Sir Alec was a member of the House of Lords as the 14th earl of Home at the time, and he had to resign his peerage and run in a by-election for the Commons in order to serve as prime minister; the idea of a prime minister serving in the Lords was no longer acceptable, despite many precedents in British history. To date Douglas-Home is the last prime minister to come from the Lords.

Despite resigning his title, Douglas-Home was a juicy target for Labour campaigners as an elitist aristocrat. Labour won the general election of 1964 by a very thin margin, ending up with 317 seats to the Conservatives' 304. Labour's leader, Harold Wilson, was one of the few postwar prime ministers to serve nonconsecutive terms. His first and longer prime ministership lasted from 1964 to 1970. Like most Labour prime ministers, Wilson, who had risen through his knowledge of statistics, had little interest in the socialist agenda of advancing workers' or even public control of industry. He was more interested in

BRITISH SCIENCE

Britons could take consolation from their economic and political decline in the fact that British science in the late 1940s and 1950s remained vital and innovative. In 1951 John Cockroft (1897–1967) and Ernest Walton (1903–95) received the Nobel Prize in physics, a recognition of their work on nuclear acceleration in the 1930s. Perhaps the best-known British scientific triumph in this period was the identification of the structure of the organic molecule DNA. This work, which took place in Cambridge, was credited to Maurice Wilkins (1916–2004) and Rosalind Franklin (1920–58), and to the partnership of the British scientist Francis Crick (1916–2004) and the American James Watson (b. 1928). In an ominous note, however, the British scientists Ernst Chain (1906–79) and Howard Florey (1898–1968), who had shared the Nobel Prize in 1945 for the development of penicillin, had to go to the United States to put the new antibiotic into mass production, as Britain lacked sufficient capital. By the end of the 1950s, C. P. Snow's famous lectures on the "Two Cultures" suggested that Britain had failed to appreciate its scientists and was in the grip of an essentially reactionary humanistic culture.

presenting Labour as a technological, modernizing force by fostering innovation—"the white heat of the technological revolution" (quoted in Pearce and Stewart 1992, 485)—as he famously phrased it, and by curbing the power of the trade unions. (Wilson has been credited with a number of phrases that became clichés; the most famous is "a week is a long time in politics.") His agenda of technological and industrial modernization had some successes but failed to reignite the lagging British economy.

The Cultural Revolts of the 1960s and 1970s

Britain in the 1960s and 1970s saw the rise of a number of new cultural and political movements, often challenging what they saw as the established order (though usually not the welfare state specifically). Youth asserted itself musically and culturally in the 1960s, as did a new youth cohort in the 1970s. A more diverse and multiracial Britain brought new voices. The women's movement reached Britain, as did newly assertive movements of sexual minorities. The very idea of Britain was challenged by Scottish and Welsh separatists, and the British state was violently assaulted by a revival of Irish nationalism.

Pop Culture

The 1960s saw an astounding renaissance of British popular culture, which had a worldwide impact. Much of this culture built on American culture or other foreign influences, but it also had distinctively British qualities. The greatest examples of this phenomenon were the Beatles, four young men from Liverpool who adapted American rock and roll into a uniquely British sound. Paul McCartney (b. 1942), John Lennon (1940–80), George Harrison (1943–2001), and Ringo Starr (b. 1940) together became the world's most popular pop music phenomenon. Their tour of the United States in 1964 was triumphant, paving the way for numerous other bands—many of them slavish imitators of "England's phenomenal pop combo," as the Beatles were identified on the cover to their first American album, *Meet the Beatles*—such as Herman's Hermits and the Dave Clark Five. The Beatles and the British bands that followed in their wake were referred to collectively in the United States as the "British Invasion" and often credited with revitalizing American rock and roll.

The other leading band of the British Invasion was the Rolling Stones, who had a more blues-influenced style and despite some personnel changes have lasted as a band well into the third millennium.

Other influential British bands of the 1960s and early 1970s included the Who, the Kinks, Pink Floyd, Led Zeppelin, and Roxy Music. Solo British artists included the virtuoso guitarist Eric Clapton (b. 1945) and the "blue-eyed soul" singer Dusty Springfield (real name Mary Isabel Catherine Bernadette O'Brien, 1939–99).

London was a particularly significant cultural center during the 1960s; the city of youth culture was referred to as "Swinging London." In addition to music, it was for the first time regarded as a center of women's fashion when designer Mary Quant (b. 1934) attained international fame as the inventor of the miniskirt (although Quant's claim is disputed), and British model Twiggy became the first supermodel with an impact on culture far beyond just wearing clothes. The television show *The Avengers* and the James Bond films (based on the novels of London-born writer Ian Fleming [1908–64]) added to the image of a youthful, exciting culture. England even won the World Cup, soccer's greatest prize, in 1966.

By the mid-1970s, the earlier British bands had either broken up, like the Beatles, or, in the feeling of many fans, had been co-opted or corrupted by success. The time was ripe for a new and energetic musical youth movement. The most significant form of cultural protest in the second half of the 1970s was punk music. A blast against the conformity of mainstream rock, punk music was loud, aggressive, and musically very simple, lacking the harmony and complex melodies of previously dominant progressive rock groups such as Jethro Tull and Yes. The punk aesthetic was deliberately crude and even disgusting. The leading group of the first wave of punk, the Sex Pistols, sported members with the pseudonyms Sid Vicious (original name John Simon Ritchie, 1957–79) and Johnny Rotten (John Lydon, b. 1956). The Sex Pistols were pure nihilists who went so far as to invoke Nazi imagery in "Belsen was a Gas," mostly for the shock value. Even more controversial was 1977's "God Save the Queen," viewed as a frontal assault on the still-sacrosanct monarchy with its memorable line "There is no future, in England's dreaming." (The assault on the monarchy was particularly relevant, as 1977 was the 25th anniversary of Elizabeth II's ascension to the throne, the object of official celebration.) The Sex Pistols were followed by more political bands, of which the most significant and influential was the Clash (whose first public gig was as an opener for the Sex Pistols), a left-wing group that incorporated Jamaican reggae beats and other influences from Caribbean and black American music. Punk music shocked and horrified many, to the delight of its performers and fans.

The band that did more than any other to inspire British punk, the Sex Pistols (l–r: Johnny Rotten, Glen Matlock, Paul Cook, Steve Jones). (AP Photo)

Immigration and the Beginning of Multiracial Britain

The fall of the British Empire was accompanied by the immigration of people from empire nations to Britain. In some cases these were British settlers, expelled or alienated from the newly independent countries they had settled and generally reassimilated into British life. However, in many other cases the immigrants were indigenous to the colonized areas, and their arrival in Britain posed profound cultural and political challenges.

Another immigrant population comprised those Eastern Europeans, particularly Poles, who were left in Britain by the end of World War II but could not or did not wish to return to their countries, now under communist regimes. Immigration from the Republic of Ireland also continued, particularly after the United States, the preferred destination of most Irish immigrants, changed to a more restrictive immigration policy in the 1950s.

However, it was the dark-skinned immigrants from the colonies and former colonies who attracted the most interest and resentment. The 1948 arrival of the *Empire Windrush,* a ship bringing hundreds of immigrants from Jamaica, is often treated as a founding date for multicultural Britain, although there were already small Caribbean immigrant communities. There were no restrictions on immigration within the empire until 1962, so migration was one solution to the poverty and political turmoil facing British colonies.

The new immigrants attracted hostility, both on purely racial grounds and on the fear that they would be a source of cheap labor, undercutting workers' wages. Sir Oswald Mosely, (1896–1980), the prewar leader of the British Union of Fascists, made an abortive attempt at a political comeback by exploiting racial resentment, running for Parliament from North Kensington in 1959 for the anti-immigrant British Movement; however, he received only 8 percent of the vote. More successful was the Conservative Peter Griffiths (b. 1928), who won a parliamentary seat on an openly racist platform in 1964. The National Front, an amalgamation of British racist and neo-Nazi groups, was founded in 1967.

The first mainstream British politician of eminence to capitalize on anti-immigrant resentment was the Conservative Enoch Powell (1912–98). Powell was a somewhat eccentric figure, better educated and more intellectual than most British politicians but never very successful in politics. He had been heartbroken by the loss of India, which caused him to switch from being a zealous imperialist to becoming a zealous anti-imperialist. His "Rivers of Blood" speech, delivered in Birmingham on April 20, 1968, denounced antiracist legislation as an infringement on personal freedom and warned of a future Britain dominated by racial conflict, like the United States. Powell was removed from the Conservative hierarchy the next day and never served in the cabinet after the speech, but he became a popular figure to many working-class white Britons. His hostility to immigration helped attract many of them to the Conservative Party and made him particularly hated among immigrants and British communities of color.

Under Harold Wilson, the British government started to establish agencies and laws to combat racism and integrate the immigrant communities into British life. The 1965 Race Relations Act forbade discrimination and racial incitement and set up a Race Relations Board; it was the first in a succession of acts bearing that name. Subsequent Race Relations Acts would become law in 1968 and 1976. The effect of these acts was limited, but they did establish the principle of nondiscrimination.

Immigrants formed their own communities, with businesses, pubs, restaurants, and places of worship. Relations between the native Britons and the new immigrant communities were often distant, even when not hostile. Relations between immigrant communities and the virtually all-white police force were a particularly sore spot in many cities. Racially motivated street violence, often carried out by skinheads or football (soccer) fans, was also on the rise.

British Feminism

After the vote had been won for women in the early 20th century, the feminist movement in Britain virtually disappeared. But feminism revived in the 1960s as part of the tendency of suppressed populations to assert themselves and under the influence of American feminism.

The Labour government of Harold Wilson saw the rise to prominence of the most important female party politician to that time: Barbara Castle (1910–2002). Although Castle identified herself politically as a socialist first and a woman second, she successfully shepherded the passing of a 1970 bill forbidding pay discrimination against women. The type of feminism Castle represented—one that maneuvered in a male-dominated polity for specific goals, often economic in nature—was challenged in the 1970s by a more radical feminism aimed at the foundations of male supremacy and often more interested in issues such as domestic abuse rather than equal pay. The Australian immigrant Germaine Greer (b. 1939) became one of Britain's—and the world's—leading feminist intellectuals; her *The Female Eunuch* (1970) became a best seller. Greer critiqued a broad range of social phenomena, from misogyny to the suppression of women's sexuality to constricting bras. *The Female Eunuch* was a powerful consciousness-raising text, drawing many women to feminism. Greer went on to have a long and varied intellectual career, sooner or later outraging just about everyone, including feminists.

Gay and Lesbian Britons

The sexual revolution of the 1960s was marked by the increasing activism and visibility of sexual minorities. Sexual minorities, particularly gay men, often faced a bleak existence in postwar Britain. Homosexuality was regarded as a mental illness, a sin, and a crime. Sex between men was illegal (although lesbian sex was not), and police frequently raided the pubs and public restrooms used by gay men to meet others for sex. Blackmail was common: An arrest for homosexuality had destroyed the career of Alan Turing (1912–54), the great computer scientist, and led to his suicide two years later.

The Wolfenden Committee, an assembly of what the British call "the great and good"—persons of established reputations and establishment connections—had convened in 1954 and suggested that homosexuality was not a mental disease. The committee had recommended the decriminalization of homosexuality, but its report, published in 1957, had produced little actual change. The hidden world of British homosexuality began to cautiously reveal itself with the founding of the London periodical *Gay News* in 1962. The key legislative change was the Sexual Offences Act of 1967, which exempted from prosecution sexual activities between no more than two men over the age of 21. (The age of consent for heterosexual sex remained 16.) The act applied only to England and Wales; homosexuality was not decriminalized in Scotland until 1980. Despite the act's fairly narrow scope, it was widely regarded as a positive development for gay men.

By the 1970s, British gay activism had become more flamboyant and less willing to accept the terms of debate offered by the straight world. The Gay Liberation Front (GLF) took a more militant and revolutionary attitude than previous gay and lesbian groups. Despite some high-profile activities, the GLF fell apart due to tensions between men and women, different political tendencies, and the London leadership and provincial branches. It left a number of successor activist organizations.

CORBETT V. CORBETT

Although cross-dressing is a staple for many British comedians and an integral part of the Christmas theatrical ritual of the panto (pantomime), life for transsexual and transgendered Britons has often been grim. Although not the first, the most high-profile transsexual in postwar Britain was April Ashley, a male-to-female transsexual who became the subject of a celebrated court case. Ashley, born into a working-class family as George Jamieson in 1935, had had sexual-reassignment surgery in France in 1960 and married the aristocratic Arthur Corbett (1919–93) in 1963. In 1970, Corbett had the marriage annulled on the grounds that Ashley, despite her surgery and the fact that she lived as a woman, was still a man. The case of *Corbett v. Corbett* was a disaster for British transsexuals, essentially preventing legal changes of sex until legislation in 2004.

Opposition to the Cultural Revolts

The rebellious behavior of youths, feminist women, and gays and lesbians did not go unopposed. Lumped together with pornography and sexual freedom under the banner of the "permissive society," they were attacked by populist conservatives, church leaders, and church-affiliated organizations. The best-known leader of this cultural reaction was Mary Whitehouse (1910–2001), who focused on popular media, particularly television, combating programming she considered objectionable through letter-writing campaigns and the courts. In 1965 she founded the National Viewers and Listeners Association, now known as Mediawatch UK. Whitehouse became a widespread figure of ridicule, particularly on satirical BBC television shows.

The Rise of Scottish and Welsh Separatism

Although some Scottish and Welsh people had always resented English domination of Great Britain, the rise of organized nationalist movements with a broad appeal was a phenomenon of the 1960s. Previously, leading Welsh and Scottish politicians such as Aneurin Bevan had been more interested in acquiring power on a national level than creating separate institutions. Welsh and Scottish nationalists tended to finish at the bottom of the poll in parliamentary elections through the 1950s.

While the Scots could look back on Scotland's history as an independent kingdom that had only ended in 1707, Welsh history showed division between numerous principalities, only rarely united and never for long. Consequently, while the Scottish National Party (SNP) always had a political agenda focused on the restoration of Scottish independence, the Welsh nationalist party, Plaid Cymru, was more focused on the preservation of the Welsh language and the advancement of Welsh cultural institutions. Many Welsh were particularly offended by the flooding of the Tryweryn valley in 1957 and 1958 and the displacement of its Welsh community in order to provide a reservoir of water for the English city of Liverpool (although Liverpool had a large Welsh population).

A principal cause for Welsh nationalism was the disrespect shown the Welsh language by the English-speaking government and national media. This was especially menacing because fewer and fewer people were learning Welsh as a first language, and an increasing number of English people were settling in Wales. The vacation homes of English people in Wales were the frequent targets of arson. Other targets included post offices, Inland Revenue (tax) offices, and television broadcasting antennas. The English names of communities were removed or defaced from road signs. (This terrorism extended only to property damage.)

Regardless of the dramatic actions and manifestos of these nationalist movements, they proved less able to gather long-term electoral support. Many nationalist firebrands were able to win election to local councils, but they proved unable to do the hard footslogging and constituency work of successful professional politicians. When referenda for devolution—the setting up of Welsh and Scottish assemblies with limited power—were put before the people on March 1, 1979, the Welsh referendum was defeated overwhelmingly while the Scottish one passed, but not by the large margin needed to go into effect.

The Irish Troubles in Britain

Following the establishment of the Irish Free State in 1922, Ireland had played a virtually negligible role in British politics. Northern Ireland, although part of the United Kingdom, had its own political system dominated by its own parties and by sectarian issues that had little resonance in the United Kingdom as a whole. This began to change with "the Troubles," starting in 1969.

The Catholic population of the north, inspired by the American Civil Rights movement, began to challenge peacefully the brutally repressive Protestant Northern Irish regime. The regime reacted harshly, eventually leading to a revival of militant Irish Catholic nationalism in the provisional Irish Republican Army, also known as the IRA or the Provos. The British government intervened violently; British troops killed 13 civil rights marchers on January 30, 1972—a date known as "Bloody Sunday." The British decision in 1972 to suspend the Northern Irish government and occupy the province militarily proved a disaster; in the ensuing violence, the police and army suffered three times more casualties than did the IRA.

The IRA, seeing the British government as the main enemy, launched a campaign of terror in England. (Because the Welsh and Scots were viewed as fellow oppressed Celts, the IRA avoided attacks on Scotland and Wales.) Among the most horrifying terrorist acts were the 1974 pub bombings in Guildford, which killed five and injured even more. The attacked pubs had been targeted because they were off-duty hangouts for British military personnel. After the bombings, three men and one woman were arrested and charged with the crime. Known as the Guildford Four, they were convicted despite a lack of evidence of guilt

229

aside from confessions made to the police, exacted under torture and fraudulently manipulated. Despite growing doubts about the verdict, the Guildford Four were not vindicated and released from prison until 1989. The IRA attacks led to growing hostility and suspicion of Irish and Irish-descended people in Britain.

Britain in the 1970s

By the 1970s the British could no longer deny the reality of economic decline. The prime ministers of the decade were the Conservative Edward Heath (1916–2005) and Labour's James Callaghan (1912–2005). Heath, prime minister from 1970 to 1974, was a different kind of Conservative from his predecessors, the aristocrats Churchill, Eden, Macmillan, and Douglas-Home. The son of a carpenter and a maid, he had risen by sheer intellectual ability. His rise was widely believed to herald a more modern, meritocratic conservatism as opposed to the old conservativism based on hereditary class.

Despite Heath's great abilities and enormous capacity for hard work, his government proved unsuccessful. The most pressing problem was the economy. Britain's balance of payments remained unfavorable, inflation was becoming a serious problem, and unemployment was growing. The general sense that Britain was falling behind economically was often blamed on the trade unions, now generally seen not as warriors for a better life for the workers but as reactionaries defending an obsolescent economic order and going on strike at the drop of a hat. The government faced long and divisive strikes by the National Union of Miners in 1972 and 1974. Other problems included rising crime and a general feeling of dissatisfaction with the postwar settlement on both the left and the right.

Heath's government was responsible for two revolutionary changes in British life. In 1973 Britain finally entered the European Common Market. The move provoked little enthusiasm among Britons. Even less popular was the redrawing of the British administrative map, which for many of the counties meant the end of their thousand-year-long histories as administrative and political units when they were replaced by larger and more uniform units. Heath's government was voted out of power in 1974, and Harold Wilson returned to 10 Downing Street, the home of the prime minister. Shortly after the fall of his government, Heath was overthrown as Conservative leader by Margaret Thatcher (b. 1925), who had been minister of education in Heath's government. Under Thatcher, the Conservatives would move, slowly at first, away from "one-nation" conservatism to a much more free-market and union-busting approach.

Wilson gave way as prime minister to James Callaghan in 1976, probably because of impaired health. Wilson and Callaghan faced many of the same problems as Heath, with different methods but little better success. Britain suffered keenly from the overall world economic slowdown of the late 1970s. In 1976 the government was forced to seek a loan from the International Monetary Fund, available only on humiliating terms involving large cuts in government expenditure. The ultimate expression of trade union power, and the great crisis for Callaghan's government, was the "winter of discontent" in 1979. Wave after wave of strikes from public- and private-sector employees greatly inconvenienced many people and led the British public to question whether the government or the trade unions were the real leaders of Britain. The election that year returned the Conservatives to power. But the Conservatives who assumed control of the government in 1979 were very different from the ones who had lost it in 1974.

10

A HOUSE DIVIDED
(1979–2009)

The period from 1979 to 2009 saw a radical and partially successful challenge to the welfare-state consensus of the mid-20th century. It was also a time of continuity at the top. While the 34 years between 1945 and 1979 had produced nine prime ministers (including the two times Harold Wilson served), the 30 years between 1979 and 2009 saw only four. Party power in Parliament was also continuous: Power only changed hands once during this period, from the Conservatives to Labour in 1997. The late 20th century also witnessed a reassertion of British power abroad, while the divisions within the country—between the rich, the middle class, and the poor; native Britons and immigrants; whites and people of color; England and the Celtic Fringe nations of Wales and Scotland; and different religious positions—grew sharper.

Margaret Thatcher and Thatcherism
The parliamentary election of 1979, held in the shadow of disruptive strikes and economic slowdown, was a rejection of Prime Minister James Callaghan's Labour Party and a strong victory for the Conservatives. The new prime minister, Margaret Thatcher (b. 1925), was the first woman to lead a major British political party and the first woman prime minister. (Thatcher's husband, Denis Thatcher, remained in the background during her prime ministership but was widely mocked anyway.) She was also the most ideological prime minister since Clement Atlee's postwar Labour government. Thatcherism was a conservatism willing to break with the postwar social compact using an aggressive, confrontational attitude to the unions, hostility to state ownership, and plans to make substantial cuts in the welfare state (but not completely abolish it). As a movement, Thatcherism was bigger than Thatcher alone. Its intellectual leader was Sir Keith Joseph (1918–94), Thatcher's close

Early in her career as prime minister, Margaret Thatcher met U.S. president Jimmy Carter.
(Marion S. Trilosko for *US News and World Report*)

friend and ally who headed the Centre for Policy Studies, a think tank founded in 1974 to promote free-market policies. Thatcherism also had followers outside the United Kingdom, as part of a global turn to the right in the late 1970s and 1980s.

Thatcherism was precipitated by the global economic slowdown after 1973, which brought into question the benefits of the welfare state and the price of those benefits to society. National competitiveness, which Thatcher claimed to be able to restore, was a particularly important concern in Britain after decades of relative decline and serious difficulties with productivity. Thatcherites believed that the high taxes necessary to support the welfare state and the high wages demanded by British unions were making British businesses less competitive. Thatcherism can be seen as a movement toward making British society more "American"—competitive, meritocratic, and self-interested. Thatcher's famous statement that "There is no society, only individuals" (quoted in Hobsbawm 1994, 337) was seen as an attack on the intellectual basis of the welfare state.

The electoral basis of Thatcherism was in the English lower-middle classes, small businesspeople (the class from which Thatcher herself came), and self-employed professionals. Thatcherism was often seen as a revolution within British conservatism, challenging the old elite, moderate conservatives often from the upper classes, and identified by Thatcher as "wets." The "wets" in Thatcher's first cabinet were largely legacies from the previous Conservative administration of Edward Heath. Throughout her tenure, Thatcher promoted a new breed of tougher, more ideological conservatism. The Thatcherite victory was a mark of Britain's changing demographics. The traditional working class, Labour's electoral bastion, was a numerically declining sector. The trade unions, the financial and organizational backbone of Labour, had increasingly alienated members of the middle class and even the working class.

Despite Thatcher's successes, there were limits on what she could accomplish, caused by the popularity of some welfare state functions and the continuing, though waning, strength of the trade unions. Even Thatcher was never able to suggest the abolition of the National Health Service (NHS) and its replacement by privatized medicine on the American model, although she cut NHS resources and moved toward privatization as much as she could.

In addition to Thatcherite economics, Thatcherism also presented itself as having a moral and philosophical component. Thatcher emphasized traditional values, or, as she sometimes called them, Victorian values. These included self-reliance, the power of hard work, and adherence to the traditional family. Although Thatcher herself was a Christian and a member of the Church of England, her calls to return to traditional values had little effect on British secularism. Thatcher's traditionalism also had the paradoxical result that Britain's first woman prime minister did little or nothing to advance either feminist causes or women within the Conservative Party or the government. Most British feminists saw Thatcher as an enemy, as did many politically active gays and lesbians.

In foreign policy Thatcherism was strongly anticommunist and emphasized the "special relationship" with the United States. When Ronald Reagan became the U.S. president in 1981, the personal connection between the U.S. president and the British prime minister was stronger than it had been since the days of Harold Macmillan and Dwight Eisenhower in the 1950s. Like Reagan, Thatcher won admiration from Russian and Eastern European dissidents, but given Britain's weaker position internationally, anticommunism was much less ideologically and politically central for Thatcherism than it was for Reaganism. One of Thatcher's most important international contributions was the role she played in the warming of Soviet-Western relations in the late 1980s under Soviet general secretary Mikhail Gorbachev. Her description of

Gorbachev as "a man we can do business with" (quoted in Pilger 2005, 289) helped win Gorbachev some credibility on the European and American right.

The Falklands War and the General Election of 1983

The most dramatic event of Margaret Thatcher's first term was the Falklands War. The Falklands are a chain of islands in the South Atlantic off the coast of Argentina. Argentina, which refers to the islands as the Malvinas, has claimed them, but they are a British colony whose population is of British descent and loyal to Britain. In March 1982, Argentine forces attacked and occupied the islands. The Argentine military dictator, General Leopoldo Galtieri (1926–2003), apparently thought that Britain would not respond, and a quick diplomatic and military triumph over a waning empire would bolster his faltering regime. Despite warnings from British naval personnel, the attack took the Thatcher government by surprise.

Taking the islands back presented many difficulties. The Argentines were fighting far closer to home and, lacking Britain's continuing global defense commitments, could commit a larger portion of their forces. The islands themselves were inhospitable, with few roads or developed harbors. American support was at first uncertain, as some of the neo-conservatives around Reagan believed it was more important to support Galtieri to bolster anticommunist forces in South America than to uphold the British Empire. However, the United States eventually came to support Britain in the conflict.

Britain began preparations for war shortly after news of the Argentine occupation reached London. After diplomatic efforts to remove the Argentine forces failed, the Falklands War began on April 2, 1982. The idea that Britain was once again resisting an aggressive dictator, as in World War II, helped make the conflict popular. Britain won, driving Argentine forces off the islands and declaring hostilities over on June 20. Victory was not without controversy, however. A British submarine sank an Argentine cruiser, the *Belgrano*, with the loss of 323 lives, about half of the total Argentine casualties in the war. Although the attack was on a legitimate military target, some claimed that since the *Belgrano* was outside the "exclusion zone" proclaimed by the Royal Navy and was heading away from the Falklands, it should not have been attacked. The war resulted in the fall of the Galtieri government and eventually the reestablishment of Argentine democracy. Argentina continues to claim the islands, although it has renounced the use of force in settling the dispute.

British triumph is widely credited with bolstering support for Thatcher, helping her win an overwhelming victory in the 1983 parliamentary election. Part of the credit for Thatcher's victory, however, must go to weak opposition. The Labour Party was torn by a struggle between leftists led by Tony Benn (b. 1925), who believed that the party had lost power because it had failed to carry out a socialist agenda, and Labour rightists who believed that the party was in danger of becoming too radical for the electorate. Many also feared that local branches of the Labour Party were being taken over by far-left radicals. Labour's manifesto was uncompromising in its support for nuclear disarmament, moving toward socialism, and higher taxes. Gerald Kaufman (b. 1930), a leader of the party's right wing, referred to it as "the longest suicide note in history" (quoted in Dale 2000, 4).

The leader of the Labour Party, Michael Foot (b. 1913), was an old leftist and intellectual, a follower and admirer of the Welsh Labour radical Aneurin Bevan (1897–1960), whose biography he had written. The aged Foot, who had first become active in politics when he denounced appeasement before World War II, seemed like a figure from another time. Labour was also weakened by the secession of four of its leaders: Roy Jenkins (1920–2003), Shirley Williams (b. 1930), David Owen (b. 1938), and William Rodgers (b. 1928). Disturbed by what they viewed as Labour's turn to the left, the "Gang of Four" formed the Social Democratic Party (SDP), with the declared goal of promoting policies similar to those of the social democratic parties of the European continent. The SDP was always more popular among the media than among the British people, but for a time there was talk of its replacing a Labour Party many viewed as discredited by leftism and failure in office. (The Social Democrats allied and eventually merged with the Liberals to form the Liberal Democrats.)

Thatcher and the Miners' Union

A great challenge to Thatcherism was the coal miners' strike in 1984 and 1985. The National Union of Miners (NUM) was one of the strongest and most radical of British unions, but mining was becoming increasingly marginal and obsolescent. The issue in the strike was pit closures—the closing of mines the government viewed as unprofitable—which devastated entire communities that were essentially left without an economy.

The strike was widely portrayed as a personal duel between Thatcher and the NUM president, Arthur Scargill (b. 1938). Scargill was a hard leftist who shared Thatcher's love of confrontation. The miners' strike initially drew support from miners and their families across the country, and for a while it looked as if Thatcher might have to back down. However, the government's careful preparation, the stockpiling of fuel, and a mild winter kept the strike from turning into a national crisis. The government also employed harsh and well-organized police tactics against mass picketers. Scargill's leadership was both a source of energy for the strikers and a handicap. He had taken the miners into the strike without a strike vote and made it difficult to cooperate with other unions. The Labour Party, which after the 1983 election had selected the Welshman Neil Kinnock (b. 1942) as its leader, was also ambivalent. Kinnock, the son of a coal miner and widely regarded as on the left of the Labour Party before his elevation, supported the strike's aims but was bitterly critical of its timing and tactics. He did not hide his contempt for what he regarded as the poor planning of the NUM leadership, who had not even rallied all miners in support. Miners in some parts of the country, such as Nottinghamshire, kept working throughout the strike. Eventually the miners backed down, and over the next few years many more pits would be closed, devastating large areas of England and Wales. The once-fearsome miners' unions were finished as a force in British politics, and so was militant trade unionism.

Northern Ireland and Irish Terrorism

The stalemate in Northern Ireland and the Provisional IRA's campaign of terror in England continued throughout the Thatcher years. Irish nationalist terrorism had already come close to Thatcher personally. The Irish National Liberation Army (INLA), an offshoot of the IRA, had killed one of her closest advisers, Airey Neave (1916–79), with a car bomb. On October 12, 1984, the IRA got even closer, bombing a hotel in Brighton where Thatcher, her husband, and many leading Conservative politicians were staying for the annual Conservative Party conference. Thatcher and her husband were uninjured, but five people were killed and many more permanently injured. The conference continued as scheduled, and Thatcher's speech the next morning was widely covered. Her popularity soared in the aftermath of the attack, while the IRA hinted at further attacks.

Thatcher began to move toward formalizing cooperation against terrorism with the government of largely Catholic Ireland. The Hillsborough Agreement of 1985 between the United Kingdom and Ireland provided for regular consultation on security matters. The agreement itself was fairly innocuous, but by providing a role for the Dublin government in Northern Irish affairs, it set off a firestorm among the Protestant Ulster Unionists, 15 of whose MPs resigned their seats. It also made Thatcher look like a more conciliatory leader on Irish affairs, important in Britain's relations with the United States.

Core and Periphery under Thatcherism

The Conservative Party has traditionally been the party of England, especially rural southern England. However, the Thatcher period saw this characteristic reach an extreme. The Conservatives virtually disappeared as a political force in Scotland and Wales, and throughout much of northern England as well. The politics of Scotland and Wales were essentially divided among Labour; the Liberals; and the nationalist parties, Scotland's Scottish National Party and Wales's Plaid Cymru. Scots were particularly concerned with the decline of Scottish industry and the Conservative government's refusal to help the unemployed Scottish population, while the closing of coal pits devastated huge areas of Wales.

Many parts of northern England shared Scotland's industrial decline and its political alienation from the Conservative government, but the northerners' English identity remained strong, and northern discontent was not expressed in separatist politics. Occasional calls for a "northern assembly" attracted little interest, while the gap between the deindustrializing north and the prosperous Thatcherite heartland of southern and eastern England grew. Conservative support was often identified with a nouveau-riche figure from the southern English county of Essex called Essex Man. (The earliest recorded appearance of the phrase is in the Conservative newspaper, the *Sunday Telegraph,* and dates from 1990 [Oring 2003, 69].) Essex Man loved Thatcher's low income taxes (although other taxes went up in the Thatcher administrations) and had a devil-takes-the-hindmost attitude to society and to Britain's deprived areas. Essex Man also owned a newly privatized council house. Although Essex Man was something of a myth, no one believed that Thatcherism had much appeal to Yorkshire Man, Selkirk Man, or Glamorganshire Man.

The great exception to Conservative dominance in southern England was London, where Thatcher faced some of her most vociferous opposition. The leading London politician of the 1980s was Ken Livingstone (b. 1945), an ardent leftist known as Red Ken. In 1981 Livingstone was elected leader of the Greater London Council, the local government authority for London and its surrounding area. An unusual combination of radical, hardball politician, and effective city manager, the irrepressible Livingstone had become one of Britain's most controversial politicians. His most stunning act was to extend an official welcome to London to the leaders of Sinn Féin, the political wing of the Provisional IRA. The meeting did not come off in London, as the Sinn Féin leaders were forbidden from entering Britain, but Livingstone went to Northern Ireland to meet them, attracting condemnation from a wide spectrum of British opinion.

Despite efforts by Conservatives and his numerous enemies in the Labour Party, Livingstone's position in London proved unassailable through conventional means. In 1986 the exasperated Conservative government forced through a dissolution of the Greater London Council (along with other municipal councils), effectively depriving London of central government and eliminating Livingstone's job. The government of London fell back on the individual boroughs. Livingstone was back the next year as a Labour MP, but he was much less influential as one of many backbench Labour MPs than he had been as the ruler of London.

Livingstone was the most spectacular example of the takeover of many metropolitan governments by the left, stigmatized in the Conservative popular press as the "loony left." Another controversial figure was Derek Hatton (b. 1948), the militant deputy leader of Liverpool City Council. Hatton was expelled from the Labour Party in 1986 for belonging to Militant Tendency, an activist group that had infiltrated many local Labour Party organizations. Opposition to Militant Tendency and the "loony left" was central to Neil Kinnock's tenure as leader of the party (1983–92).

Thatcherism and British Culture in the 1980s

Margaret Thatcher divided British culture as she did British politics. While previous prime ministers had been mocked or attacked in popular culture, few since David Lloyd George had attracted the venomous hatred that Thatcher did. In 1980, only a year after she took power, the Beat, a two-tone band including black and white Britons, had a hit with "Stand Down Margaret," calling on the prime minister to resign. Thatcher continued to be a prominent target in pop songs and literature throughout her prime ministership and long after.

Few of Thatcher's actions were more infuriating to many of Britain's cultural leaders than Clause 28. Clause 28, or Section 28, was part of the Local Government Act of 1988. It forbade local authorities from

THE HILLSBOROUGH DISASTER

Although violence and overcrowding had long been problems at British soccer (called *football* in Britain) stadiums, the greatest disaster in the history of British soccer occurred in 1989. Ninety-six fans of the Liverpool Football Club were killed in a stampede of supporters trying to get into Hillsborough Stadium in Sheffield, where Liverpool was playing a semifinal in the contest for the FA Cup, the championship of English soccer. The subsequent official report on the disaster was known as the Taylor Report after Lord Chief Justice Peter Taylor (1930–1997), who conducted the enquiry and placed much of the blame on poor police work. Since the Taylor Report appeared, new British stadiums have followed its recommendation of eliminating areas for fans to stand, and older stadiums have been remodeled into all-seated layouts.

"promoting homosexuality" and schools from "teaching . . . the acceptability of homosexuality as a pretended family relationship," although the application to schools was unclear. No one was ever actually successfully prosecuted for violating it, but the law had a chilling effect, leading to the closing of gay and lesbian student groups. The impetus for the law did not come from Thatcher but from grassroots conservatives concerned about AIDS (the first recorded Briton to die from AIDS was a man named Terry Higgins, on July 4, 1982) and the circulation of pro-gay materials, including children's books, by local councils. Section 28 also led to the founding of many new gay and lesbian political associations and lobbying groups.

Not all opposition to Thatcherism came from the left and marginalized groups. She also faced opposition from the established churches of England and Scotland as well as other Christian denominations. To many Britons, Thatcherite individualism and radical capitalism often seemed soulless as well as heartless.

The Fall of Thatcher

Although Thatcher was widely disliked in her last few years in office, it was increasing hostility among the leaders of the Conservative Party that proved her ultimate downfall. One fatal issue was the imposition of a new tax, to be leveled without regard for the ability to pay. The government called it the community charge, but it was widely referred to as a poll tax and compared to the poll tax that had ignited the Peasants' Revolt in the 14th century. The tax was imposed in Scotland in 1989 and in England and Wales in 1990, and in all areas it led to mass protests. The Scots, already strongly anti-Thatcher, were particularly unenthusiastic about being used as the guinea pigs for the new tax. The Thatcher government also went after the "third rail" of British politics, the National Health Service, proposing to allow hospitals to opt out of it, a suggestion that failed. The European Union (formerly the Common Market) was also looming larger, with the single market planned to debut in 1992, and Thatcher had never been very skillful in European politics. With the economy in doldrums and Thatcher's friend and ally Reagan retiring from the U.S. presidency in 1989, Thatcherism seemed more radical and less successful.

Conservative leaders saw that Thatcher's increasing unpopularity posed a threat to Conservative continuation in office. Consequently, she faced challenges in leadership elections at the annual meetings of the Conservative Party. In 1989 an obscure backbencher, Sir Anthony Meyer (1920–2004), won 33 votes running against Thatcher as an advocate of closer ties to Europe; this was nowhere close to victory but a large number in an election against a sitting prime minister. The following year saw a stronger, better-organized challenge, as increasing inflation, higher interest rates, and an economic down-turn seemed to threaten the survival of Conservative government. Thatcher's opponent, Michael Heseltine (b. 1933), won 152 votes to Thatcher's 202, leaving Thatcher just short of the majority and losing the confidence of the Conservative elite. On November 22, 1990, she announced her decision to withdraw from the election. The Thatcher era had ended, though hers had been the longest prime ministership in the 20th century.

Globalization and British Society in the 1980s and 1990s

Britain in the 1980s and 1990s continued to become a more diverse society, particularly in the big cities. Immigrants tended to cluster in those areas where the demand for labor was high. Although certain neighborhoods attracted a high proportion of immigrants, few British cities displayed the high degree of racial segregation characteristic of American cities. Chinese restaurants and Indian and Pakistani take-aways, often serving a combination of South Asian or Middle-Eastern–based fast food (such as the doner kebab) and traditional English fare (such as fish and chips) became ubiquitous in England, extending beyond the large cities into smaller communities, similar to the more formal Indian restaurants.

Asian and other immigrant communities continued to expand, and eventually each developed into distinctively British subcultures. Generational conflicts between conservative first-immigration immigrants and their Briticized children emerged as a common theme in literature and film. New, hybrid identities evolved: The Black British—black people whose ancestors came from the Caribbean or Africa—now defined themselves as a British community, albeit a marginalized and oppressed one. Successful Black British writers and intellectuals who emerged in the 1980s and 1990s include the academic theorist Paul Gilroy (b. 1956) and the novelist Zadie Smith (b. 1975). The Notting Hill Carnival, taking place over two days in August and dedicated to the cultures of London's Caribbean immigrants, became Britain's largest carnival and one of the largest in the world, attracting more than a million visitors in some years.

Despite many immigrant successes, people of color continued to face discrimination in many areas of British life. Although there were efforts to recruit members of ethnic minorities for the police, relations

Novelist Zadie Smith is one of the most prominent of the new multicultural wave of British authors. (AP Photo/Sang Tan)

with law enforcement remained a sore point. Tension between Afro-Caribbeans and the police contributed to a number of riots such as those in the largely black London neighborhood of Brixton in 1981, 1985, and 1995.

Although immigration from countries of the former British Empire received the most publicity, there was also substantial immigration to the United Kingdom from continental Europe. The creation of the European Union eliminated barriers to immigration among the European countries, and many poor Eastern Europeans migrated to the West. Poles were particularly well represented among European immigrants. The Republic of Ireland was also a continuing source of immigrants to Britain.

The role of immigrants in Britain continues to be controversial to this day and has led to both official multiculturalism and political racism. Immigrants have organized into political pressure groups, usually allied with the Labour Party, that have elected members of minorities to Parliament and local office. Official multiculturalism is expressed in the passage of laws against racial discrimination and incitement to racial hatred. However, despite their official endorsements of racial equality and diversity, racism plays a role in the big parties. Political racism is not exclusively associated with the right, and not with all the right: Prime Minister Thatcher liked to present herself as the defender of the hardworking immigrant family against confiscatory taxes. Both parties have on occasion taken stands against further immigration and asylum seekers.

The most important racist party is the British National Party (BNP), a slicker successor to the old National Front. The BNP's platform includes the repatriation of nonwhite immigrants and their descendants. They have elected some local counselors and Members of the European Parliament (MEPs) but never an MP. The BNP and other extreme right-wing political movements are allied with movements of street thugs, often skinheads. Sometimes lethal skinhead and other street violence has been directed against minorities—immigrants, Jews, gays, and lesbians—and each other. Violence is often connected with soccer supporters, some of whom cultivate a reputation as thugs and engage in violent rumbles with supporters of other clubs. There has been an increasing willingness in the third millennium for skinhead gangs to use explicitly Nazi motifs such as swastikas.

Besides immigrants, another ubiquitous cultural presence in modern Britain is the United States. Britain is the European state most closely tied to America by language, culture, and politics, and British political

243

leaders present themselves as Americanophiles much more often than do Continental politicians. Rightists admire the United States's free-market culture of support for business, while leftists, though skeptical of American foreign policy, sometimes invoke it as a more egalitarian society, free of Britain's class distinctions. (Research has shown that the actual social mobility of Britain and the United States is about the same, and even less than that of many continental European countries.) American corporations have dominated the British market, and American media companies have dominated film and been strongly influential in television, literature, and music. American popular-music movements such as hip-hop have attracted legions of British followers and practitioners. Britain has had some reciprocal influence on America, of course, most spectacularly demonstrated by the Harry Potter novels of J. K. Rowling (b. 1965). Rowling's works draw deeply on the English tradition of the public school story, but they have an appeal well beyond Britain and have made her one of the country's richest women.

Secular and Religious Britain

Immigrants have added to Britain's religious diversity. The most obvious examples are those religions historically not practiced in Britain, such as Hinduism and Islam, which have become increasingly prominent features on the physical landscape with the construction of large temples and mosques. However, immigrants have also brought new and different strands of Christianity. The introduction of Pentecostal Christianity to Britain was mostly the work of Caribbean immigrants.

By the start of the 21st century the greatest concern among Britons and British authorities was caused by Britain's growing Muslim communities, mostly immigrants from Pakistan and India. Radical Islamic organizers had become influential in some British Muslim communities. The strength of radical Islam in London led some to dub it "Londonistan," although others argued the phenomenon, though real, was exaggerated. In addition to extra-European issues such as the Palestinian situation, radical Muslim organizations fed on resentment of British racism and some immigrants' fear of being assimilated.

What brought the relationship of the Muslim community to the larger society to the top of the agenda was the Rushdie affair. British writer Salman Rushdie (b. 1947), an immigrant from India, wrote a novel called *The Satanic Verses* (1988), which many Muslims viewed as blaspheming Islam. Furious authorities of the Islamic Republic of Iran issued a fatwa, or decree, calling for Rushdie's death. (This led to the breaking of diplomatic relations between the United Kingdom and

THE REGENTS PARK MOSQUE

The largest mosque in Britain is the Central London mosque, more commonly known as the Regents Park mosque after its location next to London's Regents Park. Although the idea of a mosque to serve London's Muslim population goes back to the early 20th century, work on its construction began only in 1969. The mosque itself is part of a large complex that includes offices, an Islamic library and bookstore, and event space. The worship area can hold more than a thousand worshippers, with the possibility of adding more outside, and it is full to overflowing on Islamic holidays. The mosque's gold dome and 140-foot minaret have made it a London landmark, but there have also been controversies about radical Islamist preachers it has hosted, such as the woman preacher Um Amira, charged with preaching the death penalty for those who leave Islam.

Iran.) Many British Muslims attacked Rushdie verbally, called for a ban on the book, and burned copies of it. A Muslim terrorist, Mustafa Mamoud Maza, died in London in 1989 when a bomb he was preparing, allegedly to kill Rushdie, went off. Riots and demonstrations played out in public as a confrontation between Muslim immigrant communities and the British secular elite, right and left, with intellectuals from Muslim communities caught in the middle. Much of the emergence of the Muslim community as an organized community and interest group in British politics, as opposed to merely a religious and cultural grouping, was associated with the Rushdie affair. Subsequent events continued to bring Rushdie and *The Satanic Verses* back into the headlines. The Iranian fatwa has never been withdrawn, although the Iranian government eventually stated that it would neither help nor hinder attempts to kill Rushdie. In 2007 the author received a knighthood, setting off a fresh round of protests throughout the Islamic world.

While immigrants were bringing in new religions or new varieties of Christianity, there was a seemingly unstoppable rise of secularism among the indigenous British population. Today Britons have a very low rate of religious belief and church attendance. Many Church of England services are attended by a tiny number of aging Christians, and the Protestant Dissenting churches as a group are doing even worse. By the first years of the new century, militant atheists such as Oxford's

Professor Richard Dawkins (b. 1941) had become more conspicuous with their vociferous attacks on religion.

Green and Anti-Nuclear Movements

Britain participated in the rise of green politics in the 1980s. Self-identified "Greens" reject the damage done to the environment by industrialism and support the preservation of what little open space remains in Britain. Greens also strongly oppose nuclear power and support renewable energy. Unlike Germany and some other European countries, Britain has not seen an effective Green political party. It is difficult to found a national party in Britain, due to the large number of parliamentary districts or constituencies from which the House of Commons is elected and Britain's majority-takes-all electoral system. Some activists have tried to get Britain to switch to a system of proportional representation, used in many other democratic countries, in which people vote for a party rather than a candidate and votes are counted nationwide. Countries with proportional representation tend to have more parties and to make it easier to start a party; in some, such as Germany, Green activists have been elected to national legislatures. (Some in Britain have argued that proportional representation would result in candidates from racist parties such as the BNP being elected to the House of Commons.) Green action takes place outside of the electoral process and often in direct confrontation with state agencies.

The 1980s were a time when fear of nuclear war ran high, and much British radical protest focused on nuclear weapons. The Greenham Common Women's Peace Group set up a camp next to the RAF base at Greenham Common in the county of Berkshire to protest the basing of nuclear-armed cruise missiles and prevent access to the base. There was an unsuccessful attempt to evict the Greenham Common women in 1984, but the camp remained until 2000, although the missiles had actually been removed in 1991. The Faslane Peace Camp in Faslane, Scotland, open to all sexes, was set up in 1982 to protest the basing of Trident missiles at the Faslane Naval Base, and it is still in existence

John Major

Margaret Thatcher's successor as Conservative Party leader and prime minister, John Major (b. 1943), was a little-known figure when he was entrusted with the highest position in British politics; one commentator joked that he had "risen without trace" (quoted in Taylor 2006, 2). His background was truly obscure: He neither came from the traditional

Conservative gentry nor did he have the meritocratic academic career of politicians such as Edward Heath and Margaret Thatcher. A commonly told story early in his prime ministership related how he had once applied for a job as a bus driver and been turned down. Major was also one of the few Londoners to become prime minister. A less ideological and confrontational politician than Thatcher, Major offered a kind of "Thatcherism lite."

The new prime minister faced an immediate challenge with Britain's participation in the American-led coalition against Iraq in the Gulf War of 1991. British forces played a greater role than those of any other American ally, but despite British military success there was no Falklands factor, in which a British victory boosted the prime minister's popularity. However, Major did overcome many people's expectations in winning a narrow majority in his own right in his first election as prime minister. Some attributed this to his own hard campaigning, while others pointed to the continuing weakness of the Labour Party. Only a few months later, the government bungled a currency crisis. In 1990 Britain had joined the European Exchange Rate Mechanism (ERM), an agreement between European countries to keep their currencies fluctuating within a narrow range against each other rather than floating freely. The value of the pound, however, was sinking rapidly, and on September 16, 1992, Black Wednesday, the Treasury's increasingly desperate attempts to shore up the value of the pound collapsed. Later estimates showed that Britain had lost more than £3 billion, and it was forced to withdraw from the ERM. Although sterling recovered its value over the next few years, the crisis was followed by a huge drop in the Conservatives' popularity, which took the party more than a decade to make up.

The first tentative moves to a peace settlement in Northern Ireland also began under Major with secret talks between the British and Sinn Féin, as well as the "Downing Street Declaration" of December 15, 1993. Major and Irish prime minister Albert Reynolds (b. 1932) jointly declared that the people of Ireland had the right to self-determination based on consensus. Britain acknowledged that a united Ireland was possible if all Irish people wanted it, while the Irish Republic acknowledged the right of the Northern Irish Unionists to a voice in the process.

Although decolonization had been completed throughout almost the entire old British Empire by 1979, there were a few areas left during the Major era. Belize, formerly British Honduras—the last British possession on the American mainland—gained its independence in 1981. Far more economically and politically important was Hong Kong, a British colony on the south China coast. Hong Kong was a major economic center for East Asia. Some of the land had been ceded to Britain by China in the Opium Wars of the mid-19th century, but some had been leased in 1898 for a period of 99 years.

The handover of all of Hong Kong, not just the leased territories, to China on the expiration of the lease in 1997 provoked great controversy. Although there were numerous restrictions on the political rights of Hong Kong residents as British colonial subjects, the situation would worsen considerably upon Hong Kong's absorption by China's Communist regime. Given the realities of the power situation, there was little Britain could compel China to do to respect the rights of Hong Kong citizens. The British were also reluctant to accept a flood of Hong Kong refugees. The last British governor of Hong Kong, Chris Patten (b. 1944), was a Conservative politician who had lost his seat in Parliament in the general election of 1992; most previous governors

THE "CHUNNEL"

In 1994 an idea that had been floating ever since the beginning of the 19th century finally came to fruition. A tunnel under the English channel, nicknamed the "chunnel," linked France and Britain by high-speed rail. The tunnel is 31.4 miles (50.5 kilometers) long and, at its deepest, 76 feet (250 meters) deep. Construction had begun in 1988, and 10 workers, eight of them British, died during its construction.

The tunnel was controversial in Britain, as in addition to its expense it ended the millennia since the separation of Britain from Europe when the only connection between them had been by sea. (The project was far less controversial in France.) Despite the unlikelihood of another war between Britain and a Continental power, some charged that the tunnel would compromise national security. Others hoped that it would increase the economic development of Kent, where the tunnel surfaced in England. In reality, the tunnel's impact has been less dramatic than many either hoped or feared. Neither freight nor passenger traffic has met the optimistic predictions made before it was opened. The tunnel has not led to great economic development in Kent, and despite its use by some illegal immigrants to Britain, it has not compromised British national security or become a target of terrorists.

of Hong Kong had been civil servants. Patten won some popularity in Hong Kong, and received violent condemnation from the Chinese government and its political allies, by democratizing the Hong Kong legislative assembly. The eventual transfer of Hong Kong saw it retain an identity separate from the Chinese mainland, although hopes of retaining democracy there were disappointed.

In May 1997 Major faced a new Labour leader, Tony Blair (b. 1943), in the general election. Major led the Conservative Party to one of the worst defeats in British history. The Conservatives lost 178 seats to finish at 165. Labour gained 146 seats to finish at 418, plus the Speaker, who presides over the House of Commons but does not vote. Although the stumbles and failures of Major's government and Blair's charm and dynamism played roles in the disaster, the country was also simply tired of 18 years of Conservative rule. A new generation had grown up since the last Labour government in 1979, and Labour looked like a fresh alternative.

Tony Blair and New Labour

On becoming leader of the Labour Party in 1995, Tony Blair presented himself as a break with the past. The phrase most identified with Blair and his allies was *New Labour,* which they used obsessively in place of Labour Party. Among Blair's principal concerns was severing the link between the Labour Party and a socialist agenda. He and his allies wanted to present Labour as a business-friendly party. The trade unions had been weakened by Thatcherism and the decline of the British industrial economy, and they were no longer the force in the Labour Party that they had been. One of Blair's first steps upon becoming leader of the party was to take on the elimination of clause 4 in the Labour Party constitution, which called for "the common ownership of the means of production, distribution and exchange." Blair argued that the clause represented an outmoded socialism and emphasis on nationalization. The clause was replaced with a far more vague and general statement of the party's mission.

Blair, the youngest British prime minister in the 20th century, also aimed to project the image of youth both for the Labour Party and for Britain itself. Social liberalism and multiculturalism were an important part of the New Labour program, although the antigay clause 28 was not repealed until 2003. The Blair image of a dynamic, modern Britain was frequently described as *Cool Britannia.* Critics charged that Blair was a convictionless politician more concerned with image than substance. *Cool Britannia,* some claimed, was only a mask for

THE DEATH OF PRINCESS DIANA

The most dramatic event of the early years of Tony Blair's premiership was the death of Princess Diana, the ex-wife of the heir to the throne Prince Charles (b. 1948), in a car accident in Paris on August 31, 1997. Although Diana had been an increasingly marginalized figure in the years before her death, the accident was followed by a massive outpouring of national grief. Only a few conspiracy theorists blamed Diana's death on the British government or the royal family, but many were incensed at the queen and the royal family, then on holiday, for refusing to return to London immediately or engage in public displays of grief.

The death of Diana came to be seen as an important cultural moment. The flagrant emotional displays associated with mourning the princess were seen as a renunciation of the idea of the "stiff upper lip"—that is, the typically British emotional restraint. Some argued that the Diana moment would lead to the downfall of the unpopular monarchy, although Diana's children, William (b. 1982) and Henry (b. 1989), have been fairly popular and the monarchy seems about as strong as ever. The real loser in terms of publicity was probably Prince Charles. However, despite the predictions made at the time that Charles would now never be able to wed his lover, Camilla Parker-Bowles (b. 1947), the two were married in 2005. Camilla uses the title Duchess of Cornwall (Duchess of Rothesay in Scotland), rather than Princess of Wales, to avoid conflict over Diana's use of the title.

a heartless *Cruel Britannia*—the title of a book by left-wing London journalist Nick Cohen published in 2000. Ironically, Cohen himself would later move sharply to the right.

Constitutional Changes: Devolution and the House of Lords

The most radical part of Blair's program was constitutional reform. This included the creation of regional assemblies for Scotland and Wales and the abolition of the hereditary element in the House of Lords. Removing the right of hereditary peers to vote in the House of Lords was part of Labour's campaign platform in 1997. (Until the late 1980s, the Labour position had been not to reform the House of Lords but to abolish it.) The Labour government's animosity to the upper chamber was fueled by the Lords' voting down many government measures. Although the

Lords could not permanently block a government measure, with support in the Commons they could delay it, irritating the government and leading to calls for abolition of the unelected upper chamber. The House of Lords Act of 1999 was a compromise with those in the Lords who feared the massive discontinuity that would result from removing all of the hereditary peers, some of whom were highly skilled legislators. Ninety-two peers, elected by those with the hereditary right to sit in the House, remained among the life peers who comprised the rest of the reformed Lords. This was considered a transitional measure. Hereditary peers who did not sit in the Lords gained the right to run for seats in the House of Commons, ending the necessity for peers to resign their peerages in order to sit in the Commons. Although the bill was seen as the first stage in a process of fully reforming (and possibly renaming) the Lords, the problems of the composition of a new upper chamber have proved thorny, and little has changed since the 1999 bill.

The creation of assemblies for Scotland and Wales also resulted from long campaigns. The Scottish parliament, established in 1998 after a Scottish referendum the previous year approved the idea, has 129 members elected by a mixture of single-constituency, winner-take-all elections and proportional representation in the Scottish regions. The parliament meets in the Holyrood district of Edinburgh, the capital of Scotland, as an independent nation. It has powers not covering those specifically reserved to the United Kingdom parliament—the "reserved powers." The Scottish parliament has some power to vary taxation rates, although not to establish or abolish taxes. Some have argued that the establishment of the Scottish parliament is a "slippery slope" to full Scottish independence, while others believe that it is a way of satisfying Scottish demands for autonomy short of full independence and will take the energy out of the nationalist cause. The Labour Party has dominated elections to the Scottish parliament, with the Scottish Nationalists the main opposition party.

The Welsh national assembly (Cynulliad Cenedlaethol Cymru) was established to take the place of the secretary of state for Wales and the Welsh Office, central government institutions for Welsh administration. A referendum in 1998 produced a narrow majority of Welsh voters for the creation of an assembly, which is made up of 60 members, 40 elected for constituencies and 20 elected by proportional representation. The assembly's headquarters are in Cardiff Bay. The Welsh national assembly has fewer powers than the Scottish parliament. Legislative competence is limited to matters specifically named in the Government of Wales Act or devolved from the United Kingdom parliament, and it does not include the power to tax. Labour has comprised the plurality of members, with Plaid Cymru, the Welsh nationalist party, coming in second. Labour has governed in coalitions with Plaid Cymru.

With the creation of the devolved assemblies, England became the only component of the United Kingdom without its own representative body. While most English people seem content with their representation in the U.K. House of Commons, some have argued that only an English assembly can represent specifically English interests as the interests of Scotland and Wales are represented by their assemblies.

New Labour and London

Ken Livingstone proved to be nearly as big a thorn in the side of Tony Blair as he had been for Margaret Thatcher, since Livingstone's unreconstructed leftism was far from the image of New Labour. London had been without an overall governing authority since the abolition of the Greater London Council. Labour wanted to remedy this and passed a bill to establish the Greater London Authority, headed for the first time in London's history by a popularly elected mayor. (This position is distinct from that of Lord Mayor of London, a mostly ceremonial position dealing only with the ancient City of London, a small district in central London.) Livingstone defeated the official Labour candidate, Frank Dobson (b. 1940), who had had Blair's strong support. Livingstone had been expelled from the party in 2000 but was readmitted for the 2004 election, as the Labour leadership feared another humiliating defeat for a party candidate running against him. Now the official Labour candidate, Livingstone easily won reelection.

As mayor, Livingstone worked to modernize London's aging transit infrastructure and introduced congestion charges to cut down car traffic in London's central areas. The strongly pro-gay Livingstone also set up the United Kingdom's first registry for same-sex couples, a step toward Parliament's Civil Partnership Act of 2004 that provided a status for same-sex couples with many of the benefits of marriage. The mayor frequently appeared in tabloid headlines for his freewheeling denunciations of many world leaders and governments, most definitely including the United Kingdom's. In 2008 Livingstone was defeated for reelection by the Conservative Boris Johnson (b. 1964).

Ireland

One of the Blair government's most important achievements was building on the efforts of John Major to establish peace in Ireland. The Good

Friday Agreement, or Belfast Agreement, of 1998 was the product of years of negotiating. It established a devolved assembly for Northern Ireland with a power-sharing agreement for a Northern Irish government. The Republic of Ireland abandoned its constitutional territorial claim on the North, and all parties agreed that any change in Northern Ireland's political status would have to be arrived at peacefully. The Protestant and Catholic paramilitaries agreed to disarm. The agreement also partially reversed the separation of the Republic of Ireland and the United Kingdom by establishing all-Ireland and all-British Isles institutions.

Some condemned the agreement and the peace process generally as giving in to terrorism. The British government, as part of its conciliation of Irish nationalists in the North, released numerous Irish terrorists with blood on their hands from British prisons. One of the most controversial was Patrick Magee (b. 1951), who had planted the Brighton Hotel bomb. Magee had previously been sentenced to life in prison but was released in 1999 after 14 years. Despite the opposition to these early releases, overall reaction to the agreement, which led to the end of Northern Ireland–related terrorism in Britain, was very positive, and the agreement was viewed as a political triumph for Blair.

The War on Terror and Iraq

Like many other countries around the world, Britain was quick to express its support of the United States following the terrorist attacks of September 11, 2001. British troops, as part of NATO, supported the U.S. attack on the Taliban regime of Afghanistan, an ally of the terrorist group al-Qaeda.

What proved to be the greatest political challenge of Tony Blair's career was the U.S. war on Iraq. Iraq had not been involved with the 9/11 attacks, and its dictator, Saddam Hussein (1937–2006), was not ideologically sympathetic to the Islamic fundamentalists of al-Qaeda. The American decision to go to war with Iraq in the aftermath of the 9/11 attacks was viewed with puzzlement in Europe, and in many cases it was met with outright opposition. Europeans, including Britons, feared that the American claim that Saddam Hussein was developing dangerous weapons of mass destruction (WMDs—nuclear, biological, and chemical weapons) was a cover for the desire to control Middle Eastern oil. Blair earned a reputation as U.S. president George W. Bush's most important ally in Europe, or indeed anywhere.

Blair's support for Bush's war in Iraq proved an enormous political liability. The relatively quick triumph over the armies of the Iraqi state was followed by a grinding insurgency. Even more problematic

253

Tony Blair with U.S. president George W. Bush. The complex relationship of the two men would largely define Blair's prime ministership. (AP Photo/Susan Walsh)

was the fact that no evidence of weapons of mass destruction or active programs to create them was ever produced. British prewar intelligence was revealed as inaccurate or even fraudulent. Blair's association with Bush, a highly unpopular figure in Britain, was also a liability. Blair was portrayed in the British press as Bush's "poodle," sacrificing British interests and the lives of British soldiers to American folly.

On July 7, 2005, Britain reeled from terrorist attacks in London. A coordinated series of four suicide bombings rocked the London Underground and a transit bus, killing 52 passengers. The bombings were the work of Islamic terrorists, prompted in part by the British role in the Iraq war. (Spain, also part of the coalition in Iraq, had been hit with a major terrorist attack on a train the previous year.) A second wave of bombings was planned for July 21, but the bombs did not go off and no one was harmed. The second bombings did, however, further depress many British people, as it looked as if bombings were not an aberration but would be a common feature of everyday life. Unlike the 9/11 bombings, which were perpetrated by foreigners, not citizens or long-term residents, the 7/7 bombings were carried out principally by British Muslim residents. They were followed by increased suspicion and monitoring of British Muslim communities, as well as demands that British Muslims publicly repudiate terrorism. Right-wing extremist movements such as the BNP have increasingly targeted the British Muslim population, with a corresponding de-emphasis on anti-Semitism. More moderate conservatives have called for greater controls on Muslim immigration and British Muslim institutions and preachers. British Muslims themselves have reacted in many ways, some harshly denouncing terrorism as un-Islamic, others becoming more alienated from mainstream British society.

The Fall of Tony Blair

By the middle of the first decade of the new century, Britons were increasingly weary of Tony Blair. Although he won the last of his general-election victories in 2005 (becoming the only leader in Labour history to lead his party to three victories), Labour lost seats, and its share of the popular vote dropped by 5.4 percent. Opposition to the war motivated a great deal of Blair's unpopularity, but there were other factors as well. The Millennium Dome, a structure built on London's dockland to commemorate the coming of the new millennium, was widely viewed as an expensive failure and failed to attract the predicted crowds. A scandal over the possibility that large loans to the Labour Party had been made as a quid pro quo for appointments to the House of Lords as "life peers" gave Labour an aura of sleaze, even though no prosecutions were made. As Blair's poll numbers continued to drop, the Labour Party leadership pressed him to resign. Although Blair had vowed to serve a full term if elected in 2005, he resigned as prime minister on June 27, 2007, handing over the position to Chancellor of the Exchequer Gordon Brown (b. 1951), who had long coveted the office.

Brown has not been a successful prime minister. Britain has faced numerous economic problems, in part associated with the global economic decline beginning in 2008. He has also presided over a steep decline in the popularity of the Labour Party, and few expect Labour to do well at the next election in 2010. The party has done poorly in by-elections and local elections, although Brown has at least managed to nip in the bud any challenges to his leadership within the Labour Party itself. He managed to maintain a greater distance from U.S. president George Bush, whose unpopularity in Britain continued throughout his term, than did Tony Blair. British anti-Americanism, however, may be declining after the election of Barack Obama, a popular figure in Britain as throughout Europe, to the U.S. presidency in November 2008.

The Conservatives have had a difficult time recovering from their 1997 defeat. After John Major resigned as leader shortly after the election, the party selected William Hague (b. 1961), the youngest Conservative leader since William Pitt the Younger in the 18th century, hoping to compete with Blair's youthful New Labour. Although a brilliant debater in the Commons, Hague proved a failure as leader, taking the Conservatives into another rout in the general election of 2001. Hague's successor, Iain Duncan Smith (b. 1954), was a complete flop, receiving a vote of no confidence from the party in 2003. The veteran Michael Howard (b. 1941) succeeded as a caretaker leader and did a creditable job in the 2005 general election, although Labour maintained a comfortable majority. Howard retired from the leadership position that December and was succeeded by David Cameron (b. 1966). Cameron, a wealthy graduate of Eton, Britain's most elite private school, with aristocratic connections—his wife Samantha is the daughter of a baronet and a descendant of King Charles II—is a throwback to an earlier kind of Conservative leader. Some Thatcherites have attacked him as a superficial and trendy leader without much substance, even comparing him to Tony Blair. Although Cameron remains a controver-

The Millennium Dome, a monument to the Britain of the 1990s, is unlikely to last as long as Stonehenge. (Julie Brazier)

Britain, past and future—the innovative Greater London Authority Building, whose bulbous shape is designed to control energy use, and the Tower Bridge (Neil Setchfield/Lonely Planet)

sial figure within the party and the nation, under his leadership the Conservatives have gained in popularity. Whether this is a result of Cameron's policies or of Labour's decline is a subject for debate.

In the last few decades, Britain has led a more humble existence than it did as a global empire. Some challenges—like those of economic development, an increasingly multicultural society, and terrorism—are challenges it has shared with other nations of the developed world. Others, such as the challenges of Welsh and Scottish devolution or the emotional shocks delivered by the royal family, have been more uniquely British. The future will bring many more, from the threat of economic disaster facing the world in 2009, to the end of the reign of the only queen most Britons have ever known. But only a fool would count out the society that gave the world William Shakespeare, Isaac Newton, Winston Churchill, and the Industrial Revolution, to name but a few. Britain's past will continue to shape its future.

Appendix 1

BASIC FACTS ABOUT GREAT BRITAIN

Official Name
United Kingdom of Great Britain and Northern Ireland

Geography

Land area
Great Britain covers 88,787 square miles (230,000 square kilometers). It is the ninth-largest island in the world and the largest island in Europe.

Coastal borders
The island is bordered by the English Channel to the south, the Irish Sea to the west, the North Atlantic to the north, and the North Sea to the east.

Elevation
The highest point in Great Britain is the mountain of Ben Nevis (Aonach Mor) in Scotland, at 4,400 feet (1,344 meters). The lowest point is in the English fens, at 13 feet (4 meters) below sea level.

Terrain
There are level and rolling plains, hills, and low mountains mainly in Scotland and Wales.

Government
The United Kingdom is a constitutional monarchy. The British constitution is unwritten, but the government is a parliamentary democracy

in a multiparty system. The head of government is a prime minister, usually the leader of the party with the largest representation in the House of Commons, the lower chamber of Parliament and the seat of power. The members of the prime minister's cabinet are almost always drawn from members of Parliament. There are 646 seats in the House of Commons. Members are elected from local constituencies for five-year terms, although their terms can be shortened if the government calls an election before the full five years are up, or extended in a national emergency. The House of Lords currently has 618 seats, of which 92 (Lords Temporal) are elected by the House from the hereditary peers, 26 (Lords Spiritual) are bishops of the Church of England, and the rest are appointed for life (Life Peers). There is also a Scottish parliament and a Welsh national assembly, with limited powers.

Political Divisions

Capital
The capital city of the United Kingdom and of England is London, with a population of about 7.5 million. The Greater London area, with a population of about 12 million, is the largest urban area in Europe.

Other capitals
The capital city of Scotland is Edinburgh, with a population of slightly under half a million. The capital city of Wales is Cardiff, with a population of slightly more than 300,000.

People

Population
The total population is approximately 60 million. The population of Great Britain is about 57 million. It is the third most heavily populated island in the world. By far the most heavily populated area is England, with a population of about 49 million. Scotland has about 5 million people, and Wales has about 3 million people. The population of Great Britain is about 97 percent of the population of the United Kingdom.

Growth Rate
.276 percent (source: *CIA World Factbook*)

Ethnic Groups
In the 2001 census, about 87.5 percent of the population of Great Britain identified as "British" by ethnicity, 1.2 percent as Irish, and 2.6

percent as "other white." Some 4.4 percent identified as Asian or Asian British, mostly from India and Pakistan; 2.2 percent identified as black and black British, mostly from former British colonies in the Caribbean and Africa; 1.3 percent identified as mixed; .4 percent identified as Chinese; and .4 percent were from other groups.

Languages
English is the main language. Welsh and Gaelic are also spoken, as are different languages in immigrant communities.

Religions
The Church of England is the established church in England, and the Presbyterian Church of Scotland is the established church in Scotland. There is no established church in Wales. The population of Great Britain is primarily Christian or secular. About 72 percent identify as Christian, and about 22.8 percent do not identify with or declare a religion. Numerous other religions are represented among the British population, including Islam (2.8 percent), Hinduism (1 percent) and Judaism (.5 percent).

Literacy
99 percent

Age Structure (United Kingdom)
18.1 percent, under 15; 65.9 percent, 15–64; 16 percent 65 and over (Source: National Statistics Online)

Median Age (United Kingdom)
39.9 years (source: *CIA World Factbook*)

Birthrate
1.92 children per woman in England and Wales (source: National Statistics Online); 1.73 per woman in Scotland (source: General Record Office for Scotland). This is below replacement rate.

Death Rate (United Kingdom)
10.05 deaths per thousand per year (source: *CIA World Factbook*).

Infant Mortality
4.93 deaths per thousand live births (source: *CIA World Factbook*).

Life Expectancy
Male, 76.6 years; female, 81 years

Economy

Gross Domestic Product (GDP)

$2.231 trillion est. for 2009 (source: *CIA World Factbook*)

GDP Real Growth Rate

British GDP is currently declining as part of the worldwide economic crisis. GDP declined by 1.5 percent in the last quarter of 2008, by 2.4 percent in the first quarter of 2009, and by 0.8 percent in the second quarter of 2009 (source: National Statistics Online)

Currency

Pound sterling

Natural resources

Oil, coal, tin, iron

Agriculture

Cereals, oilseed, potatoes, cattle, sheep, poultry, pigs

Industries

Mining, manufacturing, petroleum, food processing

Labor force

31.2 million (source: *CIA World Factbook*)

Distribution of labor force by sector

agriculture: 1.4 percent
industry: 18.2 percent
services: 80.4 percent (2006 est.)
(source: *CIA World Factbook*)

National Anthem

"God Save the Queen" (sung as "God Save the King" when a male is reigning)

Membership in International Organizations

United Nations (permanent member of the Security Council), European Union, North Atlantic Treaty Organization (NATO), Commonwealth of Nations, International Monetary Fund, World Trade Organization, Interpol, G-8, and many others

Appendix 2

Chronology

Early Settlements, Celts, and Romans

250,000–300,000 years ago	Earliest prehuman and human archaeological finds.
11,000 years ago	British island separates from Continent.
6,500 years ago	Beginning of Neolithic Age in Britain.
ca. 3000 B.C.E.	Start of Stonehenge construction.
ca. 2000 B.C.E.	Use of Stonehenge declines.
ca. 1500 B.C.E.	Change in climate leads to sharp decline in population.
sixth century B.C.E.	Beginning of Iron Age and Celtic culture in Britain.
ca. 325 B.C.E.	Greek traveler Pytheas of Massilia circumnavigates Britain.
55 B.C.E.	First Roman invasion of Britain, under Julius Caesar.
43 C.E.	Roman invasion under Claudius followed by conquest of most of Britain.
60–61	Rebellion of Boudicca.
196	In an attempt to seize rule over the Roman Empire, Clodius Albinus launches the first recorded invasion of Europe from Britain.
306	Constantine is proclaimed emperor at York.
410	The end of Roman rule in Britain.
449	Traditional date for the arrival of the Anglo-Saxons in England.

Anglo-Saxons, Scots, and Vikings

563	Founding of the monastery of Iona in the Hebrides by the Irish monk Columba. It will serve

262

	as a center for the Christian conversion of North Britain.
597	A papal mission, led by a monk named Augustine, lands in Anglo-Saxon Kent and begins the conversion of the southern Anglo-Saxons.
664	Synod of Whitby in the kingdom of Northumbria adopts the customs of the Roman church over those of the Irish.
673	First Synod of Anglo-Saxon bishops at Hertford.
768	The Welsh church adopts Roman customs.
793	Viking raid on the great monastery of Lindisfarne, first recorded major Viking raid in Britain.
843	Traditional date for the founding of the Kingdom of Scotland by Kenneth MacAlpin.

Scotland, England, and Wales

871–899	Reign of Alfred the Great of Wessex.
927	Traditional date for the founding of the Kingdom of England by Athelstan, after he subjugates Viking Northumbria.
1066	Battle of Hastings, the start of the Norman Conquest of England (1066–75).
1154	Accession of Henry II (r. 1154–89), already ruler of Anjou and Aquitaine.
1170	The murder of Thomas Becket, archbishop of Canterbury, by supporters of King Henry II.
1192	Papal decree establishes the independence of the Scottish church from the Church of England.
1199–1216	Reign of King John sees the loss of most of the Angevin possessions in France, quarrels with the pope, and rebellions by the king's barons.
1215	Magna Carta, treaty agreed between King John and his rebellious barons, asserts some fundamental rights of free English people.
1266	The Scots take over the Hebrides and the lordship of the Isle of Man from Norway.
1267	England recognizes Gruffydd ap Llywelyn as prince of Wales.

Britain in the Late Middle Ages

1282	Conquest of Wales by English king Edward I.
1284	Declaration of Rhuddlan brings Wales under English rule.
1290	Edward I expels the Jews from England, confiscating their property; death of Margaret of Norway leads to dynastic uncertainty in Scotland, eventually prompting English attempts at conquest.
1314	Scottish victory over the English at Bannockburn.
1320	Declaration of Arbroath establishes Scottish support for independence.
1328	In the Treaty of Edinburgh, England recognizes Scottish independence.
1337–1453	Hundred Years' War between England and France.
1348	First arrival of the Black Death in Britain.
1349	The Black Death arrives in Scotland.
1351	Statute of Laborers enacted by the English parliament.
1362	The English parliament switches from French to English as the official language of its proceedings.
1371	Steward house ascends to the Scottish throne.
1381	Great Peasants' Revolt in England.
1400–1408	Welsh rebellion against the English led by Owain Glyndwyr.
1415	A small English army led by King Henry V defeats the French at Agincourt.
1453	The Hundred Years' War ends with English defeat and the loss of all territory in France except the town of Calais.
1455–1485	Wars of the Roses.
1476	First appearance of the printing press in England.
1485	Battle of Bosworth Field leads to the death of the last Yorkist king, Richard III, and the accession of Henry Tudor to the throne of England.
1507	First appearance of the printing press in Scotland.

1509–1547   Reign of Henry VIII of England.
1513   Battle of Flodden Field between Scotland and England: Overwhelming victory for the English, as James IV of Scotland is killed along with many of his nobles, the last British monarch to die in battle.

The Making of Protestant Britain

1529   First meeting of the Reformation Parliament.
1534   Act of Supremacy makes the monarch head of the English church.
1536   Act of Union between England and Wales.
1547   Death of Henry VIII, followed by the accession of his son Edward and a more strongly Protestant religious policy.
1550s   Protestant Reformation in Scotland.
1553   Death of Edward VI, followed by the accession of his Catholic sister Mary and a reversal of religious policy back to Catholicism.
1558   The English lose Calais, their last possession in France.
      Death of Queen Mary followed by the accession of her Protestant sister Elizabeth and a return to Protestantism as the official religion.
1588   Defeat of the Spanish Armada by the English.
1603   Death of Elizabeth I leads to the accession of James VI of Scotland to the English throne as James I, unifying the entire island under a single ruler.
      Final conquest of Ireland by the English.
1604   End of the Anglo-Spanish War.
1605   The Gunpowder Plot, a plan of radical Roman Catholics to blow up the Houses of Parliament during the king's visit, is frustrated.
1607   Founding of Jamestown, the first English colony in North America.
1637   Scottish Calvinists rebel against the new Anglican liturgy introduced by King Charles I.
1639–1640   Bishop's Wars between King Charles I and the Scottish rebels end with Scottish occupation of part of northern England.

1641	Irish rebellion.
1642	English Civil War begins.
1649	Execution of Charles I.
1650	Irish rebels defeated by Oliver Cromwell.
1653	Republican government overthrown, replaced by military-based rule of Oliver Cromwell.
1658	Death of Oliver Cromwell.
1660	Restoration of Charles II.
1662	Chartering of the Royal Society, Britain's pre-eminent scientific organization.
1665	Last great outbreak of the plague in Britain, centering in London.
1666	Great Fire of London.
1687	Publication of Isaac Newton's *Mathematical Principles of Natural Philosophy*.
1688	Revolution overthrows James II; he is succeeded by William of Orange and Mary.

Industry and Conquest

1701–1713	War of the Spanish Succession.
1707	Parliamentary union of England and Scotland leads to the creation of the United Kingdom of Great Britain.
1714	Death of Anne, the last Stuart monarch, followed by the accession of the House of Hanover with the reign of George I.
1715	Jacobite rising to restore the Stuarts is defeated.
1745	The last Jacobite rising defeated.
1756–1763	Seven Years' War sees overwhelming British victory, driving the French from Canada and establishing Britain as the world's premier naval and colonial power.
1783	Treaty of Paris ends the American Revolution with the loss of most British colonies in North America.
1793	The war between Britain and revolutionary France begins.
1801	Act of Union between Great Britain and Ireland creates the United Kingdom of Great Britain and Ireland.

1815	Battle of Waterloo ends the revolutionary and Napoleonic Wars with victory for Britain and its allies.
1825	First public railroad opened.
1832	The Great Reform Bill broadens the right to vote for members of Parliament.

Britain in the Age of Empire

1851	Great Exhibition, the first World's Fair, opens in the Crystal Palace in London.
1859	Publication of Charles Darwin's *On the Origin of Species,* setting forth his theory of evolution by natural selection.
1867	Second Reform Bill further broadens the right to vote.
1882	Married Women's Separate Property Act allows married women to hold property independently of their husbands.
1884	Third Reform Bill further broadens the parliamentary franchise.
1899–1902	The Boer War ends in British victory but reveals British weaknesses and adds to British global unpopularity.
1900	Formation of the Labour Representation Committee, later to be known as the Labour Party.
1904	Entente Cordiale, an alliance between Britain and France.
1907	Anglo-Russian Entente.
1911	Drastic limitations imposed on the power of the House of Lords.
1914–1918	World War I.
1918	Fourth Reform Bill gives the parliamentary vote to men over the age of 21 and women over 30.
1922	The Irish Free State is constituted as a dominion of the Crown.

An Age of Crisis

1924	Election of Britain's first Labour government.
1926	Short-lived general strike.

	Chartering of the British Broadcasting Corporation (BBC).
1929	Women get the right to vote on the same basis as men.
1931	Statute of Westminster loosens the colonies of settlement from British rule by establishing the legislative independence of the dominions.
1938	Munich agreement.
1939–1945	World War II.
1940	Chamberlain government overturned to give way to Churchill coalition government. Fall of France. Battle of Britain.
1941	Germany invades the Soviet Union. Japan enters the war with attacks on Britain and the United States. Germany declares war on the United States.
1942	Fall of Singapore to the Japanese. British victory over the Germans in North Africa at the Battle of El Alamein.
1943	British forces capture Tripoli from the Italians. Allied invasion of Sicily followed by invasion of Italy.
1944	British and Indian troops win victory over the Japanese at Imphal. Allied Normandy landings.
1945	End of World War II with Allied victory.

The Age of Consensus

1945	General election returns the Labour Party, headed by Clement Atlee. Between 1945 and 1951 the Labour government transforms the British economy with a program of nationalizations and lays the foundations of the British welfare state.
1946	"Iron Curtain" speech by Winston Churchill.
1947	India and Pakistan win their independence from Britain, while remaining members of the Commonwealth.
1948	Britain leaves Palestine.

1950–1953	Britain participates in the Korean War as a member of the United Nations.
1951	Festival of Britain on the 100th anniversary of the Great Exhibition.
1953	Coronation of Elizabeth II.
1956	The Suez Crisis leads to fall of Anthony Eden as prime minister.
1958	Founding of the Campaign for Nuclear Disarmament (CND).
1960	The British attempt to enter the Common Market (founded in 1957) is vetoed by the French. Prime Minister Harold Macmillan's "Winds of Change" speech signals British acceptance of its African colonies' moves to independence.
1961	South Africa becomes an independent republic.
1962	Formation of the Beatles.
1964	The Beatles tour America.
1969	Beginning of the Troubles in Northern Ireland.
1973	Britain enters the European Common Market.

A House Divided

1979	Margaret Thatcher becomes prime minister.
1982	The Falklands War.
1984	Irish Republican Army bombs the hotel in Brighton hosting the Conservative Party Conference.
1984–1985	Miner's strike.
1990	Faced with opposition from within the Conservative Party, Margaret Thatcher withdraws from leadership. John Major takes over as prime minister and leader of the Conservative Party.
1991	Britain fights as a U.S. ally in the Gulf War.
1997	Major government comes to an end as New Labour under Tony Blair wins an overwhelming victory in the parliamentary elections. Handover of Hong Kong to China.
1998	Establishment of the Scottish parliament. Good Friday Agreement, or Belfast Agreement, ends Irish Troubles.
1999	Establishment of the Welsh national assembly.

	House of Lords Act removes most of the hereditary element from the upper chamber of Parliament.
2000	Millennium Dome opened.
2003	Britain joins the United States in the Iraq War.
2005	Terrorist bombings in London by Muslim radicals.
2007	Resignation of Tony Blair as leader of the Labour Party and prime minister; succeeded by Gordon Brown.
2008	British financial institution Northern Rock taken under government control, as concern grows about financial crisis.
2009	British troops withdrawn from Iraq.
	European Parliament elections return two members of the British National Party, the BNP's first victory in a national election.

Appendix 3

BIBLIOGRAPHY

Adam, Isabel. *Witch Hunt: The Great Scottish Witch Trials of 1697.* London: Macmillan, 1978.

The Anglo-Saxon Chronicle According to the Several Original Authorities. 2 vols. Edited and translated by Benjamin Thorpe. London: Longman, 1861.

Aurell, Martin. *The Plantagenet Empire.* Translated by Donald Crouch. Harlow, England: Pearson Longman, 2007.

Barrow, G. S. *Kingship and Unity: Scotland 1000–1306.* 2nd ed. Edinburgh: Edinburgh University Press, 2003.

Brewer, John. *The Sinews of Power: War, Money and the English State 1688–1783.* Cambridge, Mass.: Harvard University Press, 1990.

Caesar, Julius. *Caesar's Commentaries on the Gallic and Civil Wars.* Translated by W. A. McDevitte and W. S. Bohn. New York: Harper and Row, 1870.

Carpenter, Hugh. *The Struggle for Mastery: The Penguin History of Britain, 1066–1284.* London: Penguin, 2004.

Churchill, Winston S. *The Second World War.* 6 vols. London: Cassell; Boston: Houghton Mifflin, 1948–54.

Colley, Linda. *Britons: Forging the Nation 1707–1837.* New Haven, Conn.: Yale University Press, 1992.

Dale, Iain, ed. *Labour Party General Election Manifestos.* New York: Routledge, 2000.

Ellis, Stephen G., with Christopher Maginn. *The Making of the British Isles: The State of Britain and Ireland 1450–1660.* Harlow, England: Pearson Longman, 2007.

Haigh, Christopher, ed. *The Cambridge Historical Encyclopedia of Great Britain and Ireland.* Cambridge: Cambridge University Press, 1985.

Hanawalt, Barbara A. *The Ties That Bound: Peasant Families in Medieval England.* New York: Oxford University Press, 1986.

Harvie, Christopher. *Scotland: A Short History.* Oxford and New York: Oxford University Press, 2002.

Hobsbawm, Eric. *The Age of Extremes: A History of the World, 1914–1991.* New York: Pantheon, 1994.

Hodder, Edwin. *The Life and Work of the Seventh Earl of Shaftesbury.* 3 vols. Shannon: Irish University Press, 1971.

Hutton, Ronald. *The Triumph of the Moon: A History of Modern Pagan Witchcraft.* Oxford and New York: Oxford University Press, 1999.

Inwood, Stephen. *A History of London.* New York: Carroll and Graf, 1998.

James, Robert Rhodes. *The British Revolution, 1880–1939.* New York: Knopf, 1977.

Jenkins, Geraint H. *A Concise History of Wales.* Cambridge: Cambridge University Press, 2007.

Jillings, Karen. *Scotland's Black Death: The Foul Death of the English.* Stroud, England: Tempus, 2003.

Johnson, James William. *A Profane Wit: The Life of John Wilmot, Earl of Rochester.* Rochester, N.Y.: University of Rochester Press, 2004.

Kearney, Hugh. *The British Isles: A History of Four Nations.* 2nd ed. Cambridge: Cambridge University Press, 2006.

Kipling, Rudyard. *The Writings in Prose and Verse of Rudyard Kipling.* 32 vols. New York: Charles Scribner's Sons, 1920.

Leese, Peter. *Britain since 1945: Aspects of Identity.* New York: Palgrave Macmillan, 2006.

Louis, William Roger, ed. *The Oxford History of the British Empire.* 5 vols. Oxford and New York: Oxford University Press, 1998–99.

Mackie, J. D. *A History of Scotland.* 2nd ed. Revised and edited by Bruce Lenman and Geoffrey Parker. Harmondsworth, England, and New York: Penguin, 1978.

Morgan, Kenneth O., ed. *The Oxford History of Britain.* Rev. ed. Oxford and New York: Oxford University Press, 1999.

———. *The People's Peace: British History 1945–1990.* Oxford: Oxford University Press, 1992.

Moss, Norman. *Nineteen Weeks: America, Britain, and the Fateful Summer of 1940.* Boston: Houghton Mifflin, 2003.

Oring, Elliott. *Engaging Humour.* Urbana: University of Illinois Press, 2003.

Pearce, Malcolm, and Geoffrey Stewart. *British Political History, 1867–1990: Democracy and Decline.* London and New York: Routledge, 1992.

Pilger, John, ed. *Tell Me No Lies: Investigative Journalism That Changed the World.* New York: Thunders Mouth Press, 2005.

Pugh, Martin. *The Making of Modern British Politics, 1867–1945.* Oxford: Blackwell, 2002.

Records of the Parliaments of Scotland to 1707 (RPS). University of St. Andrews. Available online. URL: http://www.rps.ac.uk/. Accessed on February 19, 2009.

Rhodes, Neil, Jennifer Richards, and Joseph Marshall, eds. *King James VI and I: Selected Writings,* Aldershot, England; Burlington, Vt.: Aldershot, 2003.

Sharpe, James A. *Instruments of Darkness: Witchcraft in Early Modern England.* Philadelphia: University of Pennsylvania Press, 1996.

Slack, Paul, and Ryk Ward, eds. *The Peopling of Britain: The Shaping of a Human Landscape: The Linacre Lectures 1999.* New York: Oxford University Press, 2002.

Snyder, Christopher A. *An Age of Tyrants: Britain and the Britons, A.D. 400–600.* University Park: Pennsylvania State University Press and Stroud: Sutton, 1998.

Starkey, David, ed. *The English Court from the Wars of the Roses to the Civil Wars.* London and New York: Longman, 1987.

Stengers, Jean, and Anne von Neck. *Masturbation: The History of a Great Terror.* Translated by Kathryn A. Hoffman. New York: Palgrave, 2001.

Suetonius. *Suetonius.* 2 vols. Translated by J. C. Rolfe. London: William Heinemann, 1920.

Tacitus, Cornelius. *The Complete Works of Tacitus.* Translated by Alfred John Church and William Jackson Brodribb. New York: Modern Library, 1942.

Taylor, A. J. P. *English History 1914–1945.* New York and Oxford: Oxford University Press, 1965.

Taylor, Robert. *Major.* London: Haus, 2006.

Weeks, Jeffrey. *Coming Out: Homosexual Politics in Britain, From the Nineteenth Century to the Present.* London and New York: Quartet, 1977.

Wesley, John. *The Works of the Reverend John Wesley.* 7 vols. Edited by John Emory. New York: 1840.

Whitelocke, Dorothy. *The Beginnings of English Society.* Harmondsworth, England: Penguin, 1952.

Wilson, A. N. *After the Victorians: The Decline of Britain in the World.* New York: Picador, 2005.

Wilson, Trevor. *The Downfall of the Liberal Party, 1914–1935.* Ithaca, N.Y.: Cornell University Press, 1966.

APPENDIX 4
SUGGESTED READING

General Surveys of British History
Ackroyd, Peter. *London: The Biography.* London: Chatto and Windus; New York: Talese, 2000.

Cain, P. J., and A. G. Hopkins. *British Imperialism 1688–2000.* New York: Longman, 2001.

Elton, G. R. *The English.* Oxford and Cambridge, Mass.: Blackwell, 1992.

Early Settlements, Celts, and Romans
Allason-Jones, Lindsay. *Women in Roman Britain.* London: British Museum Publications, 1989.

Frere, Sheppard. *Britannia: A History of Roman Britain.* 3rd edition, further revised. London: Folio Society, 1999.

Hutton, Ronald. *The Pagan Religions of the Ancient British Isles: Their Nature and Legacy.* Oxford and Cambridge, Mass.: Blackwell, 1991.

Jones, Michael E. *The Fall of Roman Britain.* Ithaca, N.Y.: Cornell University Press, 1996.

Millet, Martin. *The Romanization of Britain: An Essay in Archaeological Interpretation.* Cambridge and New York: Cambridge University Press, 1990.

Oppenheimer, Stephen. *The Origins of the British: A Genetic Detective Story: The Surprising Roots of the English, Irish, Scottish and Welsh.* New York: Carroll & Graf, 2006.

Salway, Peter. *A History of Roman Britain.* Oxford and New York: Oxford University Press, 1997.

Anglo-Saxons, Scots, and Vikings
Crawford, Barbara E. *Scandinavian Scotland.* Leicester, England: Leicester University Press and Atlantic Highlands, N.J.: Humanities Press, 1987.

Davies, Wendy. *Wales in the Early Middle Ages.* Leicester, England: Leicester University Press, 1982.

Graham-Campbell, James, and Coleen E. Batey. *Vikings in Scotland: An Archaeological Survey.* Edinburgh: Edinburgh University Press, 1998.

Higham, N. J. *The Kingdom of Northumbria: AD 350–1100.* Stroud, England, and Dover, N.H.: Alan Sutton, 1993.

Loyn, Henry. *The Vikings in Britain.* Rev. ed. Oxford: Blackwell, 1994.

Mayr-Harting, Henry. *The Coming of Christianity to England.* 3rd ed. University Park: Pennsylvania State University Press, 1991.

Neuman de Vegvar, Carol L. *The Northumbrian Renaissance: A Study in the Transmission of Style.* Selinsgrove, Pa.: Susquehanna University Press; London: Associated University Press, 1987.

Smyth, Alfred P. *Warlords and Holy Men: Scotland, AD 80–1000.* Edinburgh: Edinburgh University Press, 1989.

Stenton, F. M. *Anglo-Saxon England.* 3rd ed. Oxford and New York: Oxford University Press, 1990.

Williams, Ann. *Kingship and Government in Pre-Conquest England, ca. 500–1066.* London: Macmillan; New York: St. Martin's Press, 1999.

Scotland, England, and Wales

Barlow, Frank. *Thomas Becket.* London: Weidenfeld and Nicolson; Berkeley: University of California Press, 1986.

Davies, R. R. *The Age of Conquest: Wales 1063–1415.* Oxford and New York: Oxford University Press, 1992.

———. *The First English Empire: Power and Identities in the British Isles, 1093–1343.* Oxford and New York: Oxford University Press, 2000.

Powicke, Maurice. *The Thirteenth Century 1216–1307.* 2nd ed. Oxford: Clarendon Press, 1962.

Smyth, Alfred P. *King Alfred the Great.* Oxford and New York: Oxford University Press, 1995.

Tyerman, Christopher. *England and the Crusades, 1095–1588.* Chicago: University of Chicago Press, 1988.

Williams, Ann. *The English and the Norman Conquest.* Woodbridge, England, and Rochester, N.Y.: Boydell Press, 1995.

Wormald, Patrick. *The Making of English Law: King Alfred to the Twelfth Century.* Oxford, England, and Cambridge, Mass.: 1999.

Britain in the Late Middle Ages

Allmand, Christopher T. *The Hundred Years War: England and France at War, ca. 1300–ca. 1450.* Cambridge and New York: Cambridge University Press, 1988.

Barrow, G. S. *Robert Bruce and the Community of the Realm of Scotland.* 3rd ed. Edinburgh: Edinburgh University Press, 1988.

Chrimes, S. B. *Henry VII.* New Haven, Conn., and London: Yale University Press, 1999.

Grant, Alexander. *Independence and Nationhood: Scotland, 1306–1469.* London and Baltimore: Arnold, 1984.

Knowles, David. *The Religious Orders in England.* 3 vols. Cambridge: Cambridge University Press, 1948–1953.

Macfarlane, K. B. *The Nobility of Later Medieval England.* Oxford: Clarendon Press, 1973.

Mattingly, Garret. *Catherine of Aragon.* Boston: Little, Brown, 1941.

McSheffrey, Shannon. *Gender and Heresy: Women and Men in Lollard Communities, 1420–1530.* Philadelphia: University of Pennsylvania Press, 1995.

Starkey, David, ed. *The English Court from the Wars of the Roses to the Civil Wars.* London and New York: Longman, 1987.

Weir, Alison. *Isabella: She-Wolf of France, Queen of England.* London: Jonathan Cape, 2005.

The Making of Protestant Britain

Burns, William E. *An Age of Wonders: Prodigies, Politics and Providence in England, 1657–1727.* Manchester, England: Manchester University Press, 2002.

Force, James E., and Richard H. Popkin, eds. *The Millenarian Turn: Millenarian Contexts of Science, Politics, and Everyday Anglo-American Life in the Seventeenth and Eighteenth Centuries.* Dordrecht, Netherlands: Kluwer Academic Publishers, 2001.

Harris, Tim. *Revolution: The Great Crisis of the British Monarchy 1685–1720.* London and New York: Allen Lane, 2006.

Hill, Christopher. *God's Englishman: Oliver Cromwell and the English Revolution.* London: Weidenfeld and Nicolson, New York: Dial Press, 1970.

Kenyon, J. P. *Stuart England.* Harmondsworth, England: Penguin Books, 1978.

Marsh, Christopher. *Popular Religion in Sixteenth-Century England: Holding Their Peace.* New York: St. Martin's Press, 1998.

Memegalos, Florene. *George Goring (1608–1657): Caroline Courtier and Royalist General.* Aldershot, England, and Burlington, Vt.: Ashgate, 2007.

Mitchison, Rosalind. *Lordship to Patronage: Scotland 1603–1745.* Edinburgh: Edinburgh University Press, 1990.

Shapin, Steven. *A Social History of Truth: Civility and Science in Seventeenth-Century England*. Chicago: University of Chicago Press, 1994.

Smith, Lacey Baldwin. *Henry VIII: The Mask of Royalty*. Boston: Houghton Mifflin, London: Jonathan Cape, 1971.

Walsham, Alexandra. *Charitable Hatred: Tolerance and Intolerance in England, 1500–1700*. Manchester, England: Manchester University Press, 2006.

Williamson, Arthur H. *Scottish National Consciousness in the Age of James VI: The Apocalypse, the Union, and the Making of Scotland's Public Culture*. Edinburgh: John Donald, 1979.

Industry and Conquest

Hatton, Ragnhild. *George I: Elector and King*. London: Thames and Hudson; Cambridge, Mass.: Harvard University Press, 1978.

Hitchcock, Tim. *English Sexualities, 1700–1800*. New York: St. Martins, 1997.

Holmes, Geoffrey, and Daniel Szechi. *The Age of Oligarchy: Pre-Industrial Britain 1722–1783*. London and New York: Longman, 1993.

Hunt, Margaret R. *The Middling Sort: Commerce, Gender and the Family in England, 1680–1780*. Berkeley: University of California Press, 1996.

Jacob, Margaret C., and Larry Stewart. *Practical Matter: Newton's Science in the Service of Industry and Empire, 1687–1851*. Cambridge, Mass.: Harvard University Press, 2004.

Lenman, Bruce P. *Integration and Enlightenment: Scotland 1746–1832*. Edinburgh: Edinburgh University Press, 1992.

Pares, Richard. *King George III and the Politicians*. Oxford: Clarendon Press, 1953.

Porter, Roy. *The Creation of the Modern World: The Untold Story of the British Enlightenment*. New York: W. W. Norton, 2000.

Sher, Richard B. *Church and University in the Scottish Enlightenment: The Moderate Literati of Edinburgh*. Princeton, N.J.: Princeton University Press; Edinburgh: Edinburgh University Press, 1985.

Thompson, E. P. *The Making of the English Working Class*. London: Gollancz; New York: Vintage, 1963.

Woodward, Llewellyn. *The Age of Reform: England 1815–1870*. 2nd ed. Oxford: Oxford University Press, 1962.

Britain in the Age of Empire

Bagehot, Walter. *The English Constitution*. London: Chapman and Hall, 1867.

Dangerfield, George. *The Strange Death of Liberal England*. New York: H. Smith and R. Haas, 1935.

Holton, Sandra Stanley. *Feminism and Democracy: Women's Suffrage and Reform Politics in Britain, 1900–1918*. Cambridge and New York: Cambridge University Press, 1986.

Magnus, Philip. *King Edward VII*. London: John Murray, 1964.

Marwick, Arthur. *The Deluge: British Society and the First World War*. Boston: Little, Brown, 1965.

Matthew, H. C. G. *Gladstone 1809–1898*. Oxford: Clarendon Press; New York: Oxford University Press, 1997.

Parry, Jonathan. *The Rise and Fall of Liberal Government in Victorian Britain*. New Haven, Conn., and London: Yale University Press, 1993.

Roberts, Robert. *The Classic Slum: Salford Life in the First Quarter of the Century*. Manchester, England: Manchester University Press, 1971.

Robbins, Keith. *Nineteenth-Century Britain: England, Scotland and Wales: The Making of a Nation*. Oxford and New York: Oxford University Press, 1989.

Robinson, Ronald, and John Gallagher, with Alice Denny. *Africa and the Victorians: The Official Mind of Imperialism*. 2nd ed. London: Macmillan, 1981.

Smith, Paul. *Disraeli: A Brief Life*. Cambridge and New York: Cambridge University Press, 1996.

Sumida, Jon Tetsuro. *In Defence of Naval Supremacy: Finance, Technology and British Naval Policy, 1889–1914*. Boston: Unwin Hyman, 1989.

Weiner, Martin J. *English Culture and the Decline of the Industrial Spirit, 1850–1980*. Cambridge and New York: Cambridge University Press, 1981.

Wilson, Trevor. *The Myriad Faces of War: Britain and the Great War, 1914–1918*. Oxford and New York: Blackwell and Cambridge: Polity Press, 1986.

An Age of Crisis

Calder, Angus. *The People's War: Britain 1939–1945*. New York: Pantheon Books, 1969.

Cannadine, David. *The Decline and Fall of the British Aristocracy*. New Haven, Conn.: Yale University Press, 1990.

Marquand, David. *Ramsay Macdonald*. London: Jonathan Cape, 1977.

Medlicott, William Norton. *The Economic Blockade*. 2 vols. London: HM Stationary Office, 1952, 1959.

Orwell, George. *The Road to Wigan Pier.* London: V. Gollancz, 1937.

Pelling, Henry. *Britain and the Second World War.* London and Glasgow: Collins, 1970.

Stevenson, John. *British Society, 1914–45.* London: A. Lane, 1984.

Stevenson, John, and Chris Cook. *Britain in the Depression: Society and Politics, 1929–1939.* London and New York: Longman, 1994.

The Age of Consensus

Blythe, Ronald. *Akenfield: Portrait of an English Village.* London: Allen Lane, 1969.

Bullock, Alan. *The Life and Times of Ernest Bevin.* 3 vols. London: Heinemann, 1960–1983.

Foot, Michael. *Aneurin Bevan: A Biography.* London: New English Library, 1966.

Jeffery-Poulter, Stephen. *Peers, Queers and Commons: The Struggle for Gay Law Reform from 1950 to the Present.* London and New York: Routledge, 1991.

Lacey, Robert. *Majesty: Elizabeth II and the House of Windsor.* New York: Harcourt Brace Jovanovich; London: Hutchinson, 1977.

Lewis, Jane. *Women in Britain since 1945: Women, Family, Work and the State in the Post-war Years.* Oxford and Cambridge, Mass.: Blackwell, 1992.

Morgan, Kenneth O. *Labour in Power, 1945–1951.* Oxford: Clarendon Press, 1984.

Nairn, Tom. *The Break-up of Britain: Crisis and Neo-Nationalism.* London: NLB, 1977.

Pimlott, Ben. *Harold Wilson.* London: HarperCollins, 1992.

Savage, Jon. *England's Dreaming: Anarchy, Sex Pistols, Punk Rock and Beyond.* Rev. ed. London: Faber, 2001.

A House Divided

Bartle, John, and Anthony King, eds. *Britain at the Polls 2005.* Washington, D.C.: CQ Press, 2006.

Buford, Bill. *Among the Thugs.* New York: W. W. Norton, 1992.

Clark, Alan. *Diaries.* London: Orion Books, 1994.

Gilroy, Paul. *"There Ain't No Black in the Union Jack": The Cultural Politics of Race and Nation.* London: Hutchinson, 1987.

Hutton, Will. *The State We're In.* London: Jonathan Cape, 1995.

Luhrmann, Tanya. *Persuasions of the Witch's Craft: Ritual Magic in Contemporary England.* Cambridge, Mass.: Harvard University Press, 1989.

Seldon, Anthony, ed. *Blair's Britain, 1997–2007.* Cambridge and New York: Cambridge University Press, 2007.

Seldon, Anthony, with Lewis Baston. *Major: A Political Life.* London: Weidenfeld and Nicolson, 1997.

Turpin, Colin, and Adam Tomkins. *British Government and the Constitution: Text and Materials.* Cambridge: Cambridge University Press, 2007.

INDEX

Note: Page numbers in *italic* indicate illustrations. The letters *c* and *m* indicate chronology entry and map, respectively.